# About the cover

## Civil Rights March Past Brown Chapel in Selma, Alabama, March 1, 1965

The cover image presents a portion of the larger photograph, which appears below. When they explore American histories, scholars consider many different aspects of America's past and connect them for a rich, fresh synthesis. This photo of a civil rights march from Selma to Montgomery, Alabama, in 1965 offers a wider angle on the movement for racial equality that transformed the United States into the nation that exists today.

# EXPLORING AMERICAN HISTORIES

## A BRIEF SURVEY WITH SOURCES

### Volume 2: Since 1865

Nancy A. Hewitt

Rutgers University

Steven F. Lawson

Rutgers University

**Bedford/St. Martin's**

Boston • New York

**To Mary and Charles Takacs, Florence and Hiram Hewitt,
Sarah and Abraham Parker, Lena and Ben Lawson,
who made our American histories possible.**

**For Bedford/St. Martin's**

*Publisher for History*: Mary V. Dougherty
*Senior Executive Editor for History*: William J. Lombardo
*Director of Development for History*: Jane Knetzger
*Senior Developmental Editor*: Sara Wise
*Senior Production Editor*: Christina M. Horn
*Senior Production Supervisor*: Jennifer Peterson
*Senior Marketing Manager for U.S. History*: Amy Whitaker
*Associate Editor*: Jennifer Jovin
*Editorial Assistant*: Arrin Kaplan
*Production Assistant*: Elise Keller
*Copy Editor*: Linda McLatchie
*Map Editor*: Charlotte Miller
*Indexer*: Leoni McVey
*Cartography*: Mapping Specialists, Ltd.
*Photo Researcher*: Naomi Kornhauser
*Permissions Manager*: Kalina K. Ingham

*Senior Art Director*: Anna Palchik
*Text Designer*: Jerilyn Bockorick
*Cover Designer*: Billy Boardman
*Cover Art*: Selma civil rights march: A march to Montgomery, Alabama, in front of Brown Chapel in Selma, Alabama, March 1, 1965. © Flip Schulke/CORBIS.
*Composition*: Cenveo Publisher Services
*Printing and Binding*: RR Donnelley and Sons

*President, Bedford/St. Martin's*: Denise B. Wydra
*Presidents, Macmillan Higher Education*: Joan E. Feinberg and Tom Scotty
*Director of Marketing*: Karen R. Soeltz
*Production Director*: Susan W. Brown
*Associate Production Director*: Elise S. Kaiser
*Managing Editor*: Elizabeth M. Schaaf

Manufactured in China

7   6   5   4
f   e   d

*For information, write*: Bedford/St. Martin's, 75 Arlington Street, Boston, MA 02116   (617-399-4000)

ISBN 978-0-312-40998-2 (Combined Edition)
ISBN 978-1-4576-4194-7 (Loose-leaf Edition)
ISBN 978-0-312-41000-1 (Volume 1)
ISBN 978-1-4576-4195-4 (Loose-leaf Edition, Volume 1)
ISBN 978-0-312-41001-8 (Volume 2)
ISBN 978-1-4576-4196-1 (Loose-leaf Edition, Volume 2)

**Acknowledgments**

**Exploring American Histories** is a new kind of U.S. history survey text. Unique among textbooks, its innovative format makes a broad and diverse American history accessible to a new generation of students and instructors interested in a more active learning and teaching style. To accomplish this, our book joins an inclusive yet brief narrative text with an integrated documents reader; together, these two elements create unsurpassed opportunities for exploring American history in ways best suited for the twenty-first-century classroom.

## Format

Our extensive experience teaching American history in a wide variety of classrooms has led us to conclude that students learn history most effectively when they read historical narrative in conjunction with primary sources. Sources bring the past to life in ways that narrative alone cannot, while narrative offers the necessary framework, context, and chronology that documents by themselves do not typically provide. We believe that the most engaging entry to the past starts with individuals and how people in their daily lives connect to larger political, economic, cultural, and international developments. This approach makes the history relevant and memorable. The available textbooks left us unsatisfied, compelling us to assign additional books, readers, and documents we found on the Web. However, these supplementary texts raised costs for our students, and too often students had difficulty seeing how the different readings related to one another. Simply remembering what materials to bring to class became too unwieldy. So we decided to write our own book.

For *Exploring American Histories*, we sought to reconceive the relationship of the textbook and reader to create a mutually supportive set of course materials designed to help our students appreciate the diversity of America's history, to help instructors teach that primary sources are the building blocks of historical interpretation, and to encourage students to see that every past event can and should be considered from multiple perspectives. The people of the past experienced the events of their lifetimes in a variety of ways and from multiple vantage points, and historians debate continually among themselves and the general public about what actually happened and why it matters for us today. Consequently, there is no one story about the past; there are many stories, and so we wanted to emphasize these plural *Histories* in the book's title. Indeed, on the last day of our own survey classes, we measure our

success by how well our students can demonstrate that they understand this rich complexity that is central to the discipline, and whether they can put the multiple stories they have come to understand into the context of the larger whole. Instructors at all types of schools share our goal, and we hope that *Exploring American Histories* will help them enrich their students' understanding of events of the past.

For *Exploring American Histories*, we have selected an extensive and diverse array of primary-source materials that highlight multiple perspectives, and we have integrated them at key points as teaching moments within the narrative text. Each chapter contains numerous featured primary sources with a distinctive pedagogy designed to help students make connections between the documents and the text's big themes. Every document is clearly cross-referenced within the narrative so that students can easily incorporate them into their reading as well as reflect on our interpretation. A specially selected set of interrelated documents placed at the end of each chapter addresses an important historical question related to the chapter.

*Exploring American Histories* also opens up a new dimension to the familiar textbook format by expanding beyond its printed pages to grant students and teachers access to a wealth of online tools and resources built specifically for our text to enhance reading comprehension and promote in-depth study. Of special note, every chapter includes an additional document set that instructors can order packaged with the book; each set of documents focuses on a particular theme and is available only online. Many of these projects incorporate multimedia sources such as audio and video files that until recently were unavailable to work with in class. In addition, *Exploring American Histories* features LearningCurve, an easy-to-assign adaptive learning tool that helps students rehearse the material in the narrative so that they come to class better prepared. Students receive access to LearningCurve, described more fully below, when they purchase a new copy of the book. And because textbook prices are a big concern, our "two-in-one" survey text—a combination of brief narrative plus reader—offers attractive cost savings for students.

## Approach

During the last thirty years, scholarship in history has transformed our vision of the past, most notably by dramatically increasing the range of people historians study, and thus deepening and complicating traditional under-standings of change over time. Creating a story of the past was easier to do when it was limited to the study of great white men engaged in national politics and high-level diplomacy, but it was also stunted in its explanatory power and disconnected from the life experiences of nearly all our students. Over the last several decades, the historical profession itself has made huge strides in becoming more inclusive in membership, with teachers and scholars increasingly reflecting the diverse face of America. The range of new research has been vast, with a special focus on gender, race, ethnicity, and class, and histori-ans have produced landmark work in women's history, African American history, American Indian history, and labor history.

All of these changes in the historical profession have greatly influenced how the American history survey course is taught in two fundamental ways. First, many instructors now try to help their students see that ordinary people, from all walks of life, can and do affect the course of historical change. Second, many historians have become increasingly transparent about their methodology and have a strong desire to teach their students that history is an interpretive discipline and open to multiple perspectives. Since the 1970s, survey textbooks have changed in coverage, organization, and pedagogy, but they have struggled to get it right—becoming overwhelming in their scope, difficult to read, and losing the sense of story that makes the past accessible, engaging, and comprehensible. As more instructors have embraced teaching with documents, they have come to see these shortcomings in the available survey textbooks. Along with many of our colleagues, we came to the same conclusion ourselves. Many current texts are too long, so we've made ours brief. *Exploring American Histories* is comprehensive, but with a carefully selected amount of detail that is more in tune with what instructors can realistically expect their students to remember. Many texts include some documents, but the balance between narrative (too much) and primary sources (too few) was off-kilter, so we have included more documents and integrated them in creative ways that help students make the necessary connections and that spur them to think critically. But the most innovative aspect of *Exploring American Histories*, and what makes it a true alternative, is that its format introduces a unique textbook structure organized around the broad theme of *diversity.*

Diversity as a theme works in *Exploring American Histories* in several ways. First, diversity supports our presentation of an inclusive historical narrative, one that recognizes the American past as a series of interwoven stories made by a multiplicity of historical actors. We do this within a strong national framework that allows our readers to see how the various stories fit together and to understand why they matter. Our narrative is comple-mented by a wide variety of documents that challenge students to consider multiple points of view. In chapter 4, students hear from both a woman accused of witchcraft and a minister who defended the Salem witch trials. In chapter 25, we ask our readers to contrast an idyllic, inviting depiction of 1950s suburbia with a racially restrictive covenant of the same period.

Second, our theme of diversity allows us to foreground the role of individual agency as we push readers to consider the reasons behind historical change. Each chapter opens with a pair of American Histories, biographies that showcase indi-viduals who experienced and influenced events in a particular period, and then returns to them throughout the chapter to strengthen the connections and highlight their place in the bigger picture. These biographies cover both well-known Americans—such as Daniel Shays, Frederick Douglass, Andrew Carnegie, and Eleanor Roosevelt—and those who never gained fame or fortune—such as the activist Amy Kirby Post, organizer Luisa Moreno, and World War II internee Fred Korematsu. Introducing such a broad range of biographical subjects illuminates the many ways that individuals shaped and were shaped by historical events. This strategy also works to make visible throughout the chapter the intersections where history from the top down meets history from the bottom up and to connect social and political histories to their relation-ships with economic, cultural, and diplomatic developments. We work to show that events at the national level, shaped by elite political and economic leaders, have a direct impact on the lives of ordinary people; at the same time, we demonstrate that actions at the local level often have a significant influence on decisions made at the centers of national government and commerce. The discussions of the interrelationship among international, national, and local theaters and actors incorpo-rate the pathbreaking scholarship of the last three decades, which has focused on gender, race, class, and ethnicity in North America and the United States, and on colonization, empire, and globalization in the larger world.

## Primary Sources

The heart of *Exploring American Histories* is its primary sources, and in every chapter we supply students with numer-ous and carefully selected documents from which they can evaluate the text's interpretations and construct their own versions of history. These firsthand accounts include maps, drawings, material artifacts, paintings, speeches, sermons, letters, diaries, memoirs, newspaper articles, political cartoons, laws, wills, court cases, petitions, advertisements, photographs, and blogs. In selecting documents, we have provided multiple perspectives on critical issues, including both well-known sources and those that are less familiar. But our choices were also influenced by the kinds of primary sources that exist. For some periods of American history and some topics, the available primary sources are limited and fragmentary.

For other eras and issues, the sources are varied and abundant, indeed sometimes overwhelming, especially as we move into the twentieth century. In all time periods, some groups of Americans are far better represented in primary sources than others. Those who were wealthy, well educated, and politically powerful produced and preserved many sources about their lives. And their voices are well represented in this textbook. But we have also provided documents by American Indians, enslaved Africans, colonial women, rural residents, immigrants, working people, and young people. Moreover, the lives of those who left few sources of their own can often be illuminated by reading documents written by elites to see what information they yield, intentionally or unintentionally, about less well-documented groups.

Individual documents are embedded throughout every chapter and connected to the narrative text with **Explore** prompts, and within each chapter these documents are treated in the following three ways:

- Each chapter has one annotated textual or visual source, with questions in the margins to help students consider a specific phrase or feature and analyze the source as a whole. These questions and annotations are intended to train students in historical habits of mind. A **Put It in Context** question prompts students to consider the source in terms of the broad themes of the chapter.
- Each chapter contains **Two Views**, a paired set of documents that show contrasting perspectives. Two Views documents are introduced by a single headnote and are followed by **Interpret the Evidence** and **Put It in Context** questions that prompt students to analyze and compare both items and place them in a larger historical framework.
- Each chapter also presents one or more additional documents consisting of excerpts or images of classic or lesser-known sources. These are provided to encourage more practice working with sources and to offer additional perspectives to compare with the narrative. These documents are accompanied by informative headnotes and conclude with **Interpret the Evidence** and **Put It in Context** questions.

A **Document Project** at the end of every chapter is the capstone of our integrated primary-sources approach. Each Document Project is a collection of five or six documents focused on a critical issue central to that chapter. It is introduced by a brief overview and ends with interpretive questions that ask students to draw conclusions based on what they have learned in the chapter and read in the sources.

We understand that the instructor's role is crucial in teaching students how to analyze primary-source materials and develop interpretations. Teachers can use the documents to encourage critical thinking and also to measure students' understanding and assess their progress. The integration of the documents in the narrative should prompt students to read more closely than they usually do, as they will see more clearly the direct connection between the two. We have organized the documents to give instructors the flexibility to use them in many different ways—as in-class discussion prompts, for take-home writing assignments, and even as the basis for exam questions—and also in different combinations, as the documents throughout the chapter can be compared and contrasted with one another. An instructor's manual for *Exploring American Histories* provides a wealth of creative suggestions for using the documents program effectively (see the Versions and Supplements description on pages xiii–xvi for more information on all the available instructor resources).

## More Help for Students

We know that students often need help making sense of their reading. As instructors, all of us have had students complain that they cannot figure out what's important in the textbooks we assign. For many of our students, especially those just out of high school, their college history survey textbook is likely the most difficult book they have ever encountered. We understand the challenges that our students face, so in addition to the extensive document program, we have included the following pedagogical features designed to aid student learning:

- **Review and Relate** questions help students focus on main themes and concepts presented in each major section of the chapter.
- **Key terms** in boldface highlight important content. All terms are defined in a glossary at the end of the book.
- Clear **conclusions** help students summarize what they've read.
- A full-page **Chapter Review** lets students review key terms, important concepts, and notable events.

In addition, the book includes access to **LearningCurve**, an online adaptive learning tool that promotes engaged reading and focused review. Cross-references at the end of every major section and chapter in the text prompt students to log in and rehearse their understanding of the material they have just read. Students move at their own pace and accumulate points as they go, giving the interaction a game-like feel. Feedback for incorrect responses explains why the answer is incorrect and directs students back to the text to review before they attempt to answer the question again. The end result is a better understanding of the key elements of the text. See the inside front cover for more details.

We imagine *Exploring American Histories* as a new kind of American history textbook, one that not only offers a strong, concise narrative but also challenges students to construct their own interpretations through primary-source analysis. We are thrilled that our hopes have come to fruition, and we believe that our textbook will provide a thought-provoking and highly useful foundation for every U.S. history survey course and will benefit students and faculty alike. The numerous opportunities provided for active learning will allow teachers to engage students in stimulating ways and help them experience the past in closer connection to the present. After all, active learning is the basis for active citizenship, and teaching the survey course is our chance as historians, whose work is highly specialized, to reach the greatest number of undergraduates. We hope not only to inspire the historical imaginations of those who will create the next generation of American histories but also to spur them to consider the issues of today in light of the stories of yesterday.

## Acknowledgments

We wish to thank the talented scholars and teachers who were kind enough to give their time and knowledge to review the manuscript:

Benjamin Allen, *South Texas College*
Christine Anderson, *Xavier University*
Uzoamaka Melissa C. Anyiwo, *Curry College*
Anthony A. Ball, *Housatonic Community College*
Terry A. Barnhart, *Eastern Illinois University*
Edwin Benson, *North Harford High School*
Paul Berk, *Christian Brothers University*
Deborah L. Blackwell, *Texas A&M International University*
Thomas Born, *Blinn College*
Margaret Bramlett, *St. Andrews Episcopal High School*
Lauren K. Bristow, *Collin College*
Tsekani Browne, *Duquesne University*
Jon L. Brudvig, *Dickinson State University*
Dave Bush, *Shasta College*
Barbara Calluori, *Montclair State University*
Julia Schiavone Camacho, *The University of Texas at El Paso*
Jacqueline Glass Campbell, *Francis Marion University*
Amy E. Canfield, *Lewis-Clark State College*
Dominic Carrillo, *Grossmont College*
Mark R. Cheathem, *Cumberland University*
Laurel A. Clark, *University of Hartford*
Myles L. Clowers, *San Diego City College*
Hamilton Cravens, *Iowa State University*
Audrey Crawford, *Houston Community College*
John Crum, *University of Delaware*
Alex G. Cummins, *St. Johns River State College*
Susanne Deberry-Cole, *Morgan State University*
Julian J. DelGaudio, *Long Beach City College*

Patricia Norred Derr, *Kutztown University*
John Donoghue, *Loyola University Chicago*
Timothy Draper, *Waubonsee Community College*
David Dzurec, *University of Scranton*
Keith Edgerton, *Montana State University Billings*
Blake Ellis, *Lone Star College*
Christine Erickson, *Indiana University–Purdue University Fort Wayne*
Todd Estes, *Oakland University*
Gabrielle Everett, *Jefferson College*
Julie Fairchild, *Sinclair Community College*
Randy Finley, *Georgia Perimeter College*
Kirsten Fischer, *University of Minnesota*
Michelle Fishman-Cross, *College of Staten Island*
Jeffrey Forret, *Lamar University*
Kristen Foster, *Marquette University*
Susan Freeman, *Western Michigan University*
Nancy Gabin, *Purdue University*
Kevin Gannon, *Grand View University*
Benton Gates, *Indiana University–Purdue University Fort Wayne*
Bruce Geelhoed, *Ball State University*
Mark Gelfand, *Boston College*
Jason George, *The Bryn Mawr School*
Judith A. Giesberg, *Villanova University*
Sherry Ann Gray, *Mid-South Community College*
Patrick Griffin, *University of Notre Dame*
Aaron Gulyas, *Mott Community College*
Scott Gurman, *Northern Illinois University*
Melanie Gustafson, *University of Vermont*
Brian Hart, *Del Mar College*
Paul Hart, *Texas State University*
Paul Harvey, *University of Colorado Colorado Springs*
Woody Holton, *University of Richmond*
Vilja Hulden, *University of Arizona*
Colette A. Hyman, *Winona State University*
Brenda Jackson-Abernathy, *Belmont University*
Troy R. Johnson, *California State University–Long Beach*
Shelli Jordan-Zirkle, *Shoreline Community College*
Jennifer Kelly, *The University of Texas at Austin*
Kelly Kennington, *Auburn University*
Andrew E. Kersten, *University of Wisconsin–Green Bay*
Janilyn M. Kocher, *Richland Community College*
Max Krochmal, *Duke University*
Peggy Lambert, *Lone Star College*
Jennifer R. Lang, *Delgado Community College*
John S. Leiby, *Paradise Valley Community College*
Mitchell Lerner, *The Ohio State University*
Matthew Loayza, *Minnesota State University, Mankato*
Gabriel J. Loiacono, *University of Wisconsin Oshkosh*
John F. Lyons, *Joliet Junior College*
Lorie Maltby, *Henderson Community College*

Christopher Manning, *Loyola University Chicago*
Marty D. Matthews, *North Carolina State University*
Eric Mayer, *Victor Valley College*
Suzanne K. McCormack, *Community College of Rhode Island*
David McDaniel, *Marquette University*
J. Kent McGaughy, *Houston Community College, Northwest*
Alan McPherson, *Howard University*
Sarah Hand Meacham, *Virginia Commonwealth University*
Brian Craig Miller, *Emporia State University*
Brett Mizelle, *California State University Long Beach*
Mark Moser, *The University of North Carolina at Greensboro*
Jennifer Murray, *Coastal Carolina University*
Peter C. Murray, *Methodist University*
Steven E. Nash, *East Tennessee State University*
Chris Newman, *Elgin Community College*
David Noon, *University of Alaska Southeast*
Richard H. Owens, *West Liberty University*
David J. Peavler, *Towson University*
Laura A. Perry, *University of Memphis*
Wesley Phelps, *University of St. Thomas*
Merline Pitre, *Texas Southern University*
Eunice G. Pollack, *University of North Texas*
Kimberly Porter, *University of North Dakota*
Cynthia Prescott, *University of North Dakota*
Gene Preuss, *University of Houston*
Sandra Pryor, *Old Dominion University*
Rhonda Ragsdale, *Lone Star College*
Michaela Reaves, *California Lutheran University*
Peggy Renner, *Glendale Community College*
Steven D. Reschly, *Truman State University*
Barney J. Rickman, *Valdosta State University*
Pamela Riney-Kehrberg, *Iowa State University*
Paul Ringel, *High Point University*
Timothy Roberts, *Western Illinois University*
Glenn Robins, *Georgia Southwestern State University*
Alicia E. Rodriquez, *California State University Bakersfield*
Mark Roehrs, *Lincoln Land Community College*
Patricia Roessner, *Marple Newtown High School*
John G. Roush, *St. Petersburg College*
James Russell, *St. Thomas Aquinas College*
Eric Schlereth, *The University of Texas at Dallas*
Ronald Schultz, *University of Wyoming*
Stanley K. Schultz, *University of Wisconsin–Madison*
Sharon Shackelford, *Erie Community College*
Donald R. Shaffer, *American Public University System*
David J. Silverman, *The George Washington University*
Andrea Smalley, *Northern Illinois University*
Molly Smith, *Friends School of Baltimore*
David L. Snead, *Liberty University*
David Snyder, *Delaware Valley College*
Jodie Steeley, *Merced College*
Bryan E. Stone, *Del Mar College*

Emily Straus, *SUNY Fredonia*
Jean Stuntz, *West Texas A&M University*
Nikki M. Taylor, *University of Cincinnati*
Heather Ann Thompson, *Temple University*
Timothy Thurber, *Virginia Commonwealth University*
T. J. Tomlin, *University of Northern Colorado*
Laura Trauth, *Community College of Baltimore County–Essex*
Russell M. Tremayne, *College of Southern Idaho*
Laura Tuennerman-Kaplan, *California University of Pennsylvania*
Vincent Vinikas, *The University of Arkansas at Little Rock*
David Voelker, *University of Wisconsin–Green Bay*
Ed Wehrle, *Eastern Illinois University*
Gregory Wilson, *University of Akron*
Maria Cristina Zaccarini, *Adelphi University*
Nancy Zens, *Central Oregon Community College*
Jean Hansen Zuckweiler, *University of Northern Colorado*

We also appreciate the help the following scholars and students gave us in providing the information we needed at critical points in the writing of this text: Leslie Brown, Andrew Buchanan, Gillian Carroll, Susan J. Carroll, Paul Clemens, Dorothy Sue Cobble, Jane Coleman-Harbison, Alison Cronk, Elisabeth Eittreim, Phyllis Hunter, Tera Hunter, William Link, James Livingston, Julia Livingston, Gilda Morales, Vicki L. Ruiz, Susan Schrepfer, Bonnie Smith, Melissa Stein, Margaret Sumner, Jessica Unger, and Anne Valk. Jacqueline Castledine and Julia Sandy-Bailey worked closely with us in finding documents and creating the Document Projects. Without them, this would not be a docutext.

We would particularly like to applaud the many hardworking and creative people at Bedford/St. Martin's who guided us through the labyrinthine process of writing a textbook from scratch. No one was more important to us than the indefatigable and unflappable Sara Wise, our developmental editor. We are also deeply grateful to Patricia Rossi, who first persuaded us to undertake this project. Joan Feinberg had the vision that guided us through every page of this book. We could not have had a better team than Denise Wydra, Mary Dougherty, William Lombardo, Jane Knetzger, Christina Horn, Jennifer Jovin, Katherine Bates, Amy Whitaker, Jenna Bookin Barry, Daniel McDonough, and Arrin Kaplan. They also enlisted Naomi Kornhauser, Charlotte Miller, Linda McLatchie, Heidi Hood, Rob Heinrich, Shannon Hunt, John Reisbord, and Michelle McSweeney to provide invaluable service. Finally, we would like to thank our friends and family who have been asking us these past years, "When will you be finished?" We are very pleased to be able to respond, "The time is now."

Nancy A. Hewitt and Steven F. Lawson

Adopters of **Exploring American Histories** and their students have access to abundant resources, including documents, presentation and testing materials, volumes in the acclaimed Bedford Series in History and Culture, and much more. For more information on the offerings described below, visit the book's catalog site at bedfordstmartins.com/hewittlawson/catalog, or contact your local Bedford/St. Martin's sales representative.

## Get the Right Version for Your Class

To accommodate different course lengths and course budgets, *Exploring American Histories* is available in several different formats, including three-hole punched loose-leaf Budget books versions and e-books, which are available at a substantial discount.

- Combined edition (chapters 1–29)—available in paperback, loose-leaf, and e-book formats
- Volume 1: To 1877 (chapters 1–14)—available in paperback, loose-leaf, and e-book formats
- Volume 2: Since 1865 (chapters 14–29)—available in paperback, loose-leaf, and e-book formats

**Assign the online, interactive Bedford x-Book.**
With all the content of the print book—plus integrated LearningCurve and the 29 extra Document Projects, some with audio or video—the *x-Book for Exploring American Histories* features a robust search engine, navigation tools, easy ways to take and share notes, and interactive exercises. And with fast ways to rearrange chapters and add new pages, sections, or links, it lets teachers build just the right book for their course.

**Let students choose their e-book format.** Students can purchase the downloadable *Bedford e-Book to Go for Exploring American Histories* from our Web site or find other PDF versions of the e-book at our publishing partners' sites: CourseSmart, Barnes & Noble NookStudy; Kno; CafeScribe; or Chegg.

## Assign LearningCurve So That Your Students Come to Class Prepared

As described in the preface and on the inside front cover, students purchasing new books receive access to Learning Curve for *Exploring American Histories*, an online learning tool designed to help students rehearse content at their own pace in a nonthreatening, game-like environment. The feedback for wrong answers provides instructional coaching and sends students back to the book for review. Students answer as many questions as necessary to reach a target score, with repeated chances to revisit material they haven't mastered. Assigning LearningCurve is easy for instructors, and the reporting features help instructors track overall class trends and spot topics that are giving students trouble.

## Send Students to Free Online Resources

The book's companion site at bedfordstmartins.com/hewittlawson gives students a way to read, write, and study by providing plentiful quizzes and activities, study aids, and history research and writing help.

**FREE Online Study Guide.** Available at the companion site, this popular resource provides students with quizzes and activities for each chapter, including multiple-choice self-tests that focus on important concepts; flash cards that test students' knowledge of key terms; timeline activities that emphasize causal relationships; and map quizzes intended to strengthen students' geography skills. Instructors can monitor students' progress through an online Quiz Gradebook or receive email updates.

**FREE Research, Writing, and Anti-plagiarism Advice.** Available at the companion site, Bedford's **History Research and Writing Help** includes **History Research and Reference Sources**, with links to history-related databases, indexes, and journals; **More Sources and How to Format a History Paper**, with clear advice on how to integrate primary and secondary sources into research papers and how to cite and format sources correctly; **Build a Bibliography**, a simple Web-based tool known as The Bedford Bibliographer that generates bibliographies in four commonly used documentation styles; and **Tips on Avoiding Plagiarism**, an online tutorial that reviews the consequences of plagiarism and features exercises to help students practice integrating sources and recognize acceptable summaries.

## Take Advantage of Instructor Resources

Bedford/St. Martin's has developed a rich array of teaching resources for this book and for this course. They range from lecture and presentation materials and assessment tools to course management options. Most can be downloaded or ordered at bedfordstmartins.com/hewittlawson/catalog.

***HistoryClass* for *Exploring American Histories.*** *History-Class*, a Bedford/St. Martin's Online Course Space, puts the online resources available with this textbook in one convenient and completely customizable course space. There you and your students can access the interactive x-book; video clips, maps, images, documents, and links; chapter review quizzes; and research and writing help. In *HistoryClass* you can get all our premium content and tools, which you can assign, rearrange, and mix with your own resources. *HistoryClass* also includes LearningCurve, Bedford/St. Martin's adaptive tool for quizzing to learn, and the additional Document Project for each chapter. For more information, visit yourhistoryclass.com.

**Instructor's Resource Manual.** The instructor's manual offers both experienced and first-time instructors tools for preparing lectures and running discussions. It includes chapter-review material, teaching strategies, and a guide to chapter-specific supplements available for the text, plus suggestions on how to get the most out of LearningCurve.

**Computerized Test Bank.** The test bank includes a mix of carefully crafted multiple-choice, short-answer, and essay questions for each chapter. It also contains the Interpret the Evidence and Put It in Context questions from the text-book and model answers for each. All questions appear in Microsoft Word format and in easy-to-use test bank software that allows instructors to add, edit, re-sequence, and print questions and answers. Instructors can also export questions into a variety of formats, including WebCT and Blackboard.

***The Bedford Lecture Kit*: PowerPoint Maps, Images, Lecture Outlines, and i>clicker Content.** Look good and save time with *The Bedford Lecture Kit*. These presentation materials are downloadable individually from the Instructor Resources tab at bedfordstmartins.com/hewittlawson/catalog and are available on *The Bedford Lecture Kit* **Instructor's Resource CD-ROM.** They provide ready-made and fully customizable PowerPoint multimedia presentations that include lecture outlines with embedded maps, figures, and selected images from the textbook and extra background for instructors. Also available are maps and selected images in JPEG and PowerPoint formats; content for i>clicker, a classroom response system, in Microsoft Word and PowerPoint formats; the Instructor's Resource Manual in Microsoft Word format; and outline maps in

PDF format for quizzing or handing out. All files are suit-able for copying onto transparency acetates.

**Make History—Free Documents, Maps, Images, and Web Sites.** *Make History* combines the best Web resources with hundreds of maps and images, to make it simple to find the source material you need. Browse the collection of thousands of resources by course or by topic, date, and type. Each item has been carefully chosen and helpfully annotated to make it easy to find exactly what you need. Available at bedfordstmartins.com/makehistory.

***America in Motion*: Video Clips for U.S. History.** Set history in motion with *America in Motion*, an instructor DVD containing dozens of short digital movie files of events in twentieth-century American history. From the wreckage of the battleship *Maine*, to FDR's fireside chats, to Oliver North testifying before Congress, *America in Motion* engages students with dynamic scenes from key events and challenges them to think critically. All files are classroom-ready, edited for brevity, and easily inte-grated with PowerPoint or other presentation software for electronic lectures or assignments. An accompanying guide provides each clip's historical context, ideas for use, and suggested questions.

**Videos and Multimedia.** A wide assortment of videos and multimedia CD-ROMs on various topics in U.S. history is available to qualified adopters through your Bedford/St. Martin's sales representative.

# Package and Save Your Students Money

For information on free packages and discounts up to 50%, visit bedfordstmartins.com/hewittlawson/catalog or contact your local Bedford/St. Martin's sales representative.

**Online Document Projects for *Exploring American Histories.*** A complete set of additional 29 Document Projects—one per chapter—is available to provide students with more opportunities to work with primary sources. Each set mirrors the pedagogy in the text with overviews, headnotes, and Interpret the Evidence and Put It in Context questions, and many sets include audio and video sources. Topics include loyalists in the American Revolution, abolitionist debates, women's liberation, and the Reagan Revolution. Automatically available online to all students who purchase the x-Book or *HistoryClass* and free when packaged with the text.

**The Bedford Series in History and Culture.** More than 150 titles in this highly praised series combine first-rate scholarship, historical narrative, and important primary documents for undergraduate courses. Each book is brief, inexpensive, and focused on a specific topic or period. For a complete list of titles, visit bedfordstmartins.com/history/series. Package discounts are available.

***Rand McNally Historical Atlas of American History.*** This collection of more than 84 full-color maps illustrates key events and eras, from early exploration, settlement, expansion, and immigration to U.S. involvement in wars abroad and on U.S. soil. Introductory pages for each section include a brief overview, timelines, graphs, and photographs to quickly establish a historical context. Available for $3.00 when packaged with the print text.

***Maps in Context: A Workbook for American History.*** Written by historical cartography expert Gerald A. Danzer (University of Illinois at Chicago), this skill-building workbook helps students comprehend essential connections between geographic literacy and historical understanding. Organized to correspond to the typical U.S. survey course, *Maps in Context* presents a wealth of map-centered projects and convenient pop quizzes that give students hands-on experience working with maps. Available free when packaged with the print text.

***The Bedford Glossary for U.S. History.*** This handy supplement for the survey course gives students historically contextualized definitions for hundreds of terms—from *abolitionism* to *zoot suit*—that they will encounter in lectures, reading, and exams. Available free when packaged with the print text.

***U.S. History Matters: A Student Guide to U.S. History Online.*** This resource, written by Kelly Schrum, Alan Gevinson, and the late Roy Rosenzweig (all of George Mason University), provides an illustrated and annotated guide to 250 of the most useful Web sites for student research in U.S. history as well as advice on evaluating and using Internet sources. This essential guide is based on the acclaimed "History Matters" Web site developed by the American Social History Project and the Center for History and New Media. Available free when packaged with the print text.

**Trade Books.** Titles published by sister companies Hill and Wang; Farrar, Straus and Giroux; Henry Holt and Company; St. Martin's Press; Picador; and Palgrave Macmillan are available at a 50% discount when packaged with Bedford/St. Martin's textbooks. For more information, visit bedfordstmartins.com/tradeup.

***A Pocket Guide to Writing in History.*** This portable and affordable reference tool by Mary Lynn Rampolla, now also available as a searchable e-book, provides reading, writing, and research advice useful to students in all history courses. Concise yet comprehensive advice on approaching typical history assignments, developing critical-reading skills, writing effective history papers, conducting research, using and documenting sources, and avoiding plagiarism—enhanced with practical tips and examples throughout—have made this slim reference a best seller. Package discounts are available.

***A Student's Guide to History.*** This complete guide to success in any history course provides the practical help students need to be effective. In addition to introducing students to the nature of the discipline, author Jules Benjamin teaches a wide range of skills from preparing for exams to approaching common writing assignments, and he explains the research and documentation process with plentiful examples. Package discounts are available.

***Going to the Source: The Bedford Reader in American History.*** Developed by Victoria Bissell Brown and Timothy J. Shannon, this reader's strong pedagogical framework helps students learn how to ask fruitful questions in order to evaluate documents effectively and develop critical-reading skills. The reader's wide variety of chapter topics that complement the survey course and its rich diversity of sources—from personal letters to political cartoons—provoke students' interest as it teaches them the skills they need to successfully interrogate historical sources. Package discounts are available.

***America Firsthand.*** With its distinctive focus on ordinary people, this primary documents reader, by Anthony Marcus, John M. Giggie, and David Burner, offers a remarkable range of perspectives on American history from those who lived it. Popular Points of View sections expose students to different perspectives on a specific event or topic, and Visual Portfolios invite analysis of the visual record. Package discounts are available.

## Explore Other Docutexts from Bedford/St. Martin's

Bedford/St. Martin's has been a leader in pioneering new ways to bring primary sources into the undergraduate classroom, beginning with the Bedford Series in History and

Culture, described above. The "docutext" format of *Exploring American Histories,* which combines a brief narrative with themed collections of written and visual sources, represents another innovation in making documents accessible for students. Docutexts authored by leading historians are now available from Bedford for a variety of history courses.

**World History Survey.**  Find out about *Ways of the World: A Brief Global History with Sources,* by Robert W. Strayer, at bedfordstmartins.com/strayersources/catalog.

**African American History.**  Find out about *Freedom on My Mind: A History of African Americans, with Documents,* by Deborah Gray White, Mia Bay, and Waldo E. Martin Jr., at bedfordstmartins.com/graywhite/catalog.

**U.S. Women's History.**  Find out about *Through Women's Eyes: An American History with Documents,* by Ellen Carol DuBois and Lynn Dumenil, at bedfordstmartins.com/duboisdumenil/catalog.

**Native American History.**  Find out about *First Peoples: A Documentary Survey of American Indian History,* by Colin G. Calloway, at bedfordstmartins.com/calloway/catalog.

**Twentieth-Century European History.**  Find out about *Europe in the Contemporary World, 1900 to the Present: A Narrative History with Documents,* by Bonnie G. Smith, at bedfordstmartins.com/smitheurope/catalog.

# Brief Contents

# Contents

## 14
## Emancipations and Reconstructions
**1863–1877**   424

## 15
## Frontier Encounters
**1865–1896**   458

# 24
## The Opening of the Cold War
**1945–1954**   756

# 25
## Troubled Innocence
**1950–1961**   788

# Maps, Figures, and Tables

## Maps

# Figures and Tables

# How to Use This Book

## Start by reading the narrative and using the chapter tools to help you focus on what's important.

**LEARNINGCurve**
Check what you know.
bedfordstmartins.com/hewittlawson/LC

> Scan the **chapter outline** for a preview of the chapter's big topics and themes.

The Granger Collection, New York

The Granger Collection, New York

Sawmill in Terraville, South Dakota, 1888.

Shoe-factory worker in Lynn, Massachusetts, 1895.

> As you read, pay attention to the **boldfaced key terms**, which highlight important concepts you'll likely see on an exam. All terms are defined in the glossary of Key Terms at the end of the book.

oslavery document. Some Garrisonians a
work of the **underground railroad**, a se
ivists who assisted fugitives fleeing ensla

In 1835 Sarah and Angelina Grimké j
d soon began lecturing for the organiza
rominent South Carolina planter, they

new leisure pursuits. Many joined colleagues at restaurants, the theater, or sporting events. They also attended plays and lectures with their wives, visited museums, and took their children to the circus.

### REVIEW & RELATE

- Why did American cities become larger and more diverse in the first half of the nineteenth century?

- What values and beliefs did the emerging American middle class embrace?

> At the end of each major section, answer the **Review & Relate** questions to check your understanding of key concepts.

**LEARNINGCurve** bedfordstmartins.com/hewittlawson/LC

> Then log on to **LearningCurve** to review the section you've just read. LearningCurve lets you move at your own pace and earn points as you go.

# Use the Chapter Review to draw connections across all the sections of the narrative and identify significant historical developments.

Return to **LearningCurve** to review chapter material.

Test your knowledge of important concepts from the **Key Terms** list. See if you can not only define each term but also describe its significance.

**LEARNINGCurve**
Check what you know.
bedfordstmartins.com/hewittlawson/LC

## Chapter Review

Online Study Guide ▶ bedfordstmartins.com/hewittlawson

### KEY TERMS

separate spheres (p. 331)
deskilling (p. 333)
nativists (p. 337)
Second Great Awakening (p. 339)
temperance (p. 340)
transcendentalism (p. 341)
utopian societies (p. 344)
*Appeal . . . to the Colored Citizens* (p. 346)
Anti-Slavery Society (AASS) (p. 346)
(p. 346)
(p. 348)

Answer the **Review & Relate** questions, which repeat the chapter's end-of-section comprehension prompts.

### REVIEW & RELATE

1. Why did American cities become larger and more diverse in the first half of the nineteenth century?
2. What values and beliefs did the emerging American middle class embrace?
3. How and why did American manufacturing change over the course of the first half of the nineteenth century?
4. How did Northerners respond to the hard times that followed the panic of 1837? How did responses to the crisis vary by class, ethnicity, and religion?
5. What impact did the Second Great Awakening have in the North?
6. What new religious organizations and viewpoints emerged in the first half of the nineteenth century, *outside* of Protestant evangelical denominations?
7. How did the temperance movement reflect the range of tactics and participants involved in reform during the 1830s and 1840s?
8. What connections can you identify between utopian communities and mainstream reform movements in the first half of the nineteenth century?
9. How did the American Anti-Slavery Society differ from earlier abolitionist organizations?
10. How did conflicts over gender and race shape the development of the abolitionist movement in the 1830s and 1840s?

### TIMELINE OF EVENTS

| | |
|---|---|
| 1820–1850 | Size, number, and diversity of northern cities grow; immigration surges |
| 1823 | Textile factory town built in Lowell, Massachusetts |
| 1826 | American Temperance Society founded |
| 1827 | First workingmen's political party founded |
| 1829 | David Walker publishes *Appeal . . . to the Colored Citizens* |
| 1830 | Joseph Smith publishes *The Book of Mormon* |
| September 1830 | Charles Grandison Finney brings Second Great Awakening to Rochester, New York |
| 1833 | William Lloyd Garrison founds American Anti-Slavery Society (AASS) |
| 1837–1842 | Panic of 1837 |
| 1839 | American Anti-Slavery Society splits over the role of women in the society |
| 1840 | Liberty Party formed |
| | World Anti-Slavery Convention, L |
| 1842 | Amy Post helps found the Wester Anti-Slavery Society |
| 1843 | William Miller predicts Second Coming of Christ |
| 1844 | Congress funds construction of the first telegraph line |
| May 1844 | Anti-immigrant violence rocks Philadelphia |
| 1845 | Frederick Douglass publishes *Narrative of the Life of Frederick Douglass* |
| | Margaret Fuller publishes *Woman in the Nineteenth Century* |
| 1845–1846 | Irish potato famine |
| 1846 | Henry David Thoreau publishes *Civil Disobedience* |

Review the **Timeline of Events**, which shows the relationship among chapter events.

Visit the **free Online Study Guide**, which provides more quizzes and activities to help you master the chapter content.

# Apply these principles to your analysis of the chapter's primary sources.

Democracy cannot be based upon coercion, democracy must be based on convergence. Converge and align with us at #NatGat #occupy #OANatGat.

What will they be able to say about the author? How will they interpret the meaning of these sentences? Will they understand the abbreviations that have become a part of our everyday language?

A tweet—like a blog, a speech on YouTube, or a video of a protest—is a primary source, an original document or artifact created at or near the time of an event by people participating in or observing it. Different types of primary sources exist from different periods of history. In the seventeenth century and earlier, drawings, paintings, stone carvings, and relics were as plentiful as written sources are today. Printed texts and handwritten letters became more available from the eighteenth century on, while photographs, newspapers, typewritten letters, and recordings are widely available from the mid-nineteenth century through the twentieth and twenty-first centuries.

Many primary sources are produced by official institutions, while others are created by ordinary people who wrote and kept diaries and letters, took pictures, participated in oral interviews, or sent e-mails. Some documents such as newspapers provide information from official sources alongside letters, interviews, articles, and opinions offered by editors and political cartoonists. As with future historians who try to decode Twitter, historians have always had to make sense of documents filled with abbreviations and peculiarities of language and to decipher handwriting styles as puzzling as digital shorthand.

Historians use a wealth of primary sources to build an interpretation of the past and to set that interpretation alongside the work of other scholars. History refers to both the uncovering of facts about the past and interpretations of it. Besides presenting facts, then, this textbook provides interpretations of American history constructed by the book's authors that are based on their own primary research as well as the work of other historians. But it also offers a large array of primary sources, described on the next several pages, from which you can create your own interpretations and compare them with those offered by the authors.

To guide your analysis, begin by asking several basic questions that can be succinctly thought of as the five Ws: Who? What? Where? When? Why?

- **Who** is the author of the document and who is the intended audience?
- **What** kind of source is it—written, visual, official, unofficial—and what are the main ideas or opinions presented?
- **Where** was it created and how might that shape its meaning?
- **When** was it produced and how close to the event being recorded?
- **Why** was it created and how does that influence your interpretation of it?

Because history is interpretive, the kind of questions you ask will help shape the answers you come up with. The more questions you explore, the richer the history you produce will be.

Keep in mind that this book's narrative text and documents work together, each reinforcing the other. While the narrative helps place the documents in a larger context, the documents provide for more active engagement with an event or issue. Rather than merely receiving a collection of information, you will be able to participate in shaping an account of the past. If you consider all the primary sources in a chapter together, including those in the Document Project, you can begin to understand how historians assess and piece together diverse sources of evidence to forge a larger narrative about American history. The next pages introduce you to the types of documents you will be working with in this book.

# Get to work exploring the documents.

## Individual documents are easy to find and well integrated into every chapter.

> Red **Explore** boxes tell you where to find the source and where to return to the text to continue the story.

the issue opposing the measure. John C. Calhoun, a proslavery senator from South Carolina, refused to support any compromise that allowed Congress to decide the fate of slavery in the western territories. Meanwhile William H. Seward, an antislavery Whig senator from New York, proclaimed that in all good conscience he could not support a compromise that forced Northerners to help hunt down fugitives from slavery. Daniel Webster, a Massachusetts Whig and an elder statesman, appealed to his fellow senators to support the compromise in order to preserve the Union, but Congress adjourned with the fate of California undecided.

**Explore**

See Document 12.2 for Calhoun's final attempt to reject a compromise.

Before the Senate reconvened in the fall of 1850, however, the political landscape changed in unexpected ways. Henry Clay retired in the spring of 1850, leaving the Capitol with his last great legislative effort unfinished. On March 31, Calhoun died; his absence from the Senate made compromise more likely. In July, President Taylor died unexpectedly, and his vice president, Millard Fillmore of Buffalo, New York, was elevated to the presidency. Fillmore then appointed Webster as secretary of state, removing him from the Senate as well.

In September 1850, with President Fillmore's support, a younger cohort of senators and representatives steered the **Compromise of 1850** through Congress, one clause at a time, thereby allowing legislators to support only those parts of the compromise they found palatable. In the end, all the provisions passed, and Fillmore quickly signed the bills into law. California entered the Union as a free state, and John C. Frémont entered Congress as one of that state's first two senators. The Compromise of 1850, like the Missouri Compromise thirty years earlier, fended off a sectional crisis, but it also signaled future problems. Would popular sovereignty prevail when later territories sought admission to the Union, and would Northerners abide by a fugitive slave law that called on them to aid directly in the capture of runaway slaves?

### The Fugitive Slave Act Inspires Northern Protest

The fugitive slave laws of 1793 and 1824 mandated that all states aid in apprehending and returning runaway slaves to their owners. The **Fugitive Slave Act of 1850** was different in two important respects. First, it eliminated jury trials for alleged fugitives. Second, the law required individual citizens, not just state officials, to help return runaways or

**DOCUMENT 12.2**

### John C. Calhoun | On the Compromise of 1850, 1850

California's application for statehood in 1849 prompted another crisis over slavery. Southerners feared that admitting California as a free state would tip the balance in Congress against them. Senator Henry Clay tried to broker a compromise that would admit California as a free state but toughen the fugitive slave law. Amid vigorous congressional debate, South Carolina senator John C. Calhoun insisted that slavery be preserved. A colleague read Calhoun's address for the aging and ill senator. Calhoun's death a few weeks later helped pave the way for final passage of the Compromise of 1850.

**Explore**

How can the Union be saved? To this I answer, there is but one way by which it can be, and that is, by adopting such measures as will satisfy the States belonging to the Southern section that they can remain in the Union consistently with their honor and their safety. . . .

. . . The South asks for justice, simple justice, and less she ought not to take. She has no compromise to offer but the Constitution, and no concession or surrender to make. She has already surrendered so much that she has little left to surrender. Such a settlement would go to the root of the evil, and remove all cause of discontent, by satisfying the South that she could remain honorably and safely in the Union, and thereby restore the harmony and fraternal feelings between the sections which existed anterior to the Missouri agitation. . . .

But can this be done? Yes, easily; not by the weaker party, for it can of itself do nothing—not even protect itself—but by the stronger. The North has only to will it to accomplish it—to do justice by conceding to the South an equal right in the acquired territory, and to do her duty by causing the stipulations relative to fugitive slaves to be faithfully fulfilled—to cease the agitation of the slave question, and to provide for the insertion of a provision in the Constitution, by an amendment, which will restore to the South in substance the power she possessed of protecting herself, before the equilibrium between the sections was destroyed by the action of this Government. There will be no difficulty in devising such a provision—one that will protect the South, and which at the same time will improve and strengthen the Government, instead of impairing and weakening it.

Source: *The Congressional Globe*, 31st Cong., 2nd Sess. (1850), 453, 455.

**Interpret the Evidence**

- Calhoun objects to the Compromise of 1850 because it does not sufficiently protect southern rights. Which rights does he think need protection, and why does he think those rights are in jeopardy?
- Calhoun wants to regain the "harmony and fraternal feelings" between the sections that existed before "the Missouri agitation." Why does he pinpoint the Missouri Compromise as the moment when sectional divisions took hold?

**Put It in Context**

What developments in the 1840s led Calhoun and other southern leaders to fear that the South was becoming weaker, at least politically, compared to the North? Would northern senators have agreed?

else risk being fined or imprisoned. The act angered many Northerners who believed that the federal government had gone too far in protecting the rights of slaveholders and thereby aroused sympathy for the abolitionist cause.

Before 1850, the most well-known individuals aiding fugitives were free blacks such as David Ruggles in New

York City; Jermaine Loguen in Syracuse, New York; and, after his own successful escape, Frederick Douglass in Rochester, New York. Their main allies in this work were white Quakers such as Amy and Isaac Post in Rochester; Thomas Garrett in Chester County, Pennsylvania; and Levi and Catherine Coffin in Newport, Indiana. The work was

> Two **Interpret the Evidence** questions help you analyze the source.

> A **Put It in Context** question helps you connect the primary source to the larger historical narrative.

**Annotated documents** help you examine sources closely by breaking them down into smaller components.

**Annotations** direct you to points of interest—either specific text passages or visual details—to help you analyze the document and to model what to look for when you approach similar types of documents on your own.

---

**DOCUMENT 14.4**

### Sharecropping Agreement, 1870

Because Congress did not generally provide freedpeople with land, African Americans lacked the capital to start their own farms. At the same time, plantation owners needed labor to plant and harvest their crops for market. Out of mutual necessity, white plantation owners entered into sharecropping contracts with blacks to work their farms in exchange for a portion of the crop, such as the following contract between Willis P. Bocock and several of his former slaves. Bocock owned Waldwick Plantation in Marengo County, Alabama.

**Explore**

What are the farmers' responsibilities?

Why would Bocock want to clarify that his laborers would work equally hard throughout the year?

How might putting a lien on crops for debts owed create difficulties for the black farmer?

Contract made the 3rd day of January in the year 1870 between us the free people who have signed this paper of one part, and our employer, Willis P. Bocock, of the other part. We agree to take charge of and cultivate for the year 1870, a portion of land, say [left blank] acres or thereabouts, to be laid off to us by our employer on his plantation, and to tend the same well in the usual crops, in such proportions as we and he may agree upon. We are to furnish the necessary labor, say an average hand to every 15 acres in the crops, making in all average hands; and are to have all proper work done, ditching, fencing, repairing, etc., as well as cultivating and saving the crops of all kinds, so as to put and keep the land we occupy and tend in good order for cropping, and to make a good crop ourselves; and to do our fair share of job work about the place. . . . We are to be responsible for the good conduct of ourselves, our hands, and families, and agree that all shall be respectful to employer, owners, and manager, honest, industrious, and careful about every thing, and shall not interrupt any thing about the place, working as industriously the last part of the year as the first; and then our employer agrees that he and his manager shall treat us kindly, and help us to study our interest and do our duty. If any hand or family proves to be of bad character, or dishonest, or lazy, or disobedient, or any way unsuitable our employer or manager has the right, and we have the right, to have such turned off. . . .

For the labor and services of ourselves and hands rendered as above stated, we are to have one third part of all the crops, or their net-proceeds, made and secured, or prepared for market by our force. . . .

We are to be furnished by our employer through his manager with provisions if we call for them: not over one peck of meal or corn, and $3\frac{1}{2}$ pounds of meat or its equivalent per week, for every 15 acres of land or average hand, to be charged to us at fair market prices.

And whatever may be due by us, or our hands to our employer for provisions or any thing else, during the year, is to be a lien on our share of the crops, and is to be retained by him out of the same before we receive our part.

Source: Waldwick Plantation Records, 1834–1971, LPR174, box 1, folder 9, Alabama Department of Archives and History.

**Put It in Context**

Why would free blacks and poor whites be willing to enter into such a contract?

All annotated documents conclude with **Put It in Context** questions that ask you to figure out how the document fits in—or doesn't fit in—with the narrative you're reading.

---

**DOCUMENT 11.4**

### Drunkard's Home, 1850

Temperance societies undertook a variety of activities to publici[ze] and parades were popular venues, as were newspapers and boo[ks.] *Temperance Offering*, an 1850 publication of the Sons of Temper[ance.] 1842, the Sons of Temperance was one of the oldest temperance [societies,] mutual aid society that offered members life insurance, funeral b[enefits.]

**Explore**

How does the father's drinking seem to affect the family's economic situation?

In this illustration, what is the source of the father's violence?

How[w] me[n]

The National Temperance Offering, and Sons and Daughters of Temperance Gift (PS1265.N3 1850), University of Virginia Library

**Put It in Context**

What moral arguments did members of the temperance movement use to support their cause?

**"Two Views" comparison documents** present contrasting or complementary perspectives on a single topic so that you can form your own interpretation.

## Life in the Mills: Two Views

In the 1820s, the textile mills of Lowell, Massachusetts, provided the daughters of local farmers a way to contribute to their family incomes and experience some adventure. Soon, however, a slowing economy led to reduced wages, longer hours, and demands for increased productivity. The Lowell workers organized to protest these changes and went on strike several times during the late 1820s and the 1830s. The first selection below is from an 1844 edition of *The Lowell Offering*, a magazine to which mill workers contributed stories and poems. Factory owners controlled the content of the magazine to ensure an idealized vision of life in the mills. Still, the letter from "Susan" below does highlight the physical toll of industrial labor. Susan was a pseudonym for Harriet Farley, a weaver and the editor of *The Lowell Offering*. The selection at right is by Harriet Robinson, who entered the mills at age ten in 1834. She published a memoir in 1898 in which she recalls the growing dissatisfaction of the women workers and her critical role in a strike in 1836.

**Explore**

### 11.1 Letter from a Lowell Factory Worker, 1844

It makes my feet ache and swell to stand so much, but I suppose I shall get accustomed to that too. The girls generally wear old shoes about their work, and you know nothing is easier; but they almost all say that when they have worked here a year or two they have to procure shoes a size or two larger than before they came. The right hand, which is the one used in stopping and starting the loom, becomes larger than the left; but in other respects the factory is not detrimental to a young girl's appearance. Here they look delicate, but not sickly; they laugh at those who are much exposed, and get pretty brown; but I, for one, had rather be brown than pure white. I never saw so many pretty looking girls as there are here. Though the number of men is small in proportion there are many marriages here, and a great deal of courting. I will tell you of this last sometime. . . .

You ask if the work is not disagreeable. Not when one is accustomed to it. It tried my patience sadly at first, and does now when it does not run well; but, in general, I like it very much. It is easy to do, and does not require very violent exertion, as much of our farm work does.

You also ask how I get along with the girls here. Very well indeed.

and workingmen started joining forces throughout the North to advocate for principles of liberty and equality. Self-educated artisans like Thomas Skidmore of New York City argued for the redistribution of property and the abolition of inheritance to equalize wealth in the nation. However, most workingmen's parties focused on more practical proposals: government distribution of free land in the West, the abolition of compulsory militia service and imprisonment for debt, public funding for education, and the regulation of banks and corporations. Although the

**Explore**

### 11.2 Harriet Robinson | Reflections on the 1836 Lowell Mills Strike, 1898

My own recollection of this first strike (or "turn out" as it was called) is very vivid. I worked in a lower room, where I had heard the proposed strike fully, if not vehemently, discussed; I had been an ardent listener to what was said against this attempt at "oppression" on the part of the corporation, and naturally I took sides with the strikers. When the day came on which the girls were to turn out, those in the upper rooms started first, and so many of them left that our mill was at once shut down. Then, when the girls in my room stood irresolute, uncertain what to do, asking each other, "Would you?" or "Shall we turn out?" and not one of them having the courage to lead off, *I*, who began to think they would not go out, after all their talk, became impatient, and started on ahead, saying, with childish bravado, "I don't care what you do, I am going to turn out, whether any one else does or not"; and I marched out, and was followed by the others.

As I looked back at the long line that followed me, I was more proud than I have ever been since at any success I may have achieved, and more proud than I shall ever be again until my own beloved State gives to its women citizens the right of suffrage.

The agent of the corporation where I then worked took some small revenges on the supposed ringleaders; on the principle of sending the weaker to the wall, my mother [a landlady] was turned away from her boarding-house, that functionary saying, "Mrs. Hanson, you could not prevent the older girls from turning out, but your daughter is a child, and *her* you could control."

It is hardly necessary to say that so far as results were concerned this strike did no good. The dissatisfaction of the operatives subsided, or burned itself out, and though the authorities did not accede to their demands, the majority returned to their work, and the corporation went on cutting down the wages.

Source: Harriet H. Robinson, *Loom and Spindle; or, Life among the Early Mill Girls* (New York: Thomas Y. Crowell, 1898), 84–86.

**Interpret the Evidence** questions help you analyze the sources.

**Interpret the Evidence**
- How did life on the farm differ from life in the factory? How does "Susan" describe her own adjustment to industrial work?
- What connections does Robinson make between the strike and the larger social and political context of 1830s Massachusetts? How does she see herself and her actions?

**Put It in Context**

Were "Susan" and Robinson typical factory workers in this period? Why or why not?

Trades Union was established later that year, with delegates representing more than twenty-five thousand workers across the North. These organizations aided skilled workers but refused admission to women and unskilled men. panic of 1837, the common plight of workers became clearer. But the economic crisis made unified action nearly impossible as individuals sought to hold on to what little they had by any means available.

# A **Document Project** concludes each chapter.

Each project provides multiple perspectives on a particular issue or development along with an **introduction** and **questions** to guide you through the process of interpretation. The chapter itself offers the background material for your interpretation.

and grasses that would have kept the earth from eroding and turning into dust. Instead, dust storms brought life to a grinding halt, blocking out the midday sun. See Document Project 22: The Depression in Rural America, page 712.

As the storms continued through the 1930s, most residents—approximately 75 percent—remained on

Red **cross-references** at the relevant point in the chapter direct you to the chapter's Document Project.

### DOCUMENT 22.6
## The Life of a White Sharecropper, 1938

In 1936 workers in the WPA's Federal Writers Project began the Folklore Project. Interviewers spoke with thousands of ordinary individuals to document their home lives, education, occupations, political and religious views, and the impact of the Great Depression on their families. Folklore Project worker Claude Dunnagan collected the following story from a white sharecropping family in Longtown, North Carolina.

I guess we been hard luck renters all our lives—me and Morrison both. They was ten young'uns in my family, and I was next to the youngest. We had it awful hard. . . . We went to Yadkin County and rented an old rundown farm for a share of what we could raise. The crops wasn't any good that year, the landlord came and got what we had raised and had the auctioneers come and sell our tools and furniture. They was a bunch of people at the sale that day from all around. I was standin' there watchin' the man sell the things when I saw a good lookin' man in overalls lookin' toward me. He watched me all durin' the sale and I knew what he was thinkin'. That was the first time I ever saw Allison. I reckon he fell in love with me right off, for we was married a few days later. Allison didn't have no true father. His mother wasn't married, and he was raised up by his kin folks. Then we moved to a little farm near Longtown, about ten miles away. The owner said we could have three-fourths of what we raised. The first two years the crops turned out pretty good so we could pay off the landlord and buy a little furniture . . . a bed and table and some chairs. Then the first baby came on. That was Hildreth. He's out in the field workin' now, suckerin' [removing sprouts] tobacco. . . . By that time, we was able to get a cow, and that came in good, for the baby was awful thin and weak. . . .

Hildreth was only six, but he could help a lot, pullin' and tyin' the tobacco, and helpin' hang it in the barn. We got out more tobacco that year than any other, but when we took it to market in Winston, they wasn't payin' but about twelve cents a pound for the best grade, so when we give the landlord his share and paid the fertilizer bill, we didn't have enough left to pay the doctor and store bill. We didn't know what we was goin' to do durin' the winter. Allison had raised a few vegetables and apples, so we canned what we could and traded the rest for some cotton cloth up at the store so the children would have something to wear that winter. Allison got a job helpin' build a barn for a neighbor, but it didn't last but two days. The neighbor gave him two second hand pairs of overalls for the work. . . .

Things are a lot better for the renter today than in the past. It used to be we couldn't get enough to eat and wear. Now we got a cow, a hog, and some chickens. Allison bought a second-hand car and every Sunday afternoon we ride somewhere. It's the only time we ever get away from home.

The landlord gives us five-sixths of what we raise, so we get along pretty good when the crops are fair. Of course we have to furnish the fertilizer and livestock. This year we had seven barns of tobacco and four acres of corn. Wheat turned out pretty good, too. We raised forty-three bushels, and I hear the price is going to be fair at the roller mill. I canned about all our extra fruits and vegetables. I reckon we still got about a hundred cans in the pantry.

Source: Library of Congress, Manuscript Division, WPA Federal Writers Project Collection.

### DOCUMENT 22.5
## Ann Marie Low | Dust Bowl Diary, 1934

When massive dust storms swept through the Midwest beginning in the early 1930s, they blew away the topsoil of a once productive farm region and created hazardous living conditions. Residents needed to clean and wash repetitively to perform even simple daily tasks. Ann Marie Low, a young woman living with her family in southeastern North Dakota, describes in her diary the monotony and difficulty of life in the Dust Bowl.

*May 21, 1934, Monday . . .*
Saturday Dad, Bud, and I planted an acre of potatoes. There was so much dirt in the air I couldn't see Bud only a few feet in front of me. Even the air in the house was just a haze. In the evening the wind died down, and Cap came to take me to the movie. We joked about how hard it is to get cleaned up enough to go anywhere.

The newspapers report that on May 10 there was such a strong wind the experts in Chicago estimated 12,000,000 tons of Plains soil was dumped on that city. By the next day the sun was obscured in Washington, D.C., and ships 300 miles out at sea reported dust settling on their decks.

Sunday the dust wasn't so bad. Dad and I drove cattle to the Big Pasture. Then I churned butter and baked a ham, bread, and cookies for the men, as no telling when Mama will be back.

*May 30, 1934, Wednesday*
Ethel got along fine, so Mama left her at the hospital and came to Jamestown by train Friday. Dad took us both home.

The mess was incredible! Dirt had blown into the house all week and lay inches deep on everything. Every towel and curtain was just black. There wasn't a clean dish or cooking utensil. There was no food. Oh, there were eggs and milk and one loaf left of the bread I baked the weekend before. I looked in the cooler box down the well (our refrigerator) and found a little ham and butter. It was late, so Mama and I cooked some ham and eggs for the men's supper because that was all we could fix in a hurry. It turned out they had been living on ham and eggs for two days.

Mama was very tired. After she had fixed starter for bread, I insisted she go to bed and I'd do all the dishes. It took until 10 o'clock to wash all the dirty dishes. That's not wiping them—just washing them. The cupboards had to be washed out to have a clean place to put them.

Saturday was a busy day. Before starting breakfast I had to sweep and wash all the dirt off the kitchen and dining room floors, wash the stove, pancake griddle, and dining room table and chairs. There was cooking, baking, and churning to be done for those hungry men. Dad is 6 feet 4 inches tall, with a big frame. Bud is 6 feet 3 inches and almost as big-boned as Dad. We say feeding them is like filling a silo.

Mama couldn't make bread until I carried water to wash the bread mixer. I couldn't churn until the churn was washed and scalded. We just couldn't do anything until something was washed first. Every room had to have dirt almost shoveled out of it before we could wash floors and furniture.

We had no time to wash clothes, but it was necessary. I had to wash out the boiler, wash tubs, and the washing machine before we could use them. Then every towel, curtain, piece of bedding, and garment had to be taken outdoors to have as much dust as possible shaken out before washing. The cistern is dry, so I had to carry all the water we needed from the well.

Source: Ann Marie Low, *Dust Bowl Diary* (Lincoln: University of Nebraska Press, 1984), 96–97.

## DOCUMENT PROJECT 22

# The Depression in Rural America

During the 1930s, rural Americans' lives were devastated by the twin disasters of the Great Depression and, in the Great Plains, the most sustained drought in American history. But both problems only deepened the already difficult lives of many farmers. Agriculture in the South had long been dominated by sharecropping, a system that hampered crop diversification and left many African American tenant farmers vulnerable to exploitation by white landowners. In the Midwest, farmers had spent decades overgrazing pastures and exhausting the soil through overproduction. Prices dropped dramatically throughout the 1920s, and farmers were the only group whose incomes fell during that decade.

When the depression hit, many farmers did not have the resources to stay on their land, and farm foreclosures tripled in the early 1930s. Sharecroppers, tenant farmers, and former farm owners left their homes to find better opportunities, and a million people left the Great Plains alone. Most ended up as migrant agricultural laborers in farms and orchards on the West Coast. Feeling overrun by refugees, California passed a law in 1937 making it a misdemeanor to bring into California any indigent person who was not a state resident. This law remained in effect until 1941.

Under the New Deal, the federal government acted in a number of ways to relieve the plight of farmers around the country. The Agricultural Adjustment Act attempted to raise crop prices and stabilize agricultural incomes by encouraging farmers to cut production. The Farm Credit Act helped some farmers refinance mortgages at a lower rate, the Rural Electrification Administration brought electricity to farm areas previously without it, and the Soil Conservation Service advised farmers on how to properly cultivate their hillsides. The report of the Great Plains Committee (Document 22.10), another Roosevelt creation, details additional recommendations for helping the agricultural economy in the Midwest.

The following documents on the lives of farmers, sharecroppers, migrants, and labor organizers during the 1930s shed light on many aspects of the Great Depression. Consider what they reveal about the challenges faced by rural Americans and how different individuals and groups responded to those problems.

**DOCUMENT 22.7**

## Sharecropping Family in Washington County, Arkansas, 1935

The Resettlement Administration (later the Farm Security Administration) documented the plight of migrant farmworkers and sharecroppers in numerous photographs. The following photo, taken by the noted photojournalist Arthur Rothstein, depicts a sharecropper's wife and daughters in Washington County, Arkansas, in 1935.

**DOCUMENT 22.9**

## Frank Stokes | Let the Mexicans Organize, 1936

While union organizers made some gains in the industrial sector, they made little headway in the agricultural fields of California. Frank Stokes was a citrus grower who broke with his fellow farmers to support migrant labor organizing. In the following selection, Stokes argues in favor of unionization among migrant Mexican farmworkers.

The Mexican is to agricultural California what the Negro is to the medieval South. His treatment by the vegetable growers of the Imperial Valley is well known. What has happened to him in the San Joaquin has likewise been told. But for a time at least it appeared that the "citrus belt" was different. Then came the strike of the Mexican fruit pickers in Orange County. In its wake came the vigilantes, the night riders, the strike-breakers, the reporters whose job it was to "slant" all the stories in favor of the packers and grove owners. There followed the State Motor Patrol, which for the first time in the history of strike disorders in California set up a portable radio broadcasting station "in a secret place" in the strike area "to direct law-and-order activities." And special deputy badges blossomed as thick as Roosevelt buttons in the recent campaign.

Sheriff Jackson declared bravely: "It was the strikers themselves who drew first blood so from now on we will meet them on that basis." "This is no fight," said he, "between orchardists and pickers. It is a fight between the entire population of Orange County and a bunch of Communists." However, dozens and dozens of non-Communist Mexican fruit pickers were jailed; 116 were arrested en masse while traveling in automobiles along the highway. They were charged with riot and placed under bail of $500 each. . . . After fifteen days in jail the hearing was finally held—and the state's witnesses were able to identify only one person as having taken part in the trouble. . . . Judge Ames of the Superior Court ordered the release of all but one identified prisoner and severely criticized the authorities for holding the Mexicans in jail for so long a time when they must have known it would not be possible to identify even a small portion of the prisoners.

For weeks during the strike newspaper stories described the brave stand taken by "law-abiding citizens." These stories were adorned with such headlines as "Vigilantes Battle Citrus Strikers in War on Reds." During all this time, so far as I know, only one paper—the Los Angeles *Evening News*—defended the fruit pickers. . . .

These Mexicans were asking for a well-deserved wage increase and free transportation to and from the widely scattered groves; they also asked that tools be furnished by the employers. Finally they asked recognition of their newly formed union. Recognition of the Mexican laboring man's union, his cooperative organization formed in order that he might obtain a little more for his commodity, which is labor—here was the crucial point. The growers and packers agreed to furnish tools; they agreed to furnish transportation to and from the groves. They even agreed to a slight wage increase, which still left the workers underpaid. But recognition of the Mexican workers' union? Never! . . .

Not only in the fields are the Mexican people exploited. Not only as earners but as buyers they are looked upon as legitimate prey—for old washing machines that will not clean clothes, for old automobiles that wheeze and let down, for woolen blankets made of cotton, for last season's shop-worn wearing apparel. Gathered in villages composed of rough board shanties or drifting with the seasons from vegetable fields of the Imperial Valley to the grape vineyards of the San Joaquin, wherever they go it is the same old, pathetic story. Cheap labor!

Source: Frank Stokes, "Let the Mexicans Organize," *The Nation*, December 19, 1936, 731–32.

**DOCUMENT 22.10**

## Report of the Great Plains Committee, 1937

In 1936 President Roosevelt established the Great Plains Committee to investigate the causes of the Dust Bowl and possible solutions for the region. The committee's report, submitted the following year, outlined how federal, state, and local government agencies could work together to restore the Great Plains to economic health. One of the witnesses the committee called to testify was Otis Nation, an organizer for the Oklahoma Tenant Farmers' Union, whose testimony follows.

Much has been written of our droughts here in Oklahoma, and how they have driven the farmers from the land. But little has been said of the other tentacles that choke off the livelihood of the small owner and the tenant. We do not wish to minimize the seriousness of these droughts and their effects on the farming population. But droughts alone would not have permanently displaced these farmers. The great majority of migrants had already become share-tenants and sharecroppers. The droughts hastened a process that had already begun. We submit the following as the cases for migratory agricultural workers:

1. *High interest rates.* Often a farmer borrows money for periods of 10 months and is charged an interest rate of 10 percent. These rates are charged when crops are good and when they fail. Through such practices the farmer loses his ownership; he becomes a tenant, then a sharecropper, then a migrant.

2. *The tenant and sharecropping system.* When share tenants are charged 33⅓ percent of all corn or feed crops and 25 percent or more on cotton, plus 10 percent on all money borrowed at the bank, when sharecroppers are charged 50 to 75 percent of all he produces to the landlords, plus 10 percent for the bank's share on money invested; when these robbing practices are carried on in a community or a State, is it surprising that 33,241 farm families have left Oklahoma in the past 5 years?

3. *Land exhaustion, droughts, soil erosion, and the one-crop system of farming.* Lacking capital and equipment, small farmers have been unable to terrace their land or conduct other soil-conservation practices. The tenant and sharecropping system is chiefly responsible for the one-crop system. The landlord dictates what crops are to be planted—invariably cotton—and the tenant either plants it or gets off.

4. *Unstable markets.* Approximately a month and a half before the wheat harvest this year the price for this product was 93 cents here in Oklahoma City. But at harvest time the farmer sold his wheat for 46 cents to 60 cents per bushel, depending on the grade. . . . Kaffir [a grain sorghum] was selling for $1.30 one month ago, and yesterday we sold some for 85 cents per hundred. . . .

It is obvious to all of us that farm prices are set by speculators. The farmer's losses at the market have contributed in no small part to the farmer losing his place on the land. Higher prices for farm products are quoted when the farmer has nothing to sell.

5. *Tractor farming.* In Creek County, Okla., we have the record of one land-owner purchasing 3 tractors and forcing 31 of his 34 tenants and croppers from the land. Most of these families left the State when neither jobs nor relief could be secured. This is over 10 families per month, 10 families who must quit their profession and seek employment in an unfriendly, industrialized farming section of Arizona or California. Many of these families were even unable to become "Joads" [the fictional family in *The Grapes of Wrath*] in these other States, and had to seek relief from an unfriendly national administration and a more unfriendly State administration. . . .

At this hearing we will have all kinds of statistical material presented and arguments based on this material. But I am one of those who is more interested in the people, my people, than in mere figures. I do not agree with those who say "the no-good must always be weeded out." I say that all of these people, casually referred to in statistical sums, are 100-percent Americans. There are no more important problems facing us than the problem of stopping this human erosion and rehabilitating those unfortunates who have already been thrown off the land. Certainly it is un-American for Americans to be starved and dispossessed of their homes in our land of plenty. Those who seek to exploit and harass these American refugees, the migratory workers, are against our principles of democracy.

Source: U.S. Congress, House Select Committee to Investigate the Interstate Migration of Destitute Citizens (Washington: Government Printing Office, 1940–1941), 2102.

### Interpret the Evidence

1. What does Ann Marie Low's description of a typical day suggest about the particular challenges women faced during the Dust Bowl era (Document 22.5)?

2. Compare the living conditions described by a white southern sharecropper (Document 22.6) to those of the migrant family described by John Steinbeck (Document 22.8). How does the poverty of the two families differ? How would you explain the differences you note?

3. Compare the sharecropper's story (Document 22.6) with the photograph of the Arkansas family (Document 22.7). Do the subjects seem to react to the Great Depression in the same way? Do they seem hopeful or hopeless?

4. According to Frank Stokes, how did the fruit packers and grove owners characterize their conflict with the Mexican farmworkers (Document 22.9)? In what ways did their characterization draw on more general conservative criticisms of the New Deal?

5. According to the Great Plains Committee testimony (Document 22.10), what role did human-caused factors play in producing the misery that accompanied the dust storms of the early 1930s?

### Put It in Context

• What do these documents tell us about expectations regarding government help during the Great Depression?

background photos: pages 714 and 718, Library of Congress

# EXPLORING AMERICAN HISTORIES

Getty Images

Culver Pictures/The Art Archive at Art Resource, Inc.

Freed slaves in Richmond, Virginia, c. 1865.

Jack and Abby Landlord, freed slaves from Savannah, Georgia, 1875.

# 14
# Emancipations and Reconstructions

## 1863–1877

Schlesinger Library, Radcliffe Institute, Harvard University/The Bridgeman Art Library

● Women voting in Wyoming, 1870.

Jefferson Franklin Long spent his life improving himself and his race. Born a slave in Alabama in 1836, Long showed great resourcefulness in taking advantage of the limited opportunities available to him under slavery. His master, a tailor who moved his family to Georgia, taught him the trade, but Long taught himself to read and write. When the Civil War ended, he opened a tailor shop in Macon, Georgia. The measure of financial security he earned allowed him to turn his attention to politics and participate in the Republican Party. Elected as Georgia's first black congressman in 1870, Long was committed to fighting for the political rights of freed slaves. In his first appearance on the House floor, he spoke out against a bill that would allow former Confederate officials to return to Congress. He questioned their loyalty to the Union from which they had recently rebelled and noted that many belonged to secret societies, such as the Ku Klux Klan, that intimidated black citizens. Despite his pleas, the measure passed, and Long decided not to run for reelection.

By the mid-1880s, Long had become disillusioned with the ability of black Georgians to achieve their objectives within the electoral system. Instead, he counseled African Americans to turn to institution building as the best hope for social and economic advancement. Advocating "Christianity, morality, education, and industry," Long helped found the Union Brotherhood Lodge, a black mutual aid society, with branches throughout central Georgia, that provided social and economic services for its members. He died in 1901, during a

**425**

time of political disfranchisement and racial segregation that swept through Georgia and the rest of the South. In fact, after Long, Georgia would not elect another black congressman for a hundred years.

Jefferson Long and Andrew Johnson shared many characteristics, but their views on race led them to support decidedly different programs following the Civil War. Whereas Long fought for the right of self-determination for African Americans, Johnson believed that whites alone could decide what was best for freedmen. Born in 1808 in Raleigh, North Carolina, Andrew Johnson grew up in poverty. At the age of thirteen or fourteen, Johnson became a tailor's apprentice, but he ran away before completing his contract. Johnson settled in Tennessee in 1826 and, like Long, opened a tailor shop. The following year, he married Eliza McCardle, who taught him how to write. He began to prosper, purchasing his own home, farm, and a small number of slaves.

As he made his mark in Greenville, Tennessee, Johnson moved into politics, following fellow Tennessean Andrew Jackson into the Democratic Party. Success followed success as he advanced to higher political positions, and by the time the Civil War broke out, he was a U.S. senator. During his early political career, Johnson, a social and political outsider, championed the rights of workers and small farmers against the power of the southern aristocracy.

At the onset of the Civil War, Johnson remained loyal to the Union even when Tennessee seceded in 1861. As a reward for his loyalty, President Abraham Lincoln appointed Johnson as military governor of Tennessee. In 1864 the Republican Lincoln chose the Democrat Johnson to run with him as vice president, thereby constructing a successful unity ticket. Less than six weeks after their inauguration in March 1865, Johnson became president upon Lincoln's assassination.

Fate placed Reconstruction in the hands of Andrew Johnson. After four years, the brutal Civil War between the rebellious southern states that seceded from the Union and the northern states that fought to preserve the nation had come to a close. Yet the hard work of reunion remained. Toward this end, President Johnson oversaw the reestablishment of state legislatures in the former Confederate states. These reconstituted governments agreed to the abolition of slavery, but they passed measures that restricted black civil and political rights. Johnson accepted these results and considered the southern states as having fulfilled their obligations for rejoining the Union. Most Northerners reached a different conclusion. Having won the bloody war, they suspected that they were now losing the peace to Johnson and the defeated South. ●

both photos: Library of Congress

**T**HE AMERICAN HISTORIES of Andrew Johnson and Jefferson Long intersected in Reconstruction, the hard-fought battle to determine the fate of the postwar South and the meaning of freedom for newly emancipated African Americans. Would the end of slavery be little more than a legal technicality, as Johnson and many other white Southerners hoped, or would Long's vision of a deeper economic and racial transformation prevail? From 1865 to 1877, the period of Reconstruction, Americans of all races and from all regions participated in the resolution of this question.

## Prelude to Reconstruction

Even before Andrew Johnson became president in 1865 and emancipation freed Jefferson Long, Reconstruction had begun on a small scale. During the Civil War, blacks remaining in Union-occupied areas, such as the Sea Islands, located off the coast of South Carolina, had some experience with freedom. When Union troops arrived and most southern whites fled, the slaves chose to stay on the land. Some farmed for themselves, but most were employed by northern whites who moved south to demonstrate the profitability of newly freed black labor. The return of former plantation owners after the war generated conflicts. Rather than work for whites, freedpeople preferred to establish their own farms; but if forced to work for whites, they insisted on negotiating their wages instead of simply accepting what whites offered. Wives and mothers often refused to labor for whites at all in favor of caring for their own families. These conflicts reflected the priorities that would shape the actions of freedpeople across the South in the immediate aftermath of the war. For freedom to be meaningful, it had to include economic independence, the power to make family decisions, and the right to have some control over community issues.

## African Americans Embrace Emancipation

When U.S. troops arrived in Richmond, Virginia, in April 1865, it signaled to the city's enslaved African American population that the war was over and that freedom was, finally, theirs. African American men, women, and children took to the streets and crowded into churches to celebrate. They gathered to dance, sing, pray, and shout. Four days after Union troops arrived, 1,500 African Americans, including a large number of soldiers, packed First African Baptist, the largest of the city's black churches. During the singing of the hymn "Jesus My All to Heaven Is Gone," they raised their voices at the line "This is the way I long have sought." Elsewhere in Virginia, black schoolchildren sang "Glory Hallelujah," and house slaves snuck out of the dinner service to shout for joy in the slave quarters. As the news of the Confederacy's defeat spread, newly freed African Americans across the South experienced similar emotions. However, the news did not reach some isolated plantations in Georgia, Louisiana, South Carolina, and Texas for months. David Harris, a South Carolina planter, claimed that he did not hear about the emancipation edict until June 1865. He did not mention it to the slaves on his plantation until August, when Union troops stationed nearby made it impossible for him to keep it from his workers any longer. Whenever they discovered their freedom, blacks recalled the moment vividly. Many years later, Houston H. Holloway, a Georgia slave who had been sold three times before he was twenty years old, recalled the day of emancipation. "I felt like a bird out a cage," he reported. "Amen. Amen, Amen. I could hardly ask to feel any better than I did that day."

For southern whites, however, the end of the war brought fear, humiliation, and uncertainty. From their point of view, the jubilation of their former slaves was salt in their wounds. In many areas, blacks celebrated their release from bondage under the protection of Union soldiers. When the army moved out, freedwomen and freedmen suffered deeply for their enthusiasm. When troops departed the area surrounding Columbia, South Carolina, for example, a plantation owner and his wife vented their anger and frustration on a former slave. The girl had assisted Union soldiers in finding silverware, money, and jewelry hidden by her master and mistress. Her former owners hanged the newly emancipated slave. Other whites beat, whipped, raped, slashed, and shot blacks who they felt had been too joyous in their freedom or too helpful to the Yankee invaders. As one North Carolina freedman testified, the Yankees "tol' us we were free," but once the army left, the planters "would get cruel to the slaves if they acted like they were free."

Newly freed slaves also faced less visible dangers. During the 1860s, disease swept through the South and through the contraband camps that housed many former slaves; widespread malnutrition and poor housing heightened the problem. A smallpox epidemic that spread south from Washington, D.C., killed more than sixty thousand freedpeople.

Despite the danger of acting free, southern blacks eagerly pursued emancipation. They moved; they married; they attended school; they demanded wages; they refused to work for whites; they gathered up their families; they created black churches and civic associations; they held political meetings. Sometimes, black women and men acted on their own, pooling their resources to advance their freedom. At other times, they called on government agencies for assistance and support. The most important of these agencies was the newly formed Bureau of Refugees, Freedmen, and Abandoned Lands, popularly known as the **Freedmen's Bureau**. Created by Congress in 1865 and signed into law by President Lincoln, the bureau provided ex-slaves with economic and legal resources. Private organizations—particularly northern missionary and educational associations, most staffed by former abolitionists, free blacks, and evangelical Christians—also aided African Americans in their efforts to give meaning to freedom.

## Reuniting Families Torn Apart by Slavery

The first priority for many newly freed blacks was to reunite families torn apart by slavery. Men and women traveled across the South to find spouses, children, parents, siblings, aunts, and uncles. Well into the 1870s and 1880s, parents ran advertisements in newly established black newspapers, providing what information they knew about their children's whereabouts and asking for assistance in finding them. They sought help in their quests from government officials, ministers, and other African Americans. Milly Johnson wrote to the Freedmen's Bureau in March 1867, after failing to locate the five children she had lost under slavery. In the end, she was able to locate three of her children, but any chance of discovering the whereabouts of the other two was lost when the records of the slave trader who purchased them burned during the war. Although such difficulties were common, thousands of slave children were reunited with their parents in the aftermath of the Civil War.

Husbands and wives, or those who considered themselves as such despite the absence of legal marriage under slavery, also searched for each other. Those who lived on nearby plantations could now live together for the first time. Those whose husband or wife had been sold to distant plantation owners had a more difficult time. They wrote (or had letters written on their behalf) to relatives and friends who had been sold with their mate; sought assistance from government officials, churches, and even their former masters; and traveled to areas where they thought their spouse might reside.

Many such searches were complicated by long years of separation and the lack of any legal standing for slave marriages. In 1866 Philip Grey, a Virginia freedman, located his wife, Willie Ann, and their daughter Maria, who had been sold away to Kentucky years before. Willie Ann was eager to reunite with her husband, but in the years since being sold, she had remarried and borne three

children. Her second husband had joined the Union army and was killed in battle. When Willie Ann wrote to Philip in April 1866, explaining her new circumstances, she concluded: "If you love me you will love my children and you will have to promise me that you will provide for them all as well as if they were your own. . . . I know that I have lived with you and loved you then and love you still." Other spouses finally located their partner, only to discover that the husband or wife was happily married to someone else and refused to acknowledge the earlier relationship.

Despite these complications, most former slaves who found their spouse sought to legalize their relationship. Ministers, army chaplains, Freedmen's Bureau agents, and teachers were flooded with requests to perform marriage ceremonies. In one case, a Superintendent for Marriages for the Freedmen's Bureau in northern Virginia reported that he gave out seventy-nine marriage certificates on a single day in May 1866. In another, four couples went right from the fields to a local schoolhouse, still dressed in their work clothes, where the parson married them.

Of course, some former slaves hoped that freedom would allow them to leave an unhappy relationship. Having never been married under the law, couples could simply separate and move on. Complications arose, however, if they had children. In Lake City, Florida, in 1866, a Freedmen's Bureau agent asked for advice from his superiors on how to deal with Madison Day and Maria Richards. They refused to legalize the relationship forced on them under slavery, but both sought custody of their three children, the oldest only six years old. As with white couples in the mid-nineteenth century, the father eventually was granted custody on the assumption that he had the best chance of providing for the family financially.

## Free to Learn

Reuniting families was only one of the many ways that southern blacks proclaimed their freedom. Learning to read and write was another. The desire to learn was all but universal. Writing of freedpeople during Reconstruction, Booker T. Washington, an educator and a former slave, noted, "It was a whole race trying to go to school. Few were too young, and none too old, to make the attempt to learn." A newly liberated father in Mississippi proclaimed, "If I nebber does nothing more while I live, I shall give my children a chance to go to school, for I considers education [the] next best ting to liberty."

A variety of organizations opened schools for former slaves during the 1860s and 1870s. By 1870 nearly a quarter million blacks were attending one of the 4,300 schools established by the Freedmen's Bureau. Black and white

**Information Wanted.**

INFORMATION is wanted of my mother, whom I left in Fauquier county, Va., in 1844, and I was sold in Richmond, Va., to Saml. Copeland. I formerly belonged to Robert Rogers. I am very anxious to hear from my mother, and any information in relation to her whereabouts will be very thankfully received. My mother's name was Betty, and was sold by Col. Briggs to James French.— Any information by letter, addressed to the Colored Tennessean, Box 1150, will be thankfully received.
                    THORNTON COPELAND.
sept16–3m

**Reuniting Families**
Thornton Copeland, a former slave, placed this advertisement in the *Colored Tennessean* in Nashville in October 1865. Like other freedpeople, he was looking for relatives, in this case his mother, from whom he had been forcibly separated. Courtesy of the Tennessee State Library and Archives

**Wedding Day, 1866**

A Freedmen's Bureau minister unites a black Union soldier and his bride in Vicksburg, Mississippi. Most postwar weddings of freedpeople were less formal, but *Harper's Weekly*, a political magazine published in New York City and an ally of the Republican Party, wanted to present black families as respectable.
Library of Congress

churches and missionary societies also launched schools. Even before the war ended, the American Missionary Association called on its northern members to take the freedpeople "by the hand, to guide, counsel and instruct them in their new life." This and similar organizations sent hundreds of teachers, black and white, women and men, into the South to open schools in former plantation areas. Their attitudes were often paternalistic and the schools were segregated, but the institutions they established offered important educational resources for African Americans.

The demand for education was so great that almost any kind of building was pressed into service as a schoolhouse. A mule stable in Helena, Arkansas; a billiard room on the Sea Islands; a courthouse in Lawrence, Kansas; and a former cotton shed on a St. Simon Island plantation all attracted eager students. In New Orleans, local blacks converted a former slave pen into a school and named it after the famous activist, orator, and ex-slave Frederick Douglass.

Parents worked hard to keep their children in school during the day. Children, as they gained the rudiments of education, passed on their knowledge to mothers, fathers, and older siblings whose work responsibilities prevented them from attending school. Still, many freedpeople, having worked all day in fields, homes, or shops, then walked long distances in order to get a bit of education for themselves. In New Bern, North Carolina, where many blacks labored until eight o'clock at night, a teacher reported that they still insisted on spending at least an hour "in earnest application to study."

Freedmen and freedwomen sought education for a variety of reasons. Some, like the Mississippi father noted above, viewed it as a sign of liberation. Others knew that they must be able to read the labor contracts they signed if they were ever to be free of exploitation by whites. Some men and women were eager to correspond with relatives far away, others to read the Bible. Growing numbers hoped to participate in politics, particularly the public meetings organized by freedpeople in cities across the South following the end of the war. These gatherings met to set an agenda for the future, and nearly everyone demanded that state

**Freedmen's Bureau School**

This photograph of a one-room Freedmen's Bureau school in North Carolina in the late 1860s shows the large number and diverse ages of students who sought to obtain an education following emancipation. The teachers included white and black northern women sent by missionary and reform organizations as well as southern black women who had already received some education.    The Granger Collection, New York

legislatures immediately establish public schools for African Americans. Most black delegates agreed with A. H. Ransier of South Carolina, who proclaimed that "in proportion to the education of the people so is their progress in civilization."

Despite the enthusiasm of blacks and the efforts of the federal government and private agencies, schooling remained severely limited throughout the South. A shortage of teachers and of funding kept enrollments low among blacks and whites alike. The isolation of black farm families and the difficulties in eking out a living limited the resources available for education. Only about a quarter of African Americans were literate by 1880.

## Black Churches Take a Leadership Role

One of the constant concerns freedpeople expressed as they sought education was the desire to read the Bible and other religious material. Forced under slavery to listen to white preachers who claimed that God had placed Africans and their descendants in bondage, blacks sought to interpret the

Bible for themselves. Like many other churches, the African Methodist Episcopal Church, based in Philadelphia, sent missionaries and educators into the South. These church leaders were eager to open seminaries, such as Shaw University in Raleigh, North Carolina, to train southern black men for the ministry.

From the moment of emancipation, freedpeople gathered at churches to celebrate community events. Black Methodist and Baptist congregations spread rapidly across the South following the Civil War. In these churches, African Americans were no longer forced to sit in the back benches listening to white preachers claim that the Bible legitimated slavery. They were no longer punished by white church leaders for moral infractions defined by white masters. Now blacks filled the pews, hired black preachers, selected their own boards of deacons and elders, and invested community resources in purchasing land, building houses of worship, and furnishing them. Churches were the largest structures available to freedpeople in many communities and thus were used for a variety of purposes by a host of community organizations.

They often served as schools, with hymnals and Bibles used to teach reading. Churches also hosted picnics, dances, weddings, funerals, festivals, and other events that brought blacks together to celebrate their new sense of freedom, family, and community. Church leaders, especially ministers, often served as arbiters of community standards of morality.

One of the most important functions of black churches in the years immediately following the Civil War was as sites for political organizing. Some black ministers worried that political concerns would overwhelm spiritual devotions. Others agreed with the Reverend Charles H. Pearce of Florida, who declared, "A man in this State cannot do his whole duty as a minister except he looks out for the political interests of his people." Whatever the views of ministers, black churches were among the few places where African Americans could express their political views free from white interference.

## REVIEW & RELATE

- What were freedpeople's highest priorities in the years immediately following the Civil War? Why?

- How did freedpeople define freedom? What steps did they take to make freedom real for themselves and their children?

✓ **LEARNING***Curve* bedfordstmartins.com/hewittlawson/LC

## National Reconstructions

Presidents Abraham Lincoln and Andrew Johnson viewed Reconstruction as a process of national reconciliation. They sketched out terms by which the former Confederate states could reclaim their political representation in the nation without much difficulty. Southern whites, too, sought to return to the Union quickly and with as little change as possible. Congressional Republicans, however, had a more thoroughgoing reconstruction in mind. Like many African Americans, Republican congressional leaders expected the South to extend constitutional rights to the freedmen and to provide them with the political and economic resources to sustain their freedom. Over the next decade, these competing visions of Reconstruction played out in a hard-fought and tumultuous battle over the social, economic, and political implications of the South's defeat and of the abolition of slavery.

### Abraham Lincoln Plans for Reunion

In December 1863, President Lincoln issued the **Proclamation of Amnesty and Reconstruction**. He believed that the southern states could not have constitutionally seceded from the Union and therefore only had to meet minimum standards before they regained their political and constitutional rights. Lincoln declared that defeated southern states would have to accept the abolition of slavery and that new governments could be formed when 10 percent of those eligible to vote in 1860 (which in practice meant white southern men but not blacks) swore an oath of allegiance to the United States. Lincoln's plan granted amnesty to all but the highest-ranking Confederate officials, and the restored voters in each state would elect members to a constitutional convention and representatives to take their seats in Congress. In the next year and a half, Arkansas, Louisiana, and Tennessee reestablished their governments under Lincoln's "Ten Percent Plan."

Republicans in Congress had other ideas. They argued that the Confederates had broken their contract with the Union when they seceded and should be treated as "conquered provinces" subject to congressional supervision. In 1864 Congress passed the Wade-Davis bill, which established much higher barriers for readmission to the Union than did Lincoln's plan. For instance, the Wade-Davis bill substituted 50 percent of voters for the president's 10 percent requirement. Lincoln put a stop to this harsher proposal by using a pocket veto—refusing to sign it within ten days of Congress's adjournment.

Although Lincoln and his fellow Republicans in Congress disagreed about many aspects of postwar policy, Lincoln was flexible, and his actions mirrored his desire both to heal the Union and to help southern blacks. For example, the president supported the **Thirteenth Amendment**, abolishing slavery, which passed Congress in January 1865 and was sent to the states for ratification. In March 1865, Lincoln signed the law to create the Freedmen's Bureau. That same month, the president also expressed his sincere wish for reconciliation between the North and the South. "With malice toward none, with charity for all," Lincoln declared in his second inaugural address, "let us strive on to finish the work . . . to bind up the nation's wounds." Lincoln would not, however, have the opportunity to shape Reconstruction with his balanced approach. When he was assassinated in April 1865, it fell to Andrew Johnson, a very different sort of politician, to lead the country through the process of national reintegration.

### Andrew Johnson and Presidential Reconstruction

The nation needed a president who could transmit northern desires to the South with clarity and conviction and ensure that they were carried out. Instead, the nation got a president who substituted his own aims for those of the North, refused to engage in meaningful compromise even with sympathetic opponents, misled the South into believing that he could achieve restoration quickly, and subjected himself to political humiliation. Like his mentor, Andrew Jackson,

Andrew Johnson was a staunch Union man. He proved his loyalty by serving diligently as military governor of Union-occupied Tennessee from 1862 to 1864. In the 1864 election, Lincoln chose Johnson, a Democrat, as his running mate in a thinly veiled effort to attract border-state voters. The vice presidency was normally an inconsequential role, so it mattered little to Lincoln that Johnson, a southern Democrat, was out of step with many Republican Party positions.

As president, however, Johnson's views took on profound importance. Born into rural poverty, Johnson had no sympathy for the southern aristocracy. Johnson had been a slave owner himself for a time, so his political opposition to slavery was not rooted in moral convictions. Instead, it sprang from the belief that slavery gave plantation owners inordinate power and wealth, which came at the expense of the majority of white Southerners who owned no slaves. He saw emancipation as a means to "break down an odious and dangerous [planter] aristocracy," not to empower blacks. Consequently, he was unconcerned with the fate of African Americans in the postwar South. He saw no reason to punish the South or its leaders because he believed that the end of slavery would doom the southern aristocracy. He hoped to bring the South back into the Union as quickly as possible and then let Southerners take care of their own affairs.

Johnson's views, combined with a lack of political savvy and skill, left him unable to work constructively with congressional Republicans, even the moderates who constituted the majority, such as Senators Lyman Trumbull of Illinois, William Pitt Fessenden of Maine, and John Sherman of Ohio. Moderate Republicans shared the prevalent belief of their time that whites and blacks were not equal, but they argued that the federal government needed to protect newly emancipated slaves. Senator Trumbull warned that without national legislation, ex-slaves would "be tyrannized over, abused, and virtually reenslaved." They expected southern states, where 90 percent of African Americans lived, to extend basic civil rights to the freedpeople, including equal protection and due process of law, and the right to work and hold property.

Nearly all Republicans shared these positions. The Radical wing of the party, however, wanted to go still further. Led by Senator Charles Sumner of Massachusetts and Congressman Thaddeus Stevens of Pennsylvania, this small but influential group advocated suffrage, or voting rights, for African American men as well as the redistribution of southern plantation lands to freed slaves. Stevens called on the federal government to provide freedpeople "a homestead of forty acres of land," which would give them some measure of economic independence. Nonetheless, whatever disagreements the Radicals had with the moderates, all Republicans believed that Congress should have a strong voice in determining the fate of the former Confederate states. From May to December 1865,

with Congress out of session, they waited to see what Johnson's restoration plan would produce, ready to assert themselves if his policies deviated too much from their own.

At first, it seemed as if Johnson would proceed as they hoped. He appointed provisional governors to convene new state constitutional conventions and urged these conventions to ratify the Thirteenth Amendment abolishing slavery, revoke the states' ordinances of secession, and refuse to pay Confederate war debts, which the victorious North did not consider legitimate because repayment would benefit southern bondholders who financed the rebellion. He also allowed the majority of white Southerners to obtain amnesty and a pardon by swearing their loyalty to the U.S. Constitution, but he required those who had held more than $20,000 of taxable property—the members of the southern aristocracy—to petition him for a special pardon to restore their rights. Republicans expected him to be harsh in dealing with his former political foes. Instead, Johnson relished the reversal of roles that put members of the southern elite at his mercy. As the once prominent petitioners paraded before him, the president granted almost all of their requests for pardons.

By the time Congress convened in December 1865, Johnson was satisfied that the southern states had fulfilled his requirements for restoration. Moderate and Radical Republicans disagreed, seeing few signs of change or contrition in the South. As a result of Johnson's liberal pardon policy, many former leaders of the Confederacy won election to state constitutional conventions and to Congress. Indeed, Georgians elected Confederate vice president Alexander H. Stephens to the U.S. Senate. In addition, although most of the reconstituted state governments ratified the Thirteenth Amendment, South Carolina and Mississippi refused to repudiate the Confederate debt, and Mississippi rejected the Thirteenth Amendment.

Far from providing freedpeople with basic civil rights protection, the southern states passed a variety of **black codes** intended to reduce blacks to a condition as close to slavery as possible. Some laws prohibited blacks from bearing arms; others outlawed intermarriage and excluded blacks from serving on juries. Many of these laws were designed to ensure that white landowners had a supply of black labor now that slavery had ended. The codes made it difficult for blacks to leave plantations unless they proved they could support themselves. Many southern whites contended that they were acting no differently than their northern counterparts who used vagrancy laws to maintain control over workers.

Northerners viewed this situation with alarm. In their eyes, the postwar South looked very similar to the Old South, with a few cosmetic adjustments. If the black codes prevailed, one Republican proclaimed, "then I demand to know of what practical value is the amendment abolishing slavery?" Others wondered what their wartime sacrifices

**Mourning at Stonewall Jackson's Gravesite, 1866**

Many Northerners were concerned that the defeat of the Confederacy did not lessen white Southerners' devotion to the "Lost Cause" of a society based on the domination of African Americans. Women, who led the efforts to memorialize Confederate soldiers, are shown at the gravesite of General Stonewall Jackson in Lexington, Virginia. Virginia Military Institute Archives

had been for if the South admitted no mistakes, was led by the same people, and continued to oppress its black inhabitants. The *Chicago Tribune* declared that Northerners would not allow the black codes to "disgrace one foot of soil in which the bones of our soldiers sleep and over which the flag of freedom waves." **See Document Project 14: Testing and Contesting Freedom, page 449.**

## Johnson and Congressional Resistance

Faced with growing opposition in the North, Johnson stubbornly held his ground. He insisted that the southern states had followed his plan and were entitled to resume their representation in Congress. Republicans objected, and in December 1865 they barred the admission of southern lawmakers, an action that Johnson denounced as illegitimate. Up to this point, it was still possible for Johnson and Congress to work together, if Johnson had been willing to compromise. He was not. Instead, Johnson pushed moderates into the Radical camp with a series of legislative vetoes that challenged the fundamental tenets of Republican policies toward African Americans and the South. In January 1866, the president

refused to sign a bill passed by Congress to extend the life of the Freedmen's Bureau for another two years. A few months later, he vetoed the Civil Rights Act, which Congress had passed to protect freedpeople in the South from the restrictions placed on them by the black codes. These bills represented a consensus among moderate and Radical Republicans on the government's responsibility toward former slaves.

**Explore**

See Documents 14.1 and 14.2 for two perspectives on the Freedmen's Bureau.

Johnson justified his vetoes on both constitutional and personal grounds. Along with Democrats, he contended that so long as Congress refused to admit southern representatives, it could not legally pass laws affecting the South. The chief executive also condemned the Freedmen's Bureau bill because it infringed on the rights of states to handle their internal affairs concerning education and economic matters. Johnson's vetoes exposed his racism and his lifelong belief that the evil of slavery lay in the harm it did to poor white Southerners, not to enslaved blacks. Johnson

# Debating the Freedmen's Bureau: Two Views

From the start, the Freedmen's Bureau generated controversy. To its Republican supporters, it helped southern blacks make the transition from slavery to freedom. For most white Southerners and many northern Democrats, however, the bureau was little more than an expensive social welfare program that rewarded idleness in blacks. Both points of view are represented in the following documents. In a report written to the Congressional Joint Committee on Reconstruction, Colonel Eliphalet Whittlesey, the assistant head of the Freedmen's Bureau in North Carolina, outlined the bureau's initial accomplishments. The anti-bureau cartoon reprinted here was created during the height of the conflict over Reconstruction between the Republican Congress and President Andrew Johnson; it was intended to support the election of a Democratic candidate for governor of Pennsylvania, an ally of Johnson.

**Explore**

## 14.1 Colonel Eliphalet Whittlesey | Report on the Freedmen's Bureau, 1865

All officers of the bureau are instructed—

To aid the destitute, yet in such a way as not to encourage dependence.

To protect freedmen from injustice.

To assist freedmen in obtaining employment and fair wages for their labor.

To encourage education, intellectual and moral. Under these four divisions the operations of the bureau can best be presented. . . .

The statistical reports prepared by Captain Almy, commissary of subsistence, forwarded herewith, will show a steady and healthy decrease of the number of dependents from month to month.

July there were issued 215,285 rations, valued at $44,994.56; August there were issued 156,289 rations, valued at $32,664.40; September there were issued 137,350 rations, valued at $28,706.15.

Should no unforeseen trouble arise, the number will be still further reduced. But we have in our camps at Roanoke island and Newbern, many women and children, families of soldiers who have died in the service, and refugees from the interior during the war, for whom permanent provision must be made. . . . The reports prepared by Surgeon Hogan will show the condition of freedmen hospitals. In the early part of the summer much suffering and mortality occurred for want of medical attendance and supplies. This evil is now being remedied by the employment of surgeons by contract. . . .

Contrary to the fears and predictions of many, the great mass of colored people have remained quietly at work upon the plantations of their former masters during the entire summer. The crowds seen about the towns in the early part of the season had followed in the wake of the Union army, to escape from slavery. After hostilities ceased these refugees returned to their homes, so that but few vagrants can now be found. In truth, a much larger amount of vagrancy exists among the whites than among the blacks. It is the almost uniform report of officers of the bureau that freedmen are industrious.

The report is confirmed by the fact that out of a colored population of nearly 350,000 in the State, only about 5,000 are now receiving support from the government. Probably some others are receiving aid from kind-hearted men who have enjoyed the benefit of their services from childhood. To the general quiet and industry of this people there can be no doubt that the efforts of the bureau have contributed greatly.

Source: *The Reports of the Committees of the House of Representatives Made during the First Session, Thirty-ninth Congress, 1865–1866* (Washington, D.C.: Government Printing Office, 1866), 186–87, 189.

**Explore**

**14.2  Democratic Flier Opposing the Freedmen's Bureau Bill, 1866**

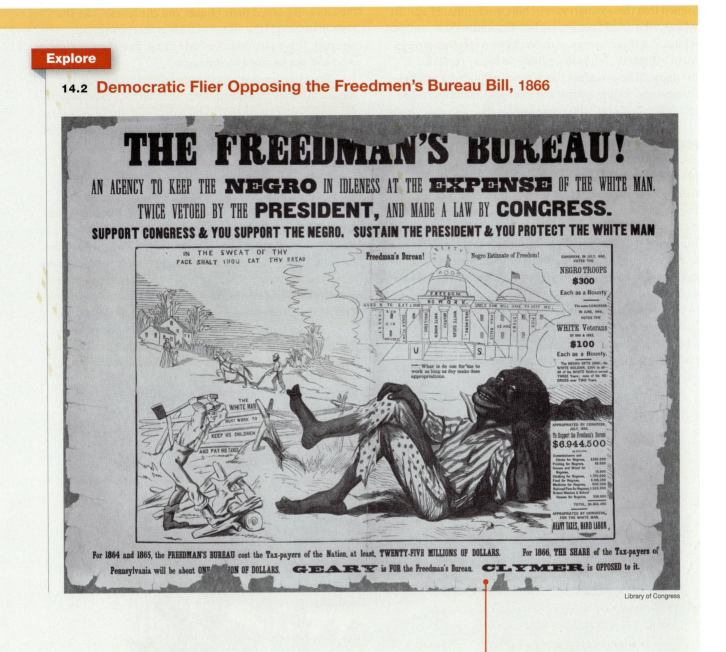

Library of Congress

**Interpret the Evidence**

- Why was there a need for the Freedmen's Bureau? How did Colonel Whittlesey measure its success?
- How is the Freedmen's Bureau portrayed in the poster? Why might its argument have appealed to some northern whites?

**Put It in Context**

How did prevailing racial assumptions shape both the cartoon and the report?

argued that these congressional bills discriminated against whites, who would receive no benefits under them, and put whites at a disadvantage with blacks who received government assistance. Johnson's private secretary recorded in his diary, "The president has at times exhibited a morbid distress and feeling against the Negroes," including those like Jefferson Long, who spoke out for their full civil rights.

Johnson's actions united moderates and Radicals against him. In April 1866, Congress repassed both the Freedmen's Bureau extension and Civil Rights Act over the president's vetoes. In June, lawmakers adopted the **Fourteenth Amendment**, which incorporated many of the provisions of the Civil Rights Act, and submitted it to the states for ratification (see Appendix). Reflecting its confrontational dealings with the president, Congress wanted to ensure more permanent protection for African Americans than simple legislation could provide. Lawmakers also wanted to act quickly, as the situation in the South seemed to be deteriorating rapidly. The previous month, a race riot had broken out in Memphis, Tennessee. For a day and a half, white mobs, egged on by local police, went on a rampage, during which they terrorized black residents of

the city and burned their houses and churches. "The late riots in our city," the editor of a Memphis newspaper asserted, "have satisfied all of one thing, that the *southern man* will not be ruled by the *negro*."

The Fourteenth Amendment defined citizenship to include African Americans, thereby nullifying the ruling in the *Dred Scott* case of 1857, which declared that blacks were not citizens. It extended equal protection and due process of law to all persons and not only citizens. The amendment repudiated Confederate debts, which some state governments had refused to do, and it barred Confederate officeholders from holding elective office unless Congress removed this provision by a two-thirds vote. Although most Republicans were upset with Johnson's behavior, at this point they were not willing to embrace the Radical position entirely. Rather than granting the right to vote to black males at least twenty-one years of age, the Fourteenth Amendment gave the states the option of excluding blacks and accepting a reduction in congressional representation if they did so.

Johnson remained inflexible. Instead of counseling the southern states to accept the Fourteenth Amendment, which would have sped up their readmission to the Union,

**Memphis Race Riot**

A skirmish between white policemen and black Union veterans on May 1, 1866, resulted in three days of rioting by white mobs that attacked the black community of Memphis, Tennessee. Before federal troops restored peace, numerous women had been raped, and forty-six African Americans and two whites had been killed. This illustration from *Harper's Weekly* depicts the carnage.    Courtesy of the Tennessee State Library and Archives

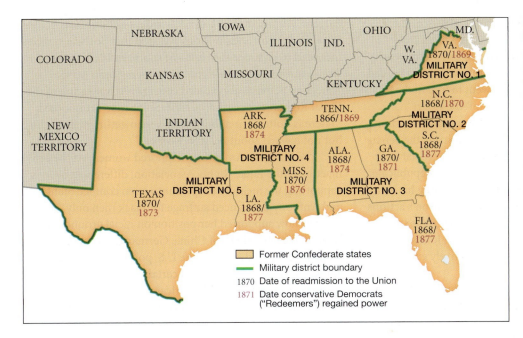

**MAP 14.1   Reconstruction in the South**

In 1867, Congress enacted legislation dividing the former Confederate states into five military districts. All the states were readmitted to the Union by 1870 and white, conservative Democrats (Redeemers) had replaced Republicans in most states by 1875. Only in Florida, Louisiana, and South Carolina did federal troops remain until 1877.

he encouraged them to reject it. Ironically, Johnson's home state of Tennessee ratified the amendment, but the other states refused. In the fall of 1866, Johnson decided to take his case directly to northern voters before the midterm congressional elections. Campaigning for candidates who shared his views, he embarked on a swing through the Midwest. Clearly out of touch with northern public opinion, Johnson attacked Republican lawmakers and engaged in shouting matches with audiences. On election day, Republicans increased their majorities in Congress and now controlled two-thirds of the seats, providing them with greater power to override presidential vetoes.

## Congressional Reconstruction

When the Fortieth Congress convened in 1867, Republican lawmakers charted a new course for Reconstruction. With moderates and Radicals united against the president, Congress intended to force the former Confederate states not only to protect the basic civil rights of African Americans but also to grant them the vote. Moderates now agreed with Radicals that unless blacks had access to the ballot, they would not be able to sustain their freedom. Extending the suffrage to African Americans also aided the fortunes of the Republican Party in the South by adding significant numbers of new black voters. By the end of March, Congress enacted three Military Reconstruction Acts. Together they divided ten southern states into five military districts, each under the supervision of a Union general and his troops (Map 14.1). The male voters of each state, regardless of race, were to elect delegates to a constitutional convention; only former Confederate officials were disfranchised.

The conventions were required to draft constitutions that guaranteed black suffrage and ratified the Fourteenth Amendment. Within a year, North Carolina, South Carolina, Florida, Alabama, Louisiana, and Arkansas had fulfilled these obligations and reentered the Union.

Having ensured congressional Reconstruction in the South, Republican lawmakers turned their attention to disciplining the president. Johnson continued to resist congressional policy and used his power as commander in chief to order generals in the military districts to soften the intent of congressional Reconstruction. In response, Congress passed the Command of the Army Act in 1867, which required the president to issue all orders to army commanders in the field through the General of the Army in Washington, D.C., Ulysses S. Grant. The Radicals had won over Grant and knew they could count on him to carry out their policies. Even more threatening to presidential power, Congress passed the **Tenure of Office Act**, which prevented Johnson from firing cabinet officers sympathetic to congressional Reconstruction. This measure barred the chief executive from removing from office any appointee that the Senate had ratified previously without returning to the Senate for approval.

Johnson sincerely believed that the Tenure of Office Act violated his presidential prerogative to remove subordinates he considered disloyal or incompetent. He may have had a legitimate constitutional point. However, the quick-tempered Johnson chose to confront the Radical Republicans directly rather than find a way to maneuver around a congressional showdown. In February 1868, Johnson fired Secretary of War Edwin Stanton, a Lincoln appointee and a Radical sympathizer, without Senate approval. In response, congressional Radicals prepared articles of impeachment on eleven counts of misconduct, including willful violation of the Tenure of Office Act.

In late February, the House voted 126 to 47 to impeach Johnson, the first president ever to be impeached, or charged with unlawful activity. The case then went to trial in the Senate, where the chief justice of the Supreme Court presided and a two-thirds vote was necessary for conviction and removal from office. After a six-week hearing, the Senate fell one vote short of convicting Johnson. Most crucial for Johnson's fate were the votes of seven moderate Republicans who refused to find the president guilty of violating his oath to uphold the Constitution, convinced that Johnson's actions were insufficient to merit the enormously significant step of removing a president from office. Although Johnson narrowly remained in office, Congress effectively ended his power to shape Reconstruction policy.

Not only did the Republicans restrain Johnson but they also won the presidency in 1868. Ulysses S. Grant, the popular Civil War Union general, ran against Horatio Seymour, the Democratic governor of New York. Although an ally of the Radical Republicans, Grant called for reconciliation with the South. He easily defeated Seymour, winning nearly 53 percent of the popular vote and 73 percent of the electoral vote.

## The Struggle for Universal Suffrage

In February 1869, Congress passed the **Fifteenth Amendment** to protect black suffrage, which had initially been guaranteed by the Military Reconstruction Acts. A compromise between moderate and Radical Republicans, the amendment prohibited voting discrimination based on race, but it did not deny states the power to impose qualifications based on literacy, payment of taxes, moral character, or any other standard that did not directly relate to race. Subsequently, the wording of the amendment provided loopholes for white leaders to disfranchise African Americans and any other "undesirable" elements. The amendment did, however, cover the entire nation, including the North, where several states, such as Connecticut, Kansas, Michigan, New York, Ohio, and Wisconsin, still excluded blacks from voting.

The Fifteenth Amendment sparked serious conflicts not only within the South but also among old abolitionist allies. The American Anti-Slavery Society disbanded with abolition, but many members believed that important work still remained to be done to guarantee the rights of freedpeople. They formed the **American Equal Rights Association** immediately following the war. Members of this group divided over the Fifteenth Amendment.

Women's rights advocates, such as Elizabeth Cady Stanton and Susan B. Anthony, had earlier objected to the Fourteenth Amendment because it inserted the word *male* into the Constitution for the first time when describing citizens. Although they had been ardent abolitionists before the war, Stanton and Anthony worried that postwar policies intended to enhance the rights of southern black men would further limit the rights of women. Some African American activists also voiced concern. At a meeting of the Equal Rights Association in 1867, Sojourner Truth noted, "There is quite a stir about colored men getting their rights, but not a word about colored women."

The Fifteenth Amendment ignored women. At the 1869 meeting of the Equal Rights Association, differences over supporting the measure erupted into open conflict. Stanton and Anthony denounced suffrage for black men only, and Stanton now supported her position on racial grounds. She claimed that the "dregs of China, Germany, England, Ireland, and Africa" were degrading the U.S. polity and argued that white, educated women should certainly have the same rights as immigrant and African American men. Black and white supporters of the Fifteenth Amendment, including Frances Ellen Watkins Harper, Wendell Phillips, Abby Kelley, and Frederick Douglass, denounced Stanton's bigotry. Believing that southern black men urgently needed suffrage to protect their newly won freedom, they argued that the ratification of black men's suffrage would speed progress toward the achievement of suffrage for black and white women.

> **Explore**
>
> See Document 14.3 for one activist's views on ratifying suffrage for black men.

This conflict led to the formation of competing organizations committed to women's suffrage. The **National Woman Suffrage Association**, established by Stanton and Anthony, allowed only women as members and opposed ratification of the Fifteenth Amendment. The **American Woman Suffrage Association**, which attracted the support of women and men, white and black, supported ratification. Less than a year later, in the spring of 1870, the Fifteenth Amendment was ratified and went into effect. However, the amendment did not grant the vote to either white or black women. As a result, women suffragists turned to the Fourteenth Amendment to achieve their goal. In 1875 Virginia Minor, who had been denied the ballot in Missouri, argued that the right to vote was one of the "privileges and immunities" granted to all citizens under the Fourteenth Amendment. In *Minor v. Happersatt*, the Supreme Court ruled against her.

### REVIEW & RELATE

- What was President Johnson's plan for reconstruction? How were his views out of step with those of most Republicans?

- What characterized congressional Reconstruction? What priorities were reflected in congressional Reconstruction legislation?

**DOCUMENT 14.3**

## Frances Ellen Watkins Harper | On Suffrage, 1869

Born a free person of color in Baltimore, Maryland, Frances Ellen Watkins Harper distinguished herself as a poet, a teacher, and an abolitionist. After the Civil War, she became a staunch advocate of women's suffrage and a supporter of the Fifteenth Amendment, which set her at odds with the suffragists Susan B. Anthony and Elizabeth Cady Stanton. In this discussion at the May 1869 American Equal Rights Association meeting, she argues for ratification of the Fifteenth Amendment.

**Explore**

When it was a question of race, she [black women] let the lesser question of sex go. But the white women all go for sex, letting race occupy a minor position. She liked the idea of working women, but she would like to know if it was broad enough to take colored women? . . . [When I] was at Boston there were sixty women who left work because one colored woman went to gain a livelihood in their midst. If the nation could only handle one question, I would not have the black women put a single straw in the way, if only the men of the race could obtain what they wanted.

Source: Susan B. Anthony, Elizabeth Cady Stanton, and Matilda Joslyn Gage, eds., *History of Women's Suffrage, 1861–1876* (Rochester, NY: Susan B. Anthony, 1882), 2:391–92.

**Frances Ellen Watkins Harper**   Image courtesy of Documenting the American South, The University of North Carolina at Chapel Hill Libraries

### Interpret the Evidence

- According to Frances Harper, why do black and white women differ on support for black male suffrage?
- How does Harper's experience in Boston influence her opinion?

### Put It in Context

Why was it important for black men to gain the right to vote even if it meant delaying women's suffrage?

*Economic
↑ opportunity*

# Remaking the South

With President Johnson's power effectively curtailed, reconstruction of the South moved quickly. However, despite the fears of southern whites and their supporters in the North, the results were neither extreme nor revolutionary. Although African Americans for the first time participated extensively in electoral politics and made unprecedented gains, whites retained control of the majority of the region's wealth and political power. In contrast to revolutions and civil wars in other countries, only one rebel was executed for war crimes (the commandant of Andersonville Prison in Georgia); only one high-ranking official went to prison (Jefferson Davis); no official was forced into exile, though some fled voluntarily; very little land was confiscated and redistributed; and most rebels regained voting rights and the ability to hold office within seven years after the end of the rebellion.

## Whites Reconstruct the South

During the first years of congressional Reconstruction, two groups of whites occupied the majority of elective offices in the South. A significant number of native-born Southerners joined Republicans in forming postwar constitutions and governments. Before the war, some had belonged to the Whig Party and opposed secession from the Union. Many mountain dwellers in Alabama, Georgia, North Carolina, and Tennessee had demonstrated a fiercely independent strain and had remained loyal to the Union. As a white resident of the Georgia mountains commented, "Now is the time for every man to come out and speak his principles publickly and vote for liberty as we have been in bondage long enough." Small merchants and farmers who detested large plantation owners also threw their lot in with the Republicans. Even a few ex-Confederates, such as General James A. Longstreet, decided that the South must change and allied with the Republicans. The majority of whites who continued to support the Democratic Party viewed these whites as traitors. They showed their distaste by calling them **scalawags**, an unflattering term meaning "scoundrels."

At the same time, northern whites came south to support Republican Reconstruction. They had varied reasons for making the journey, but most considered the South a new frontier to be conquered culturally, politically, and economically. Some had served in the Union army during the war, liked what they saw of the region, and decided to settle there. Some came to help provide education and assist the freedpeople in adjusting to a new way of

life. As a relatively underdeveloped area, the South also beckoned fortune seekers and adventurers who saw in the South an opportunity to get rich building railroads, establishing factories, and selling consumer goods. Southern Democrats denounced such northern interlopers as **carpetbaggers**, suggesting that they invaded the region with all their possessions in a satchel, seeking to plunder it and then leave. This characterization applied to some, but it did not accurately describe the motivations of most transplanted Northerners. While they did seek economic opportunity, they were acting as Americans always had in settling new frontiers and pursuing dreams of success. In dismissing them as carpetbaggers, their political enemies employed a double standard because they did not apply this demeaning label to those who traveled west—from both the North and the South—in search of economic opportunity at the expense of Indians and Mexicans settled there. Much of the negative feelings directed toward carpetbaggers resulted primarily from their attempts to ally with African Americans in reshaping the South.

## Black Political Participation and Economic Opportunities

As much as the majority of southern whites detested scalawags and carpetbaggers, the primary targets of white hostility were African Americans who attempted to exercise their hard-won freedom. Blacks constituted a majority of voters in five states—Alabama, Florida, South Carolina, Mississippi, and Louisiana—while in Georgia, North Carolina, Texas, and Virginia they fell short of a majority. They did not use their ballots to impose black rule on the South as many white Southerners feared. Only in South Carolina did African Americans control the state legislature, and in no state did they manage to elect a governor. Nevertheless, for the first time in American history, blacks won a wide variety of elected positions. More than six hundred blacks served in state legislatures; another sixteen, including Jefferson F. Long, held seats in the U.S. House of Representatives; and two from Mississippi were chosen to serve in the U.S. Senate.

Officeholding alone does not indicate the enthusiasm that former slaves had for politics. African Americans considered politics a community responsibility, and in addition to casting ballots, they held rallies and mass meetings to discuss issues and choose candidates. Although they could not vote, women attended these gatherings and helped influence their outcome. Covering a Republican convention in Richmond in October 1867, held in the African First Baptist Church, the *New York Times* reported that "the entire colored population of Richmond" attended. Freedpeople also formed associations to promote education, economic advancement, and social welfare programs, all of which they saw as deeply intertwined with politics. These included organizations like Richmond's Mutual Benefit Society, a group formed by single mothers, and the Independent Order of St. Luke, a mutual aid society for black women and men. African American women led both.

The efforts of southern blacks to bolster their freedom included building alliances with sympathetic whites. The resulting interracial political coalitions produced considerable reform in the South. These coalitions created a public school system where none had existed before the war; provided funds for social services, such as poor relief and state hospitals; upgraded prisons; and rebuilt the South's transportation system by supporting railroads and construction projects. Moreover, the state constitutions that the Republicans wrote brought a greater measure of political democracy and equality to the South by extending the right to vote to poor white men as well as black men. Some states allowed married women greater control over their property and liberalized the criminal justice system. In effect, these Reconstruction governments brought the South into the nineteenth century.

Obtaining political representation was one way in which African Americans defined freedom. Economic independence constituted a second. Without government-sponsored land redistribution, however, the options for southern blacks remained limited. Lacking capital to start farms, they entered into various forms of tenant contracts with large landowners. **Sharecropping** proved the most common arrangement. Blacks and poor whites became sharecroppers for much the same economic reasons. They received tools and supplies from landowners and farmed their own plots of land on the plantation. In exchange, sharecroppers turned over a portion of their harvest to the owner and kept some for themselves. Crop divisions varied but were usually explained in detail on written agreements. To make this system profitable, sharecroppers concentrated on producing staple crops such as cotton and tobacco that they could sell for cash.

The benefits of sharecropping proved more valuable to black farmers in theory than in practice. To tide them over during the growing season, croppers had to purchase household provisions on credit from a local merchant, who was often also the farmers' landlord. At the mercy of store owners who kept the books and charged high interest rates, tenants usually found themselves in considerable debt at the end of the year. To satisfy the debt, merchants devised a crop lien system in which tenants pledged a portion of their yearly crop to satisfy what they owed. Most indebted tenants found themselves bound to the landlord because falling prices in agricultural staples during this period meant that they did not receive sufficient return on their produce to get out of debt. For many African Americans, sharecropping turned into a form of virtual slavery.

> **Explore**
>
> See Document 14.4 for an example of a sharecropping agreement.

The picture for black farmers was not all bleak, however. About 20 percent of black farmers managed to buy their own land. Through careful management and extremely hard work, black families planted gardens for household consumption and raised chickens for eggs and food. Despite its pitfalls, sharecropping provided a limited measure of labor independence and allowed some blacks to accumulate small amounts of cash.

Following the war's devastation, many of the South's white, small farmers known as yeomen also fell into sharecropping. Yet planters, too, had changed. Many sons of planters abandoned farming and became lawyers, bankers, and merchants. Despite these changes, one thing remained the same: White elites ruled over blacks and poor whites, and they kept these two economically exploited groups from uniting by fanning the flames of racial prejudice.

Economic hardship and racial bigotry drove many blacks to leave the South. In 1879 former slaves pooled their resources to create land companies and purchase property in Kansas on which to settle. They created black towns that attracted some 25,000 African American migrants from the South, known as **Exodusters**. Kansas was ruled by the Republican Party and had been home to the great antislavery martyr John Brown. As one hopeful freedman from Louisiana wrote to the Kansas governor in 1879, "I am anxious to reach your state . . . because of the sacredness of her soil washed in the blood of humanitarians for the cause of black freedom." Exodusters did not find the Promised Land, however, as poor-quality land and unpredictable weather made farming on the Great Plains a hard and often unrewarding experience. Nevertheless, for many African American migrants, the chance to own their own land and escape the oppression of the South was worth the hardships. In 1880 the census counted 40,000 blacks living in Kansas.

## White Resistance to Congressional Reconstruction

Despite the Republican record of accomplishment during Reconstruction, white Southerners did not accept its legitimacy. They accused interracial governments of conducting a spending spree that raised taxes and encouraged corruption. Indeed, taxes did rise significantly, but mainly because of the need to provide new educational

## DOCUMENT 14.4

# Sharecropping Agreement, 1870

Because Congress did not generally provide freedpeople with land, African Americans lacked the capital to start their own farms. At the same time, plantation owners needed labor to plant and harvest their crops for market. Out of mutual necessity, white plantation owners entered into sharecropping contracts with blacks to work their farms in exchange for a portion of the crop, such as the following contract between Willis P. Bocock and several of his former slaves. Bocock owned Waldwick Plantation in Marengo County, Alabama.

**Explore**

**What are the farmers' responsibilities?**

**Why would Bocock want to clarify that his laborers would work equally hard throughout the year?**

**How might putting a lien on crops for debts owed create difficulties for the black farmer?**

Contract made the 3rd day of January in the year 1870 between us the free people who have signed this paper of one part, and our employer, Willis P. Bocock, of the other part. We agree to take charge of and cultivate for the year 1870, a portion of land, say [left blank] acres or thereabouts, to be laid off to us by our employer on his plantation, and to tend the same well in the usual crops, in such proportions as we and he may agree upon. We are to furnish the necessary labor, say an average hand to every 15 acres in the crops, making in all average hands; and are to have all proper work done, ditching, fencing, repairing, etc., as well as cultivating and saving the crops of all kinds, so as to put and keep the land we occupy and tend in good order for cropping, and to make a good crop ourselves; and to do our fair share of job work about the place. . . . We are to be responsible for the good conduct of ourselves, our hands, and families, and agree that all shall be respectful to employer, owners, and manager, honest, industrious, and careful about every thing, and shall not interrupt any thing about the place, working as industriously the last part of the year as the first; and then our employer agrees that he and his manager shall treat us kindly, and help us to study our interest and do our duty. If any hand or family proves to be of bad character, or dishonest, or lazy, or disobedient, or any way unsuitable our employer or manager has the right, and we have the right, to have such turned off. . . .

For the labor and services of ourselves and hands rendered as above stated, we are to have one third part of all the crops, or their net-proceeds, made and secured, or prepared for market by our force. . . .

We are to be furnished by our employer through his manager with provisions if we call for them: not over one peck of meal or corn, and $3\frac{1}{2}$ pounds of meat or its equivalent per week, for every 15 acres of land or average hand, to be charged to us at fair market prices.

And whatever may be due by us, or our hands to our employer for provisions or any thing else, during the year, is to be a lien on our share of the crops, and is to be retained by him out of the same before we receive our part.

Source: Waldwick Plantation Records, 1834–1971, LPR174, box 1, folder 9, Alabama Department of Archives and History.

**Put It in Context**

Why would free blacks and poor whites be willing to enter into such a contract?

**Exodusters**

This photograph of two black couples standing on their homestead was taken around 1880 in Nicodemus, Kansas. These settlers, known as Exodusters, had migrated to northwest Kansas following the end of Reconstruction. They sought economic opportunity free from the racial repression sweeping the South.　Library of Congress

and social services. Corruption, where building projects and railroad construction were concerned, was common during this time. Still, it is unfair to single out Reconstruction governments and especially black legislators as inherently depraved, as their Democratic opponents did. Economic scandals were part of American life after the Civil War. As enormous business opportunities arose and the pent-up energies that had gone into battles over slavery exploded into desires to accumulate wealth, many business leaders and politicians made unlawful deals to enrich themselves.

Most Reconstruction governments had only limited opportunities to transform the South. By the end of 1870, civilian rule had returned to all of the former Confederate states, and they had reentered the Union. Republican rule did not continue past 1870 in Virginia, North Carolina, and Tennessee and did not extend beyond 1871 in Georgia and 1873 in Texas. In 1874 Democrats deposed Republicans in Arkansas and Alabama; two years later, Democrats triumphed in Mississippi. In only three states—Louisiana, Florida, and South Carolina—did Reconstruction last until 1877.

The Democrats who replaced Republicans trumpeted their victories as bringing "redemption" to the South. Of course, these so-called **Redeemers** were referring to the white South. For black Republicans and their white allies, redemption meant defeat, not resurrection. Democratic victories came at the ballot boxes, but violence, intimidation, and fraud usually paved the way. It was not enough for Democrats to attack Republican policies. They also used racist appeals to divide poor whites from blacks and backed them up with force. In 1865 in Pulaski, Tennessee, General Nathan Bedford Forrest organized Confederate veterans into a social club called the **Knights of the Ku Klux Klan (KKK)**. The name came from the Greek word *kuklos*, meaning "circle." Spreading throughout the South, the KKK did not function as an ordinary social association; its followers donned robes and masks to hide their identities and terrify their victims. Ku Kluxers wielded rifles and guns and rode on horseback to the homes and

### Visit of the Ku Klux Klan

This 1872 wood engraving by the noted magazine illustrator Frank Bellew appeared at the height of Ku Klux Klan violence against freed blacks in the South. This image depicts a black family seemingly secure in their home in the evening while masked Klansmen stand in their doorway ready to attack with rifles.   Library of Congress

churches of black and white Republicans to keep them from voting. When threats did not work, they murdered their victims. In 1871, for example, 150 African Americans were killed in Jackson County in the Florida Panhandle. A black clergyman lamented, "That is where Satan has his seat." Here and elsewhere, many of the individuals targeted had managed to buy property, gain political leadership, or in other ways defy white stereotypes of African American inferiority. Local rifle clubs, hunting groups, and other white supremacist organizations joined the Klan in waging a reign of terror. During the 1875 election in Mississippi, which toppled the Republican government, armed terrorists killed hundreds of Republicans and scared many more away from the polls.

To combat the terror unleashed by the Klan and its allies, Congress passed three Force Acts in 1870 and 1871. These measures empowered the president to dispatch officials into the South to supervise elections and prevent voting interference. Directed specifically at the KKK, one law barred secret organizations from using force to violate equal protection of the laws. In 1872 Congress established a joint committee to probe Klan tactics, and its investigations produced thirteen volumes of vivid testimony about the horrors perpetrated by the Klan. Elias Hill, a freedman

from South Carolina who had become a Baptist preacher and teacher, was one of those who appeared before Congress. He and his brother lived next door to each other. The Klansmen went first to his brother's house, where, as Hill testified, they "broke open the door and attacked his wife, and I heard her screaming and mourning [moaning]. . . . At last I heard them have [rape] her in the yard. She was crying and the Ku-Klux were whipping her to make her tell where I lived." When Klansmen finally discovered Elias Hill, they dragged him out of his house, accused him of preaching against the Klan, beat and whipped him, and threatened to kill him. On the basis of such testimony, the federal government prosecuted some 3,000 Klansmen. Only 600 were convicted, however. As the Klan disbanded in the wake of federal prosecutions, other vigilante organizations arose to take its place.

## REVIEW & RELATE

What role did black people play in remaking southern society during Reconstruction?

How did southern whites fight back against Reconstruction? What role did terrorism and political violence play in this effort?

**LEARNINGCurve** bedfordstmartins.com/hewittlawson/LC

# The Unmaking of Reconstruction

The violence, intimidation, and fraud perpetrated by Redeemers against black and white Republicans in the South does not fully explain the unmaking of Reconstruction. Although Republicans in Congress enacted legislation combating the KKK and racial discrimination in public facilities, by the early 1870s white Northerners had grown weary of the struggle to protect the rights of freedpeople. In the minds of many, white Northerners had done more than enough for black Southerners, and it was time to focus on other issues. Growing economic problems intensified this feeling. More and more northern whites came to believe that any debt owed to black people for northern complicity in the sin of slavery had been wiped out by the blood shed during the Civil War. By the early 1870s, burying and memorializing the Civil War dead emerged as a common concern among white Americans, in both the North and the South. White America was once again united, if only in the shared belief that it was time to move on, consigning the issues of slavery and civil rights to history.

## The Republican Retreat

Most northern whites shared the racial views of their counterparts in the South. Although they had supported protection of black civil rights and suffrage, they still believed that African Americans were inferior to whites, and social integration was no more tolerable to them than it was to white Southerners. They began to sympathize with racist complaints voiced from the South that blacks were not capable of governing honestly and effectively.

In 1872 a group calling themselves **Liberal Republicans** challenged the reelection of President Grant, the Civil War general who had won the presidency on the Republican ticket in 1868. Financial scandals had racked the Grant administration. This high-level corruption reflected the get-rich-quick schemes connected to economic speculation and development following the Civil War. Outraged by these misdeeds and the rising level of immoral behavior in government and business, Liberal Republicans nominated Horace Greeley, editor of the *New York Tribune*, to run against Grant. They linked government corruption to the expansion of federal power that accompanied Reconstruction, and called for the removal of troops from the South and amnesty for former Confederates. They also campaigned for civil service reform in order to establish a merit system for government employment and for abolition of the "spoils system"—in which the party in power rewarded loyal supporters with political

appointments—that had been in place since the administration of Andrew Jackson.

The Democratic Party believed that Liberal Republicans offered the best chance to defeat Grant, and it endorsed Greeley. Despite the scandals that surrounded him, Grant remained popular. Moreover, the main body of Republicans "waved the bloody shirt," reminding northern voters that a ballot cast for the opposition tarnished the memory of brave Union soldiers who had died during the war. With the newly created national cemeteries, particularly the one established in Arlington, Virginia, providing a vivid reminder of the hundreds of thousands of soldiers killed, the "bloody shirt" remained a potent symbol. The president won reelection with an even greater margin than he had four years earlier. Nevertheless, the attacks against Grant foreshadowed the Republican retreat on Reconstruction. Among the Democrats sniping at Grant was Andrew Johnson. Johnson had returned to Tennessee, and in 1874 the state legislature chose the former president to serve in the U.S. Senate. He continued to speak out against the presence of federal troops in the South until his death in 1875.

## Congressional and Judicial Retreat

By the time Grant began his second term, Congress was already considering bills to restore officeholding rights to former Confederates who had not yet sworn allegiance to the Union. Black representatives, such as Georgia congressman Jefferson Long, as well as some white lawmakers, remained opposed to such measures, but in 1872 Congress removed the penalties placed on former Confederates by the Fourteenth Amendment and permitted nearly all rebel leaders the right to vote and hold office. Two years later, for the first time since the start of the Civil War, the Democrats gained a majority in the House of Representatives and prepared to remove the remaining troops from the South.

Economic concerns increasingly replaced racial considerations as the top priority for northern Republican leaders. Northerners and Southerners began calling more loudly for national unity and reconciliation. In 1873 a financial panic resulting from the collapse of the Northern Pacific Railroad triggered a severe economic depression lasting late into the decade. Tens of thousands of unemployed workers across the country worried more about finding jobs than they did about blacks in the South. Businessmen, too, were plagued with widespread bankruptcy. As workers looked to labor unions for support, business leaders looked to the federal government for assistance. When strikes erupted across the country in 1877, most notably the Great Railway Strike, employers asked the U.S. government to remove troops from the

South and dispatch them against strikers in the North and the West.

While Northerners sought a way to extricate themselves from Reconstruction, the Supreme Court weakened enforcement of the civil rights acts. In 1873 the *Slaughterhouse* cases defined the rights that African Americans were entitled to under the Fourteenth Amendment very narrowly. Reflecting the shift from moral to economic concerns, the justices interpreted the amendment as extending greater protection to corporations in conducting business than that extended to blacks. As a result, blacks had to depend on southern state governments to protect their civil rights, the same state authorities that had deprived them of their rights in the first place. In *United States v. Cruikshank* (1876), the high court narrowed the Fourteenth Amendment further, ruling that it protected blacks against abuses only by state officials and agencies, not by private groups such as the Ku Klux Klan. Seven years later, the Court struck down the Civil Rights Act of 1875, which had extended "full and equal treatment" in public accommodations for persons of all races.

## The Presidential Compromise of 1876

The presidential election of 1876 set in motion events that officially brought Reconstruction to an end. The Republicans nominated Rutherford B. Hayes, a Civil War officer and governor of Ohio. A supporter of civil service reform, Hayes was chosen, in part, because he was untainted by the corruption that plagued the Grant administration. The Democrats selected their own crusader against bribery and graft, Governor Samuel J. Tilden of New York, who had prosecuted political corruption in New York City.

The outcome of the election depended on twenty disputed electoral votes, nineteen from the South and one from Oregon. Tilden won 51 percent of the popular vote, but Reconstruction political battles in Florida, Louisiana, and South Carolina put the election up for grabs. In each of these states, the outgoing Republican administration certified Hayes as the winner, while the incoming Democratic regime declared for Tilden.

The Constitution assigns Congress the task of counting and certifying the electoral votes submitted by the states. Normally, this is merely a formality, but 1876 was different. Democrats controlled the House, Republicans controlled the Senate, and neither branch would budge on which votes to count. Hayes needed all twenty for victory; Tilden needed only one. To break the logjam, Congress created a fifteen-member **Joint Electoral Commission**, composed of seven Democrats, seven Republicans, and one independent (five members of the House, five U.S. senators, and five Supreme Court justices). As it turned out, the independent commissioner, Justice David Davis,

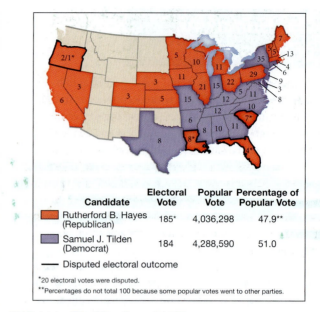

| Candidate | Electoral Vote | Popular Vote | Percentage of Popular Vote |
|---|---|---|---|
| Rutherford B. Hayes (Republican) | 185* | 4,036,298 | 47.9** |
| Samuel J. Tilden (Democrat) | 184 | 4,288,590 | 51.0 |
| — Disputed electoral outcome | | | |

*20 electoral votes were disputed.
**Percentages do not total 100 because some popular votes went to other parties.

**MAP 14.2   The Election of 1876**

The presidential election of 1876 got swept up in Reconstruction politics. Democrats defeated Republicans in Florida, Louisiana, and South Carolina, but both parties claimed the electoral votes for their candidates. A federal electoral commission set up to investigate the twenty disputed votes, including one from Oregon, awarded the votes and the election to the Republican, Rutherford B. Hayes.

resigned, and his replacement, Justice Joseph P. Bradley, voted with the Republicans to count all twenty votes for Hayes, making him president (Map 14.2).

Still, Congress had to ratify this count, and disgruntled southern Democrats in the Senate threatened a filibuster—unlimited debate—to block certification of Hayes. With the March 4, 1877, date for the presidential inauguration creeping perilously close and no winner officially declared, behind-the-scenes negotiations finally helped settle the controversy. A series of meetings between Hayes supporters and southern Democrats led to a bargain. According to the agreement, Democrats would support Hayes in exchange for the president appointing a Southerner to his cabinet, withdrawing the last federal troops from the South, and endorsing construction of a transcontinental railroad through the South. This **compromise of 1877** averted a crisis over presidential succession, underscored increased southern Democratic influence within Congress, and marked the end to strong federal protection for African Americans in the South.

## REVIEW & RELATE

- Why did northern interest in Reconstruction wane in the 1870s?

- What common values and beliefs among white Americans were reflected in the compromise of 1877?

## Conclusion: The Legacies of Reconstruction

Reconstruction was, in many ways, profoundly limited. African Americans did not receive the landownership that would have provided them with the economic independence to bolster their freedom from the racist assaults of white Southerners. The civil and political rights that the federal government conferred did not withstand Redeemers' efforts to disfranchise and deprive the freedpeople of equal rights. The Republican Party shifted its priorities elsewhere, and Democrats gained enough political power nationally to short-circuit federal intervention, while numerous problems remained unresolved in the South. Northern support for racial equality did not run very deep, so white Northerners, who shared many of the prejudices of white Southerners, were happy to extricate themselves from further intervention in southern racial matters. Nor was there sufficient support to give women, white and black, the right to vote. Finally, federal courts, with growing concerns over economic rather than social issues, sanctioned Northerners' retreat by providing constitutional legitimacy for abandoning black Southerners and rejecting women's suffrage in court decisions that narrowed the interpretation of the Fourteenth and Fifteenth Amendments.

Despite all of this, Reconstruction did transform the country. As a result of Reconstruction, slavery was abolished, and the legal basis for freedom was enshrined in the Constitution. Indeed, blacks exercised a measure of political and economic freedom during Reconstruction that never entirely disappeared over the decades to come. In many areas, freedpeople, as exemplified by Congressman Jefferson Franklin Long among many others, asserted what they could never have during slavery—control over their lives, their churches, their labor, and their families. What they could not practice during their own time because of racial discrimination, their descendants would one day revive through the promises codified in the Fourteenth and Fifteenth Amendments.

African Americans transformed not only themselves; they transformed the nation. The Constitution became much more democratic and egalitarian through inclusion of the Reconstruction amendments. Reconstruction lawmakers took an important step toward making the United States the "more perfect union" that the nation's Founders had pledged to create. Reconstruction established a model for expanding the power of the federal government to resolve domestic crises that lay beyond the abilities of states and ordinary citizens. It remained a powerful legacy for those elected officials in the future who dared to invoke it. And Reconstruction transformed the South to its everlasting benefit. It modernized state constitutions, expanded educational and social welfare systems, and unleashed the repressed potential for industrialization and economic development that the preservation of slavery had restrained. Ironically, Reconstruction did as much for white Southerners as it did for black Southerners in liberating them from the past.

**LEARNINGCurve**
Check what you know.
bedfordstmartins.com/hewittlawson/LC

# Chapter Review

Online Study Guide ▶ bedfordstmartins.com/hewittlawson

## KEY TERMS

## REVIEW & RELATE

1. What were freedpeople's highest priorities in the years immediately following the Civil War? Why?

2. How did freedpeople define freedom? What steps did they take to make freedom real for themselves and their children?

3. What was President Johnson's plan for reconstruction? How were his views out of step with those of most Republicans?

4. What characterized congressional Reconstruction? What priorities were reflected in congressional Reconstruction legislation?

5. What role did black people play in remaking southern society during Reconstruction?

6. How did southern whites fight back against Reconstruction? What role did terrorism and political violence play in this effort?

7. Why did northern interest in Reconstruction wane in the 1870s?

8. What common values and beliefs among white Americans were reflected in the compromise of 1877?

## TIMELINE OF EVENTS

| | |
|---|---|
| 1863 | Lincoln issues Proclamation of Amnesty and Reconstruction |
| 1865 | Ku Klux Klan formed |
| | Freedmen's Bureau established |
| | Congress passes Thirteenth Amendment |
| April 1865 | Lincoln assassinated; Andrew Johnson becomes president |
| May–December 1865 | Presidential Reconstruction under Andrew Johnson |
| 1866 | Congress passes extension of Freedmen's Bureau and Civil Rights Act over Johnson's presidential veto |
| | Congress passes Fourteenth Amendment |
| 1867 | Military Reconstruction Acts divide the South into military districts |
| | Congress passes Command of the Army and Tenure of Office Acts |
| 1868 | Andrew Johnson impeached |
| 1869 | Congress passes Fifteenth Amendment |
| | Women's suffrage movement splits over support of Fifteenth Amendment |
| 1870 | 250,000 blacks attend schools established by the Freedmen's Bureau |
| | Civilian rule reestablished in all former Confederate states |
| 1870–1871 | Jefferson Long serves as a Republican congressman from Georgia |
| 1870–1872 | Congress takes steps to curb KKK violence in the South |
| 1872 | Liberal Republicans challenge reelection of President Grant |
| 1873 | Financial panic sparks depression lasting until the late 1870s |
| 1873–1883 | Supreme Court limits rights of African Americans |
| 1875 | Congress passes Civil Rights Act outlawing discrimination in public accommodations, which the Supreme Court rules unconstitutional in 1883 |
| 1877 | Republicans and southern Democrats reach compromise resulting in the election of Rutherford B. Hayes as president and the end of Reconstruction |
| 1879 | Black Exodusters migrate from South to Kansas |

# DOCUMENT PROJECT 14

# Testing and Contesting Freedom

Nine months after the Civil War ended in April 1865, twenty-seven states ratified the Thirteenth Amendment, abolishing slavery throughout the United States. Freedom, however, did not guarantee equal rights or the absence of racial discrimination. Immediately following the North's victory, white southern leaders enacted black codes, which aimed to prevent the former slaves from improving their social and economic status. Although Lincoln's successor, Andrew Johnson, himself a Southerner, did not support the codes, he did nothing to overturn them. An advocate of limited government, Johnson clashed repeatedly with Congress over Reconstruction, vetoing renewal of the Freedmen's Bureau bill and opposing ratification of the Fourteenth Amendment. In 1867 the Republican majority in Congress passed the Military Reconstruction Acts, which placed the South under military rule and forced it to extend equal political and civil rights to African Americans.

The Military Reconstruction Acts, followed by the ratification of the Fifteenth Amendment in 1870, extended suffrage to black men. In alliance with white Republicans, blacks won election to a variety of public offices, including seats on local and state governmental bodies. When these interracial legislatures provided funds for public education of blacks—for the first time in the South—and for black hospitals and other social services, their opponents attacked them for fraud, corruption, wasteful spending, and imposing "Black Rule." Opponents also created vigilante groups like the Ku Klux Klan to intimidate black and white Republicans through scare tactics backed up by violence and bloodshed. By 1877 the attempt of white southern Democrats, or Redeemers, had succeeded, leaving African Americans struggling to retain the freedom they had enjoyed during Reconstruction.

As you read the following documents, consider these general questions: How did blacks and whites view freedom? How essential was it for the federal government to supervise the movement from slavery to freedom? Why didn't southern whites accept the extension of civil rights for blacks, if only in a limited way? How did views about Reconstruction change over time?

**DOCUMENT 14.5**

## Mississippi Black Code, 1865

Southern legislatures created black codes primarily to limit the rights of free blacks after emancipation and return them to a condition as close as possible to slavery. Mississippi was one of the first states to enact a black code. Although its laws did legalize marriage for blacks and allowed them to own property and testify in court, its primary intent was to limit freedpeople's mobility and economic opportunities. New vagrancy laws required blacks to provide written proof of residency and employment or else risk arrest, while other sections limited where they could live, restricted the terms of their employment, and banned intermarriage.

*An Act to Confer Civil Rights on Freedmen, and for other Purposes*

SECTION 1. All freedmen, free negroes and mulattoes may sue and be sued . . . in all the courts of law and equity of this State, and may acquire personal property, and choses in action [right to bring a lawsuit to recover chattels, money, or a debt], by descent or purchase, and may dispose of the same in the same manner and to the same extent that white persons may: Provided, That the provisions of this section shall not be so construed as to allow any freedman, free negro or mulatto to rent or lease any lands or tenements except in incorporated cities or towns, in which places the corporate authorities shall control the same.

SECTION 2. All freedmen, free negroes and mulattoes may intermarry with each other, in the same manner and under the same regulations that are provided by law for white persons: Provided, that the clerk of probate shall keep separate records of the same.

SECTION 3. All freedmen, free negroes or mulattoes who do now and have herebefore lived and cohabited together as husband and wife shall be taken and held in law as legally married, and the issue shall be taken and held as legitimate for all purposes; and it shall not be lawful for any freedman, free negro or mulatto to intermarry with any white person; nor for any person to intermarry with any freedman, free negro or mulatto; and any person who shall so intermarry shall be deemed guilty of felony, and on conviction thereof shall be confined in the State penitentiary for life; and those shall be deemed freedmen, free negroes and mulattoes who are of pure negro blood, and those descended from a negro to the third generation, inclusive, though one ancestor in each generation may have been a white person.

SECTION 4. In addition to cases in which freedmen, free negroes and mulattoes are now by law competent witnesses, freedmen, free negroes or mulattoes shall be competent in civil cases, when a party or parties to the suit, either plaintiff or plaintiffs, defendant or defendants; also in cases where freedmen, free negroes and mulattoes is or are either plaintiff or plaintiffs, defendant or defendants. They shall also be competent witnesses in all criminal prosecutions where the crime charged is alleged to have been committed by a white person upon or against the person or property of a freedman, free negro or mulatto. . . .

SECTION 5. Every freedman, free negro and mulatto shall, on the second Monday of January, one thousand eight hundred and sixty-six, and annually thereafter, have a lawful home or employment, and shall have written evidence thereof as follows, to wit: if living in any incorporated city, town, or village, a license from that mayor thereof; and if living outside of an incorporated city, town, or village, from the member of the board of police of his beat, authorizing him or her to do irregular and job work; or a written contract, as provided in SECTION 6 in this act; which license may be revoked for cause at any time by the authority granting the same.

Section 6. All contracts for labor made with freedmen, free negroes and mulattoes for a longer period than one month shall be in writing, and a duplicate, attested and read to said freedman, free negro or mulatto by a beat, city or county officer, or two disinterested white persons of the county in which the labor is to [be] performed, of which each party shall have one: and said contracts shall be taken and held as entire contracts, and if the laborer shall quit the service of the employer before the expiration of his term of service, without good cause, he shall forfeit his wages for that year up to the time of quitting. . . .

*An Act to Amend the Vagrant Laws of the State . . .*

Section 2. All freedmen, free negroes and mulattoes in this State, over the age of eighteen years, found on the second Monday in January, 1866, or thereafter, with no lawful employment or business, or found unlawful[ly] assembling themselves together, either in the day or night time, and all white persons assembling themselves with freedmen, free negroes or mulattoes, or usually associating with freedmen, free negroes or mulattoes, on terms of equality, or living in adultery or fornication with a freed woman, freed negro or mulatto, shall be deemed vagrants, and on conviction thereof shall be fined in a sum not exceeding, in the case of a freedman, free negro or mulatto, fifty dollars, and a white man two hundred dollars, and imprisonment at the discretion of the court, the free negro not exceeding ten days, and the white man not exceeding six months. . . .

Section 6. The same duties and liabilities existing among white persons of this State shall attach to freedmen, free negroes or mulattoes, to support their indigent families and all colored paupers; and that in order to secure a support for such indigent freedmen, free negroes, or mulattoes, it shall be lawful, and is hereby made the duty of the county police of each county in this State, to levy a poll or capitation tax on each and every freedman, free negro, or mulatto, between the ages of eighteen and sixty years, not to exceed the sum of one dollar annually to each person so taxed, which tax, when collected, shall be paid into the county treasurer's hands, and constitute a fund to be called the Freedman's Pauper Fund, which shall be applied by the commissioners of the poor for the maintenance of the poor of the freedmen, free negroes and mulattoes of this State, under such regulations as may be established by the boards of county police in the respective counties of this State.

Source: *Laws of the State of Mississippi, Passed at a Regular Session of the Mississippi Legislature, Held in the City of Jackson, October, November, and December, 1865* (Jackson, MS, 1866), 82–86, 165–67.

**DOCUMENT 14.6**

# Richard H. Cain | Federal Aid for Land Purchase, 1868

Richard H. Cain, a free black minister raised in Ohio, went to South Carolina after the war and served as a Republican member of the U.S. House of Representatives for two terms in the 1870s. The following excerpt comes from a speech Cain made in 1868 as a representative to the South Carolina constitutional convention. Cain proposed that the convention petition Congress for a $1 million loan to purchase land that could be resold to freedmen at a reasonable price.

I BELIEVE THE BEST MEASURE to be adopted is to bring capital to the State, and instead of causing revenge and unpleasantness, I am for even-handed justice. I am for allowing the parties who own lands to bring them into the market and sell them upon such terms as will be satisfactory to both sides. I believe a measure of this kind has a double effect: first, it brings capital, what the people want; second, it puts the people to work; it gives homesteads, what we need; it relieves the Government and takes away its responsibility of feeding the people; it inspires every man with a noble manfulness, and by the thought that he is the possessor of something in the State; it adds also to the revenue of the country. By these means men become interested in the country as they never were before. It was said that five and one-seventh acres were not enough to live on. If South Carolina, in its sovereign power, can devise any plan for the purchase of the large plantations in this State now lying idle, divide and sell them out at a reasonable price, it will give so many people work. I will guarantee to find persons to work every five acres. I will also guarantee that after one year's time, the Freedman's Bureau will not have to give any man having one acre of land anything to eat. This country has a genial clime, rich soil, and can be worked to advantage. The man who can not earn a living on five acres, will not do so on twenty-five.

I regret that another position taken by gentlemen in the opposition, is that they do not believe that we will get what we ask for. I believe that the party now in power in the Congress of the United States, will do whatever they can for the welfare of the people of this State and of the South. I believe that the noble men who have maintained the rights of the freedmen before and since their liberation, will continue to do everything possible to forward these great interests. I am exceedingly anxious, if possible, to allay all unpleasant feeling—I would not have any unpleasant feeling among ourselves.

I would not have any unpleasant feelings between the races. If we give each family in the State an opportunity of purchasing a home, I think they will all be better satisfied.

But it is also said that it will disturb all the agricultural operations in the State. I do not believe if the Congress of the United States shall advance one million of dollars to make purchase of lands, the laborers will abandon their engagement and run off. I have more confidence in the people I represent. I believe all who have made contracts will fulfill those contracts, and when their contracts have expired, they will go on their own lands, as all freemen ought to go.

Source: *Proceedings of the South Carolina Constitutional Convention of 1868* (Charleston, SC, 1868), 420–21.

**DOCUMENT 14.7**

# Ellen Parton | Testimony on Klan Violence, 1871

In March 1871, white mobs killed some thirty African Americans in Meridian, Mississippi. Later that month, a joint committee of the Mississippi legislature held hearings on the violence, which included the following testimony by Ellen Parton of Mississippi, a former slave and domestic worker. The Klan suspected that Parton's husband was involved in the Union League, a southern affiliate of the Republican Party. Congress also conducted hearings on the vigilante violence against blacks throughout the South.

Ellen Parton, being sworn, states:

I reside in Meridian; have resided here nine years; occupation, washing and ironing and scouring; Wednesday night was the last night they came to my house; by "they" I mean bodies or companies of men; they came on Monday, Tuesday, and Wednesday. On Monday night they said that they came to do us no harm. On Tuesday night they said they came for the arms; I told them there was none, and they said they would take my word for it. On Wednesday night they came and broke open the wardrobe and trunks, and committed rape upon me; there were eight of them in the house; I do not know how many there were outside; they were white men; there was a light in the house; I was living in Marshal Ware's house; there were three lights burning. Mr. Ware has been one of the policemen of this town. He was concealed at the time they came; they took the claw hammer and broke open the pantry where he was lying; he was concealed in the pantry under some plunder, covered up well; I guess he covered himself up. A man said "here is Marshal's hat, where is Marshal?" I told him "I did not know"; they went then into everything in the house, and broke open the wardrobe; I called upon Mr. Mike Slamon, who was one of the crowd, for protection; I said to him "please protect me tonight, you have known me for a long time." This man covered up his head then; he had a hold of me at this time; Mr. Slamon had an oil-cloth and put it before his face, trying to conceal himself, and the man that had hold of me told me not to call Mr. Slamon's name any more. He then took me in the dining room, and told me that I had to do just what he said: I told him I could do nothing of that sort; that was not my way, and he replied "by God, you have got to," and then threw me down. This man had a black eye, where some one had beaten him; he had a black velvet cap on. After he got through with me he came through the house, and said that he was after the Union Leagues; I yielded to him because he had a pistol drawn; when he took me down he hurt me of course; I yielded to him on that account.

Source: *Report of the Joint Select Committee [of Congress] to Inquire into the Condition of Affairs in the Late Insurrectionary States, Mississippi* (Washington, D.C.: Government Printing Office, 1872), 1:38–39.

## DOCUMENT 14.8
### The Force Act, 1871

As testimony of antiblack violence mounted, Congress passed the Force Act (also known as the Ku Klux Klan Act) in April 1871. A federal response to stop the terror and intimidation of southern black and white Republicans by their opponents, the act provided both civil relief for damages and criminal penalties. It was rooted in the Fourteenth Amendment's guarantees of the rights and privileges of U.S. citizenship. The federal government dispatched troops to enforce the law and prosecuted hundreds of Klan members, often before predominantly black juries, resulting in the breakup of the Klan within a few years.

Be it enacted . . . That any person who, under color of any law, statute, ordinance, regulation, custom, or usage of any State, shall subject, or cause to be subjected, any person within the jurisdiction of the United States to the deprivation of any rights, privileges, or immunities secured by the Constitution of the United States, shall, any such law, statute, ordinance, regulation, custom, or usage of the State to the contrary notwithstanding, be liable to the party injured in any action at law, suit in equity, or other proper proceeding for redress; such proceeding to be prosecuted in the several district or circuit courts of the United States, with and subject to the same rights of appeal, review upon error, and other remedies provided in like cases in such courts, under the provisions of the [Civil Rights Act of 1866], and the other remedial laws of the United States which are in their nature applicable in such cases. . . .

SEC. 3. That in all cases where insurrection, domestic violence, unlawful combinations, or conspiracies in any State shall so obstruct or hinder the execution of the laws thereof, and of the United States, as to deprive any portion or class of the people of such State of any of the rights, privileges, or immunities, or protection, named in the Constitution and secured by this act, and the constituted authorities of such State shall either be unable to protect, or shall, from any cause, fail in or refuse protection of the people in such rights, such facts shall be deemed a denial by such State of the equal protection of the laws to which they are entitled under the Constitution of the United States; and in all such cases, or whenever any such insurrection, violence, unlawful combination, or conspiracy shall oppose or obstruct the laws of the United States or the due execution thereof, or impede or obstruct the due course of justice under the same, it shall be lawful for the President, and it shall be his duty to take such measures, by the employment of the militia or the land and naval forces of the United States, or of either, or by other means, as he may deem necessary for the suppression of such insurrection, domestic violence, or combinations. . . .

SEC. 6. That any person or persons, having knowledge that any of the wrongs conspired to be done and mentioned in the second section of this act are about to be committed, and having power to prevent or aid in preventing the same, shall neglect or refuse to do so, and such wrongful act shall be committed, such person or persons shall be liable to the person injured, or his legal representatives, for all damages caused by any such wrongful act which such first-named person or persons by reasonable diligence could have prevented.

Source: George P. Sanger, ed., *Statutes at Large and Proclamations of the United States of America from March 1871 to March 1873* (Boston: Little, Brown, 1873), 13–15.

**DOCUMENT 14.9**

## Thomas Nast | Colored Rule in a Reconstructed (?) State, 1874

Thomas Nast began drawing for the popular magazine *Harper's Weekly* in 1859. Nast initially used his illustrations to rouse northern public sentiment for the plight of blacks in the South after the Civil War. By 1874, however, many Northerners had become disillusioned with federal efforts to enforce Reconstruction. Like them, Nash accepted the white southern point of view that "Black Reconstruction" was a recipe for corruption and immorality. This cartoon imagines a raucous scene in the South Carolina legislature, where black legislators have taken over the floor and call each other "thieves, liars, rascals, and cowards." Note the figure of Columbia (at the top right), who represents the nation, chastising black lawmakers with a switch. Nast highlights Columbia's message in the caption: "You are Aping the lowest Whites. If you disgrace your Race in this way you had better take Back Seats."

**DOCUMENT 14.10**

# What the Centennial Ought to Accomplish, 1875

The following editorial appeared in the northern periodical *Scribner's Journal*. A year before the celebration of the nation's centennial, Northerners as well as Southerners were calling for national unity and reconciliation, and thus a true end to Reconstruction. Rather than dwelling on the "Lost Cause," the magazine's editors remind southern readers of the glories of the old nation as celebrated by former Confederate president Jefferson Davis in recalling the national unity during the victorious Mexican-American War.

WE ARE TO HAVE grand doings next year. There is to be an Exposition. There are to be speeches, and songs, and processions, and elaborate ceremonies and general rejoicings. Cannon are to be fired, flags are to be floated, and the eagle is expected to scream while he dips the tip of either pinion in the Atlantic and the Pacific, and sprinkles the land with a new baptism of freedom. . . .

. . . Before we begin our celebration of this event, would it not be well for us to inquire whether we have a nation? In a large number of the States of this country there exists not only a belief that the United States do not constitute a nation, but a theory of State rights which forbids that they ever shall become one. We hear about the perturbed condition of the Southern mind. We hear it said that multitudes there are just as disloyal as they were during the civil war. This, we believe, we are justified in denying. . . . They are not actively in rebellion, and they do not propose to be. They do not hope for the re-establishment of slavery. They fought bravely and well to establish their theory, but the majority was against them; and if the result of the war emphasized any fact, it was that *en masse* the people of the United States constitute a nation—indivisible in constituents, in interest, in destiny. The result of the war was without significance, if it did not mean that the United States constitute a nation which cannot be divided; which will not permit itself to be divided; which is integral, indissoluble, indestructible. . . . The great point with them is to recognize the fact that, for richer or poorer, in sickness and health, until death do us part, these United States constitute a nation; that we are to live, grow, prosper, and suffer together, united by bands that cannot be sundered.

Unless this fact is fully recognized throughout the Union, our Centennial will be but a hollow mockery. If we are to celebrate anything worth celebrating, it is the birth of a nation. If we are to celebrate anything worth celebrating, it should be by the whole heart and united voice of the nation. If we can make the Centennial an occasion for emphasizing the great lesson of the war, and universally assenting to the results of the war, it will, indeed, be worth all the money expended upon and the time devoted to it. . . .

A few weeks ago, Mr. Jefferson Davis, the ex-President of the Confederacy, was reported to have exhorted an audience to which he was speaking to be as loyal to the old flag of the Union now as they were during the Mexican War. If the South could know what music there was in these words to Northern ears—how grateful we were to their old chief for them—it would appreciate the strength of our longing for a complete restoration of the national feeling that existed when Northern and Southern blood mingled in common sacrifice on Mexican soil. This national feeling, this national pride, this brotherly sympathy *must be restored*; and accursed be any Northern or Southern man, whether in power or out of power, whether politician, theorizer, carpet-bagger, president-maker, or plunderer, who puts obstacles in the way of such a restoration. Men of the South, we want you. Men of the South, we long for the restoration of your peace and your prosperity. We would see your cities thriving, your homes happy, your plantations teeming with plenteous harvests, your schools overflowing, your wisest statesmen leading you, and all causes and all memories of discord wiped out forever. You do not believe this? Then you do not know the heart of the North. Have you cause of complaint against the politicians? Alas! so have we. Help us, as loving and loyal American citizens, to make our politicians better. Only remember and believe that there is nothing that the North wants so much to-day, as your recognition of the fact that the old relations between you and us are forever restored—that your hope, your pride, your policy, and your destiny are one with ours. Our children will grow up to despise our childishness, if we cannot do away with our personal hates so far, that in the cause of an established nationality we may join hands under the old flag.

To bring about this reunion of the two sections of the country in the old fellowship, should be the leading object of the approaching Centennial. A celebration of the national birth, begun, carried on, and finished by a section, would be a mockery and a shame. The nations of the world might well point at it the finger of scorn. The money expended upon it were better sunk in the sea, or devoted to repairing the waste places of the war. Men of the South, it is for you to say whether your magnanimity is equal to your valor—whether you are as reasonable as you are brave, and whether, like your old chief, you accept that definite and irreversible result of the war which makes you and yours forever members of the great American nation with us. Let us see to it, North and South, that the Centennial heals all the old wounds, reconciles all the old differences, and furnishes the occasion for such a reunion of the great American nationality, as shall make our celebration an expression of fraternal good-will among all sections and all States, and a corner-stone over which shall be reared a new temple to national freedom, concord, peace, and prosperity.

Source: "What the Centennial Ought to Accomplish," *Scribner's Monthly*, August 1875, 509–10.

## Interpret the Evidence

1. How did the black codes (Document 14.5) attempt to reimpose bondage on former slaves?
2. Why did African Americans consider property holding a fundamental right (see Document 14.6)?
3. Under what circumstances did the Force Act (Document 14.8) authorize federal prosecutions?
4. Contrast the image of South Carolina's black politicians as presented in Richard Cain's speech (Document 14.6) and Thomas Nast's cartoon (Document 14.9).
5. Despite Ku Klux Klan intimidation and the fear it produced in African Americans, what does the testimony of Ellen Parton (Document 14.7) reveal about black attempts to resist it?
6. What sources of unity existed between the North and the South that would bring Reconstruction to an end (see Document 14.10)?

## Put It in Context

- How much did Reconstruction transform the South and the nation? What were its limitations?

background photo: page 451, Library of Congress

Private Collection/Peter Newark American Pictures/The Bridgeman Art Library

Library of Congress

Railroad construction crew, 1886.

Lone Wolf and his wife Etla, Kiowa Indians, c. 1860.

# 15
# Frontier Encounters
## 1865–1896

Nebraska family in front of sod house with cow on the hillside that forms the roof, 1887.

## AMERICAN HISTORIES

As an adult, Phoebe Ann Moses embodied the excitement and adventure of the mythical American West. Her childhood, however, was one of poverty and hardship. Born in 1860, Phoebe Ann grew up east of the Mississippi, seventy miles north of Cincinnati, Ohio. One of seven surviving children, she was sent to an orphanage at the age of nine, after her father died and her mother could not care for all her children. After working for a farm family, she ran away at the age of twelve and found a new home with a recently remarried widow. Over the next four years, Phoebe Ann learned to ride and hunt and became an expert shot with a rifle. At fifteen, she entered a shooting contest and defeated a professional marksman, Frank Butler. The competition sparked a romance, and the two married in 1876. Phoebe Ann changed her professional name to "Annie Oakley," and she and Butler went on tour throughout the Midwest in an act that featured precision shooting.

In 1884 Oakley and Butler met William F. "Buffalo Bill" Cody in New Orleans. Cody had been a buffalo hunter on the Great Plains and an army scout during the Indian wars of the 1870s. In 1883, as the western frontier began to recede and the U.S. government relocated Native Americans who lived there, Cody attempted to recapture and reinvent the frontier experience by staging "Wild West" shows. A year later, he hired Oakley, with Butler serving as her manager. For the next fifteen years, the diminutive Oakley was the star of the show. Wearing a fringed skirt, an embroidered blouse, and a broad felt hat emblazoned with a star, she stood atop her horse and

**459**

**Annie Oakley
and Geronimo**

shot the lights out of a revolving wheel of lit candles and took dead aim at other targets tossed in the air. Oakley toured Europe and fascinated heads of state and audiences alike with her version of "western authenticity." Fans at home and overseas displayed great nostalgia for a fast-diminishing era. When the census of 1890 reported that no open land was left to settle and thus no western frontier was left to conquer, Oakley's popularity soared. She continued performing in Wild West shows until her death in 1926.

While Annie Oakley portrayed the Wild West, Geronimo had lived it. Born to a Chiricahua Apache family in what was then northern Mexico (present-day Arizona and New Mexico), Geronimo led Apaches in a constant struggle against Spain, Mexico, and the United States. Driven to the hills of Arizona and New Mexico by Spanish conquistadors centuries before Geronimo was born, Apaches raided settlements to support themselves. In 1851 a band of Mexicans raided an Apache camp, murdering Geronimo's mother, wife, and three children. After fighting Mexicans, Geronimo clashed with U.S. troops and evaded capture until 1877, when an Indian agent arrested him in New Mexico. Sent to a reservation, Geronimo escaped and for eight years engaged in daring raids against his foes. In 1886 two Chiricahua scouts recruited by General Nelson Miles led the military to Geronimo. Against an army of five thousand soldiers, the Apache warrior, with a band of eighteen fighters and some women and children, finally surrendered and was eventually relocated by the U.S. government to Fort Sill, Oklahoma.

The once-elusive warrior decided to take advantage of his legendary reputation. With Buffalo Bill cashing in on America's fascination with the mythic West and "savage" Indians, Geronimo, like Annie Oakley, exploited this appeal. He sold photos of himself and pieces of his clothing; he appeared at the 1904 World's Fair in St. Louis, selling bows and arrows and autographs; and in 1905 he rode in President Theodore Roosevelt's inaugural parade as an example of a "tamed" Indian. Although he converted to Christianity, Geronimo, ever the rebel, was later expelled from his church for gambling. Crass commercialism and religious conversion aside, Geronimo never gave up the idea of returning to his birthplace. As long as the U.S. government prohibited him from going back to his ancestral lands in the Southwest, he considered himself a "prisoner of war." And so he remained until his death in 1909. ●

photos: Beinecke Rare Book and Manuscript Library, Yale University; Library of Congres

**A**S PROFOUNDLY DIFFERENT as Annie Oakley's and Geronimo's individual histories were, they both contributed to the creation of a shared story, the myth of the American West. The West has great fascination in American culture. Stories about the frontier have romanticized both cowboys and Indians. These stories have also glorified individualism, self-help, and American ingenuity and minimized cooperation, organization, and the role of foreign influence in developing the West. As the American histories of Annie Oakley and Geronimo make clear, reality presents a more complicated picture of a diverse region initially inhabited by native peoples who were pushed aside by the arrival of white settlers and immigrants. In the areas known as the Great Plains and the far West, women took on new roles, and new cities emerged to accommodate the influx of miners, ranchers, and farmers.

**460**

# Opening the West

The lands west of the Mississippi were not hospitable to farmers and other adventurers lured by the appeal of cheap land and a fresh start. These pioneers faced many challenges with rugged determination; however, they could not have settled the West on their own. Federal policy and foreign investment played a large role in encouraging and financing the development of the West. Railroads were essential in transforming the region (Map 15.1).

## The Great Plains

In the mid-nineteenth century, the western frontier lay in the **Great Plains**. This region spreads through present-day North and South Dakota, Nebraska, Kansas, Oklahoma, Texas, Montana, Wyoming, Colorado, New Mexico, Idaho, Utah, Arizona, and Nevada. Lying on both sides of the Rocky Mountains, the Great Plains plateau was a semiarid territory with an average yearly rainfall of twenty inches, enough to sustain short grasslands but not many trees. Bison, pronghorn antelope, jack rabbits, and prairie dogs roamed over great distances to nourish themselves on the sparse vegetation that grew in this delicate ecosystem.

Grasshoppers and locusts periodically swarmed into the area. Indian hunters in the very dry central and southern plains—Apache, Arapaho, Cheyenne, Comanche, Kiowa—opened up these lands to human habitation and survived by hunting and cultivating the grasslands.

Prospects for sedentary farmers in this dry region did not appear promising. In 1878 geologist John Wesley Powell issued a report that questioned whether the land beyond the easternmost portion of the Great Plains could support small farming. Lack of rainfall, he argued, would make it difficult or even impossible for homesteaders to support themselves on family farms of 160 acres. Instead, he recommended that for the plains to prove economically sustainable, settlers would have to work much larger stretches of land, around 2,560 acres (4 square miles). This would provide ample room to raise livestock under dry conditions.

Powell's words of caution did little to diminish Americans' conviction, dating back to Thomas Jefferson, that small farmers would populate the territories brought under U.S. jurisdiction and renew democratic values as they ventured forth. Charles Dana Wilber, a booster of settlement in Nebraska, summed up the view of those who saw no barriers to the expansion of small farmers in the plains. Rejecting the idea that either a Divine Creator or nature had determined that these lands should remain a "perpetual desert," Wilber asserted that "in reality

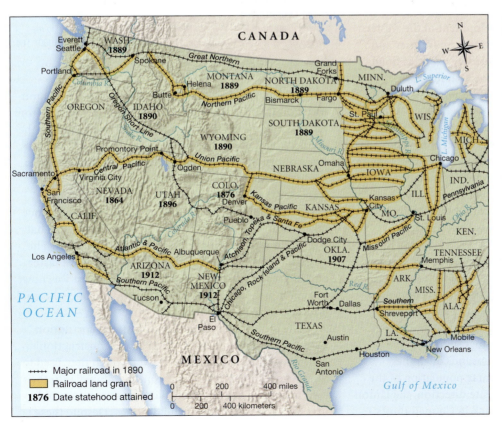

**MAP 15.1 The American West, 1860–1900**

Railroads played a key role in the expansion and settlement of the American West. The network of railroads running throughout the West opened the way for extensive migration from the East and for the development of a national market. None of this would have been possible without the land grants provided to the railroads by the U.S. government.

there is no desert anywhere except by man's permission or neglect." Along with millions of others, he had great faith in Americans' ability to turn the Great Plains into a place where Jefferson's republican vision could take root and prosper.

## Federal Policy and Foreign Investment

Despite the popular association of the West with individual initiative and self-sufficiency, the federal government played a huge role in facilitating the settlement of the West. National lawmakers enacted legislation offering free or cheap land to settlers and to mining, lumber, and railroad companies. The U.S. government also provided subsidies for transporting mail and military supplies, recruited soldiers to subdue the Indians who stood in the way of expansion, and appointed officials to govern the territories.

Along with federal policy, foreign investment helped fuel development of the West. Lacking sufficient funds of its own, the United States turned to Europe to finance the sale of public bonds and private securities. European financial houses held a majority ownership in the United States Mortgage Company and the Equitable Trust Company of New York, both of which bought and sold mortgages. European firms also invested in American mines, with the British leading the way. In 1872 an Englishman wrote that mines in Nevada were "more British than American." The development of the western cattle range—the symbol of the American frontier and the heroic cowboy—was also funded by overseas financiers. At the height of the cattle boom in the 1880s, British firms supplied some $45 million to underwrite ranch operations.

The largest share of money that flowed from Europe to the United States came with the expansion of the railroads, the most important ingredient in opening the West (Figure 15.1). The economist Joseph Schumpeter concluded that it was "primarily English (and other European) capital which took the responsibility for a great part of the $2 billion which are said to have been expended on American railroads from 1867 to 1873."

The **transcontinental railroad** became the gateway to the West. In 1862 the Republican-led Congress appropriated vast areas of land that railroad companies could use to lay their tracks or sell to raise funds for construction. The Central Pacific Company built from west to east, starting in Sacramento, California. The construction project attracted thousands of Chinese railroad workers, boosting the sparse population of the western territory. From the opposite direction, the Union Pacific Company began laying track in Council Bluffs, Iowa, and hired primarily Irish workers. In May 1869, the

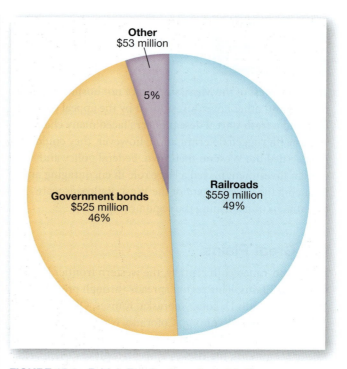

**FIGURE 15.1  British Foreign Investment in the United States, 1876**

British investment was an important source of funding for westward expansion following the Civil War. Nearly half of all British loans went toward financing railroad construction, which required large capital expenditures. The British also invested heavily in government bonds and to a lesser extent in cattle ranching and mining enterprises.

Source: Data from Mina Wilkins, *The History of Foreign Investment in the United States to 1914* (Cambridge, MA: Harvard University Press, 1989), 164.

Central Pacific and Union Pacific crews met at Promontory Point, Utah, amid great celebration. Workmen from the two companies drove a golden spike to complete the connection. For many Americans recovering from four years of brutal civil war and still embroiled in southern reconstruction (see chapter 14), the completion of the transcontinental railroad renewed their faith in the nation's ingenuity and destiny. A wagon train had once taken six to eight weeks to travel across the West. That trip could now be completed by rail in seven days. The railroad allowed both people and goods to move faster and in greater numbers than before. The West was now open not just to rugged pioneers but to anyone who could afford a railroad ticket.

The building of the railroads fostered corruption. Union Pacific promoters created a fake construction company called the Crédit Mobilier, which they used to funnel government bond and contract money into their own pockets. They also bribed congressmen to avoid investigation into their sordid dealings. Despite these efforts, in 1872 Congress exposed these wrongdoings.

### Railroad Construction Crew

Chinese and other immigrant groups were instrumental in the construction of the transcontinental railroad. This Union Pacific construction crew includes a Chinese laborer standing in the center next to African American workers and a white foreman in the front left. The boulders in the rear show the massive rock formations and rugged terrain they had to blast through.  Denver Public Library, Western History Collection, E. & H. T. Anthony, Call Number Z-3335

## REVIEW & RELATE

- What role did the federal government play in opening the West to settlement and economic exploitation?

- Explain the determination of Americans to settle in land west of the Mississippi River despite the challenges the region presented.

✔ *LEARNINGCurve* bedfordstmartins.com/hewittlawson/LC

## Conquest of the Frontier

American pioneers may have thought they were moving into a wilderness, but the West was home to large numbers of American Indians. Before pioneers and entrepreneurs could go west to pursue their economic dreams, the U.S. government would have to remove this unwelcome obstacle to American expansion. Through treaties—most of which Americans broke—and war, white Americans conquered the Indian tribes inhabiting the Great Plains during the nineteenth century. After the native population was largely subdued, those who wanted to reform Indian policy focused on carving up tribal lands and forcing Indians to assimilate into American society.

## Indian Civilizations

Long before white settlers appeared, the frontier was already home to diverse peoples. The many native groups who inhabited the West spoke distinct languages, engaged in different economic activities, and competed with one another for power and resources. The descendants of Spanish conquistadors had also lived in the Southwest and California since the late sixteenth century, pushing the boundaries of the Spanish empire northward from Mexico. Indeed, Spaniards established the city of Santa Fe as the territorial capital of New Mexico years before the English landed at Jamestown, Virginia, in 1607. The United States then acquired the New Mexican and California territories as spoils of the Mexican-American War in 1848.

By the end of the Civil War, around 350,000 Indians were living west of the Mississippi. They constituted the surviving remnants of the 1 million people who had occupied the land for thousands of years before Europeans set foot in America. Nez Percé, Ute, and Shoshone Indians lived in the Northwest and the Rocky Mountain region; Lakota, Cheyenne, Blackfoot, Crow, and Arapaho tribes occupied the vast expanse of the central and northern plains; and Apaches, Comanches, Kiowas, Navajos, and Pueblos made up the bulk of the population in the Southwest. Some of the tribes, such as the Cherokee, Creek, and Shawnee, had been forcibly removed from the East during Andrew

Jackson's presidency in the 1830s. The tribes each adapted in unique ways to the geography and climate of their home territories, spoke their own language, and had their own history and traditions. Some were hunters, others farmers; some nomadic, others sedentary. In New Mexico, the Apaches, including Geronimo, were expert horsemen and fierce warriors, while the Pueblo Indians built homes out of adobe and developed a flourishing system of agriculture. The lives of all Indian peoples were affected by the arrival of Europeans, but the consequences of cross-cultural contact varied considerably depending on the history and circumstances of each tribe (Map 15.2).

Given the rich assortment of Indian tribes, it is difficult to generalize about Indian culture and society. Pueblo Indians cultivated the land through methods of irrigation that foreshadowed modern practices. The Pawnees

periodically set fire to the land to improve game hunting and the growth of vegetation. Indians on the southern plains gradually became enmeshed in the market economy for bison robes, which they sold to American traders. Indians were not pacifists, and they engaged in warfare with their enemies in disputes over hunting grounds, horses, and honor. However, the introduction of guns by European and American traders had transformed Indian warfare into a much more deadly affair than had existed previously. And by the mid-nineteenth century, some tribes had become so deeply engaged in the commercial fur trade with whites that they had depleted their own hunting grounds.

Native Americans had their own approach toward nature and the land they inhabited. Most tribes did not accept private ownership of land, as white pioneers did. Indians recognized the concept of private property in

**MAP 15.2 The Indian Frontier, 1870**

Western migration posed a threat to the dozens of Indian tribes and the immense herds of bison in the region. The tribes had signed treaties with the U.S. government recognizing the right to live on their lands. The presence of U.S. forts did not protect the Indians from settlers who invaded their territories.

ownership of their horses, weapons, tools, and shelters, but they viewed the land as the common domain of their tribe, for use by all members. "The White man knows how to make everything," the Hunkpapa Lakota chieftain Sitting Bull remarked, "but he does not know how to distribute it." This communitarian outlook also reflected native attitudes toward the environment. They considered human beings not as superior to the rest of nature's creations, but rather as part of an interconnected world of animals, plants, and natural elements. Chief Joseph, leader of the Nez Percé Indians, explained to whites who tried to encroach on his land: "The country was made without lines of demarcation, and it's no man's business to divide it. . . . I see whites all over the country gaining wealth, and see their desire to give us lands that are worthless. . . . The earth and myself are of one mind. The measure of the land and the measure of our bodies are the same." According to this view, all plants and animals were part of a larger spirit world, which flowed from the power of the sun, the sky, and the earth.

The bison played a central role in Indian religion and society. By the mid-nineteenth century, approximately thirty million bison (commonly known as buffalo) grazed on the Great Plains. Before acquiring guns, Indians used a variety of means to hunt their prey, including bows and arrows and spears. Some rode their horses to chase bison and stampede them over cliffs. The meat from the buffalo provided food; its hide provided material to construct tepees and make blankets and clothes; bones were crafted into tools, knives, and weapons; even bison dung served a purpose—after it dried and hardened, "buffalo chips" became an excellent source of fuel. It is therefore not surprising that the Plains Indians dressed up in colorful outfits, painted their bodies, and danced to the almighty power of the buffalo and the spiritual presence within it.

Indian hunting societies contained gender distinctions, primarily around the use of horses to pursue bison. The task of riding horses to hunt bison became men's work; women waited for the hunters to return and then prepared the buffalo hides. Nevertheless, women refused to think of their role as passive: They saw themselves as sharing in the work of providing food, shelter, and clothing for the members of their tribe. Similarly, the religious belief that the spiritual world touched every aspect of the material world gave women an opportunity to experience this transcendent power without the mediation of male leaders, including the revered medicine men.

## Changing Federal Policy toward Indians

The U.S. government started out by treating western Indians as autonomous nations, thereby recognizing their stewardship over the land they occupied. In 1851 the **Treaty of Fort Laramie** confined tribes on the northern plains to designated areas in an attempt to keep white

**Buffalo Hunting**

This pictograph from around 1875 depicts a Shoshone man on a buffalo hunt, affirming the personal connection between Indians and the buffalo. The successful hunter shows his skill as a horseman in this drawing made on his buffalo skin robe. The garment also includes a brightly ornamented quillwork strip at the top.  © Werner Forman/TopFoto/The Image Works

settlers from encroaching on their land. A treaty two years later applied these terms to tribes on the southern plains. Indians kept their part of the agreement, but white miners racing to strike it rich did not. They roamed through Indian hunting grounds in search of ore and faced little government enforcement of the existing treaties. In fact, the U.S. military made matters considerably worse. On November 29, 1864, a peaceful band of 700 Cheyennes and Arapahos under the leadership of Chief Black Kettle gathered at Sand Creek, Colorado, supposedly under guarantees of U.S. protection. Instead, Colonel John M. Chivington and his troops launched an attack, despite a white flag of surrender hoisted by the Indians, and brutally scalped and killed some 270 Indians, mainly women and children. A congressional investigation later determined that the victims "were mutilated in the most horrible manner." Although there was considerable public outcry over the incident, as evidenced by the congressional investigation, the government did nothing to increase enforcement of its treaty obligations. In almost all disputes between white settlers and Indians, the government sided with the whites, regardless of the Indians' legal rights.

The duplicity of the U.S. government was not without consequences. The Sand Creek massacre unleashed Indian wars throughout the central plains, where the Lakota Sioux led the resistance from 1865 to 1868. In 1866 they killed eighty soldiers under the command of Captain William J. Fetterman in Wyoming. After two years of fierce fighting, both sides signed a second Treaty of Fort Laramie, which gave northern tribes control over the "Great Reservation" set aside in parts of present-day Montana, Wyoming, North Dakota, and South Dakota. Another treaty placed the southern tribes in a reservation carved out of western Oklahoma.

One of the tribes that wound up in Oklahoma was the Nez Percé. Originally settled in the corner where Washington, Oregon, and Idaho meet, the tribe was forced to sign a treaty ceding most of its land to the United States and to relocate onto a reservation. In 1877 Chief Joseph led the Nez Percé out of the Pacific Northwest, directing his people in an excruciating but daring march of 1,400 miles over mountains into Montana and Wyoming as federal troops pursued them. Intending to flee to Canada, the Nez Percé were finally intercepted in the mountains of northern Montana, just thirty miles from the border. Exhausted by the incredible journey, they surrendered. Subsequently, the government relocated these northwestern Indians to the southwestern territory of Oklahoma. In 1879 Chief Joseph pleaded with lawmakers in Congress to return his people to their home and urged the U.S. government to live up to the original intent of the treaties. His words carried some weight, and the Nez Percé returned under armed escort to a reservation in Washington.

The treaties did not produce a lasting peace. Though most of the tribes relocated onto reservations, some refused. The Apache chief Victorio explained why he would not resettle his people on a reservation. "We prefer to die in our own land under the tall cool pines," he declared. "We will leave our bones with those of our people. It is better to die fighting than to starve." General William Tecumseh Sherman, commander of the military forces against the Indians, issued orders to "push his measures for the utter destruction and subjugation of all who are outside the reservations in a hostile attitude." He went on to propose that the army "shall prosecute the war with vindictive earnestness against all hostile Indians till they are obliterated or beg for mercy." In November 1868, Lieutenant Colonel George Armstrong Custer took Sherman at his word and assaulted a Cheyenne village, killing more than one hundred Indians. Nearly a decade later, in 1876, the Indians, this time Lakota Sioux, exacted revenge by killing Custer and his troops at the **Battle of the Little Big Horn** in Montana. Yet this proved to be the final victory for the Lakota nation, as the army mounted an extensive and fierce offensive against them that shattered their resistance.

Among the troops that battled the Indians were African Americans. Known as "**buffalo soldiers**," a name given to them by the Indians but whose origin is unclear, they represented a cross section of the postwar black population looking for new opportunities that were now available after their emancipation. One enlisted man recalled: "I got tired of looking mules in the face from sunrise to sunset. Thought there must be a better livin' in this world." Some blacks enlisted to learn how to read and write; others sought to avoid unpleasant situations back home. Cooks, waiters, painters, bakers, teamsters, and farmers signed up for a five-year stint in the army at $13 a month. A few gained more glory than money. In May 1880, Sergeant George Jordan of the Ninth Cavalry led troops under his command to fend off Apache raids in Tularosa, New Mexico, for which he was awarded the Congressional Medal of Honor.

## Indian Defeat

By the late 1870s, Indians had largely succumbed to U.S. military supremacy. The tribes, as their many victories demonstrated, contained agile horsemen and skilled warriors, but the U.S. army was backed by the power of an increasingly industrial economy. Telegraph lines and railroads provided logistical advantages in the swift deployment of U.S. troops and the ability of the central command to communicate with field officers. Although Indians had acquired firearms over the years from American traders as well as from defeated enemies on the battlefield, the army boasted an essentially unlimited supply of superior weapons. The diversity of Indians and historic rivalries among tribes also made it difficult for them to unite against their common enemy. The federal government exploited these divisions by hiring Indians to serve as army scouts against their traditional tribal foes.

In addition to federal efforts to subdue Indians, other disasters devastated native peoples in the second half of the nineteenth century. Even before the Civil War, many Indians had died of diseases such as smallpox, cholera, scarlet fever, and measles, for which they lacked the immunity that Europeans and white Americans had acquired. Moreover, Indian policy was fundamentally flawed by cultural misunderstanding. Even the most sensitive white administrators of Indian affairs considered Indians a degraded race, in accordance with the scientific thinking of the time. At most, whites believed that Indians could be lifted to a higher level of civilization, which in practice meant a withering away of their traditional culture and heritage. See Document Project 15: American Indians and Whites on the Frontier, page 484.

The wholesale destruction of the bison was the final blow to Indian independence. As railroads pushed their tracks beyond the Mississippi, they cleared bison from their path by sending in professional hunters with high-powered rifles to shoot the animals. Buffalo Bill Cody built his reputation by working as a crack sharpshooter for the Kansas Pacific Railroad. At the same time, buffalo products such as shoes, coats, and hats became fashionable in the East. By the mid-1880s, hunters had killed more than thirteen million bison. As a result of the relentless move of white Americans westward and conspicuous consumption back east, bison herds were almost annihilated.

Faced with decimation of the bison, broken treaties, and their opponents' superior military technology, Native Americans' capacity to wage war collapsed. Indians had little choice but to settle on shrinking reservations that the government established for them. The absence of war, however, did not necessarily bring them security. In the late 1870s, gold discoveries in the Black Hills of North Dakota ignited another furious rush by miners who swooped into the sacred lands supposedly guaranteed to the Lakota people. Rather than honoring its treaties, the U.S. government forced the tribes to relinquish still more land. Government officials continued to encourage western expansion by white settlers despite previous agreements with the Indians. General Custer's Seventh Cavalry was part of the military force trying to push Indians out of this mining region, when it was annihilated at the Little Big Horn in 1876. Elsewhere, Congress opened up a portion of western Oklahoma to white homesteaders in 1889. Although this land had not been assigned to specific tribes relocated in Indian Territory, more than eighty thousand Indians from various tribes lived there. This government-sanctioned land rush only added to the pressure from homesteaders and others to acquire more land at the expense of the Indians. A decade later, Congress officially ended Indian control of Indian Territory.

## Reforming Indian Policy

As reservations continued to shrink under expansionist assault and government acquiescence, a movement arose to reform Indian policy. Largely centered in the East where few Indians lived, reformers came to believe that the future welfare of Indians lay not in sovereignty but in assimilation. In 1881 Helen Hunt Jackson published *A Century of Dishonor*, her exposé of the unjust treatment the Indians had received, including broken promises and fraudulent activities by government agents. Roused by this depiction of the Indians' plight, groups such as the Women's National Indian Association joined with ministers and philanthropists to advocate the transformation of native peoples into full-fledged Americans.

From today's vantage point, these well-intentioned reformers could be viewed as contributing to the demise of the Indians by trying to eradicate their cultural heritage. Judged by the standards of their own time, however, they truly wanted to save the Indians from the brutality and corrupt behavior they had endured, and they honestly believed they were acting in the Indians' best interests. The most advanced thinking among anthropologists at the time offered an approach that supported assimilation as the only alternative to extinction. The influential Lewis Morgan, author of *Ancient Society* (1877), concluded that all cultures evolved through three stages: savagery, barbarism, and civilization. Indians occupied the lower rungs, but reformers argued that by adopting white values they could become civilized. In effect, this would mean the cultural extermination of the Indians, but reformers such as Richard Henry Pratt, the founder of the Carlisle Indian School, stressed salvation as their motive. "Do not feed America to the Indian, which is tribalizing and not an Americanizing process," he wrote, "but feed the Indian to America, and America will do the assimilating and annihilate the problem."

Reformers such as Pratt faced opposition from white Americans who doubted that Indian assimilation was possible. For many Americans, secure in their sense of their own superiority, the decline and eventual extinction of the Indian peoples was an inevitable consequence of what they saw as Indians' innate inferiority. For example, a Wyoming newspaper predicted: "The same inscrutable Arbiter that decreed the downfall of Rome has pronounced the doom of extinction upon the red men of America." And it warned: "To pretend to defer this by mawkish sentimentalism . . . is unworthy of the age."

Reformers found their legislative spokesman in Senator Henry Dawes of Massachusetts. As legislative director of the Boston Indian Citizenship Association, Dawes shared Christian reformers' belief that becoming a true American would save both the Indians and the soul of the nation. "Soon I trust," Dawes remarked, "we will wipe out the disgrace of our past treatment and lift the [Indian] up into citizenship and manhood and cooperation with us to the glory of the country." A Republican who had served in Congress since the Civil War, Dawes had the same paternalistic attitude toward Indians as he had toward freed slaves. He believed that if both degraded groups worked hard and practiced thrift and individual initiative in the spirit of Dawes's New England Puritan forebears, they would succeed. The key for Dawes was private ownership of land.

Passed in 1887, the **Dawes Act** ended tribal rule and divided Indian lands into 160-acre parcels. The act allocated one parcel to each family head. The government held the lands in trust for the Indians for twenty-five years; at the end of this period, the Indians would receive American citizenship. In return, the Indians had to abandon their religious and cultural rites and practices, including storytelling and the use of medicine men. Whatever lands remained after this reallocation—and the amount was considerable—would be sold on the open market, and the profits from the sales would be placed in an educational fund for Indians.

Unfortunately, like most of the policies it replaced, the Dawes Act proved detrimental to Native Americans. Indian families received inferior farmlands and inadequate tools to cultivate them, while speculators reaped profits from the sale of the "excess" Indian lands. A little more than a decade after the Dawes Act went into effect, Indians controlled 77 million acres of land, down sharply from the 155 million acres they held in 1881. Additional legislation in 1891 forced Indian parents to send their children to boarding schools or else face arrest. At these educational institutions, Indian children were given "American" names, had their long hair cut, and wore uniforms in place of their native dress. The program for boys provided manual and vocational training and that for girls taught domestic skills, so that they could emulate the gender roles in middle-class American families. However, this schooling offered few skills of use in an economic world undergoing industrial transformation. The students "found themselves in a twilight world," one historian claimed. "They were not equipped or allowed to enter American society as equals, yet they had been subjected to sufficient change as to make returning to the reservations difficult and sometimes traumatic."

## Indian Assimilation and Resistance

Not all Indians conformed to the government's attempt at forced acculturation. Some refused to abandon their traditional social practices, and others rejected the white man's version of private property and civilization. Many displayed more complicated approaches to survival in a world that continued to view Indians with prejudice. Geronimo and Sitting Bull participated in pageants and Wild West shows but refused to disavow their heritage. Ohiyesa, a Lakota also known as Charles Eastman, went to boarding school, graduated from Dartmouth College, and earned a medical degree from Boston University. He supported passage of the Dawes Act, believed in the virtues of an American education, and worked for the Bureau of Indian Affairs. At the same time, he spoke out against government corruption and fraud perpetrated against Indians. Reviewing his life in his later years, Eastman/Ohiyesa reflected: "I am an Indian and while I have learned much from civilization . . . I have never lost my Indian sense of right and justice."

Disaster loomed for those who resisted assimilation and held on too tightly to the old ways. In 1888 the prophet Wovoka, a member of the Paiute tribe in western Nevada, had a vision that Indians would one day regain control of the world and that whites would disappear. He believed that the

Creator had provided him with a **Ghost Dance** that would make this happen. The dance spread to thousands of Lakota Sioux in the northern plains. Seeing the Ghost Dance as a sign of renewed Indian resistance, the army attempted to put a stop to the revival. On December 29, 1890, the Seventh Cavalry, Custer's old regiment, chased three hundred ghost dancers to Wounded Knee Creek on the Pine Ridge Reservation in present-day South Dakota. In a confrontation with the Lakota leader Big Foot, a gunshot accidentally rang out during a struggle with one of his followers. The cavalry then turned the full force of their weaponry on the Indians. When the hail of bullets ceased, about 250 Native Americans, many of them women and children, lay dead.

The message of the massacre at Wounded Knee was clear for those who raised their voices against Americanization. As Black Elk, a spiritual leader of the Oglala Lakota tribe, asserted: "A people's dream died there. . . . There is no center any longer, and the sacred tree is dead." It may not have been the policy of the U.S. government to exterminate the Indians as a people, but it was certainly U.S. policy to destroy Indian culture and society once and for all.

### REVIEW & RELATE

How and why did federal Indian policy change during the nineteenth century?

Describe some of the ways that Indian peoples responded to federal policies. Which response do you think offered their greatest chance for survival?

✔ **LEARNING***Curve* bedfordstmartins.com/hewittlawson/LC

## The Mining Frontier

Among the settlers pouring into Indian Territory in the Rocky Mountains were miners in search of gold and silver. These prospectors envisioned instant riches that would come from a lucky strike. The vast majority found only backbreaking work, danger, and frustration. Miners continued to face hardship and danger as industrial mining operations took over from individual prospectors, despite the efforts of some miners to fight for better wages and working conditions. By 1900 the mining rush had peaked, and many of the boomtowns that had cropped up around the mining industry had emptied out.

### The Business of Mining

The discovery of gold in California in 1848 had set this mining frenzy in motion. Over the next thirty years, successive waves of gold and silver strikes in Colorado, Nevada,

Washington, Idaho, Montana, and the Dakotas lured individual prospectors with shovels and wash pans. One of the biggest finds came with the **Comstock Lode** in the Sierra Nevada. All told, miners extracted around $350 million worth of silver from this source. Two of those who came to share in the wealth were Samuel Clemens and his brother Orion. Writing from Carson City, Nevada, Samuel described his new surroundings to his family: "The country is fabulously rich in gold, silver, copper, lead . . . thieves, murderers, desperadoes, ladies . . . lawyers, Christians, Indians, Chinamen, Spaniards, gamblers, sharpers, coyotes . . . poets, preachers, and jackass rabbits." He did not find his fortune in Nevada and soon turned his attention to writing, finally achieving success as the author called Mark Twain.

Like Twain, many of those who flocked to the Comstock Lode and other mining frontiers were men. Nearly half were foreign-born, many of them coming from Mexico or China. Using pans and shovels, prospectors could find only the ore that lay near the surface of the earth and water. Once these initial discoveries were played out, individual prospectors could not afford to buy the equipment needed to dig out the vast deposits of gold and silver buried deep in the earth. As a result, western mining operations became big businesses run by men with the financial resources necessary to purchase industrial mining equipment.

**Explore**

See Document 15.1 for a description of a gold rush town.

When mining became an industry, prospectors became wageworkers. In Virginia City, Nevada, miners labored for $4 a day, which was a decent wage for the time, but one that barely covered the monthly expenses of life in a mining boomtown. Moreover, the work was extremely dangerous. Mine shafts extended down more than a thousand feet, and working temperatures regularly exceeded 100 degrees Fahrenheit. Noxious fumes, fires, and floods of scalding water flowing through the shafts posed a constant threat. Between 1863 and 1880, at least three hundred miners died on the job, and accidents were a daily occurrence, leaving many men disabled and out of work with no compensation.

Struggling with low pay and dangerous work conditions, western miners sought to organize. In the mid-1860s, unions formed in the Comstock Lode areas of Virginia City and Gold Hill, Nevada. Although these unions had some success, they also provoked a violent backlash from mining companies determined to resist union demands. Companies hired private police forces to help break strikes. Such forces were often assisted by state militias deployed by elected officials with close ties to the companies. For example, in 1892 the governor of Idaho crushed an unruly strike by calling up the National Guard, a confrontation that resulted in the deaths of seven strikers. A year later, mine workers formed one of the most militant labor organizations in the nation, the Western Federation of Miners. Within a decade, it had attracted fifty thousand members. However, union solidarity did not extend to all races and ethnicities. The union was made up of members from Irish, English, Italian, Slavic, and Greek backgrounds but excluded Chinese, Mexican, and Indian workers from its ranks.

## Life in the Mining Towns

Men worked the mines, but women flocked to the area as well. In Storey County, Nevada, the heart of the Comstock Lode, the 1875 census showed that women made up about half the population. Most employed women worked long hours as domestics in boardinghouses, hotels, and private homes. Prostitution, which was legal, accounted for the single largest segment of the female workforce. Most prostitutes were between the ages of nineteen and twenty-four, and they entered this occupation because few other well-paying jobs were available to them. The demand for their services remained high among the large population of unmarried men. Yet prostitutes faced constant danger, and many were victims of physical abuse, robbery, and murder.

Boomtowns like Virginia City sported a wild assortment of miners. They sought relief in taverns, brothels, and opium

**Prostitution on the Frontier**

Prostitution was one of the main sources of employment for women in frontier mining towns. A legal enterprise, it paid better than other work such as domestic service and teaching. In 1875 in the Comstock region of Nevada, 307 women plied their trade in brothels and saloons similar to the saloon shown here.

The Art Archive/Bill Manns/Art Resource, NY

**DOCUMENT 15.1**

# Granville Stuart | Gold Rush Days, 1925

When the gold rush began in the West, Granville Stuart and his brother were among those who flooded into Montana in 1863 and struck it rich. News of their discovery set off a stampede of prospectors seeking their fortune. A second Virginia City sprang up in Montana to house the miners and the assortment of business people who served them. Gold dust, valued at $18 an ounce, became the medium of exchange. Stuart published his journals and reminiscences from his gold rush days sixty-two years later in 1925.

**Explore**

About the middle of January, 1864, a regular stampede craze struck Virginia City. The weather had been quite cold and work in the mines was temporarily suspended. A large number of idle men were about town and it required no more than one man with an imaginative mind to start half the population off on a wild goose chase. Somebody would say that somebody said, that somebody had found a good thing and without further inquiry a hundred or more men would start out for the reported diggings. . . .

Late in the evening on January 22, a rumor started that a big discovery had been made on Wisconsin creek, a distance of thirty miles from Virginia City. The report said that as much as one hundred dollars to the pan had been found; and

away the people flew all anxious to be first on the ground, where they could "just shovel up gold." Virginia City was almost deserted: men did not stop for horses, blankets, or provisions, the sole aim was to get there first and begin to shovel it out at the rate of one hundred to the pan. Fortunately the distance was not great and the weather was mild. Robert Dempsey had a ranch nearby and the stampeders got a supply of beef from him to last them back to town. It is needless to say that they found no diggings and all returned to Virginia [City] in a few days.

Source: Granville Stuart, *Forty Years on the Frontier as Seen in the Journals and Reminiscences of Granville Stuart, Gold-Miner, Trader, Merchant, Rancher, and Politician*, ed. Paul C. Phillips (Cleveland: Arthur H. Clark, 1925), 1:270–71.

**Interpret the Evidence**

- How did the expectations of newly arrived prospectors differ from reality?
- How would you characterize Stuart's attitude toward the scenes he describes?

**Put It in Context**

As western towns grew more crowded and the mining process became more complex, who profited from the frenzied atmosphere of mining regions?

dens. In Butte, Montana, miners frequented bars with such colorful names as "Bucket of Blood," "The Cesspool," and "Graveyard." They boarded in houses run by characters nicknamed "Mag the Rag," "Take-Five Annie," "Ellen the Elephant," and "The Racehorse." A folk tune described Butte's annual gala event, the "Hopheads' [drug addicts'] Ball":

All the junkies were invited
Yes every gink [skinny man] and muff [prostitute]
Not a single one was slighted
If they were on the stuff [opium].

Invitations were presented
To every hustler and her man.
They even sent up invites
To the hopheads in the can [jail].

As early as the 1880s, gold and silver discoveries had played out in the Comstock Lode. Boomtowns, which had sprung up almost overnight, now became ghost towns as gold and silver deposits dwindled. Even more substantial places like Virginia City, Nevada, experienced a severe decline as the veins of ore ran out. One revealing sign of the city's plummeting fortunes was the drop in the number of prostitutes, which declined by more than half by 1880. The mining frontier then shifted from gold and silver to copper, lead, and zinc, centered in Montana and Idaho. As with the early prospectors in California and Nevada, these miners eventually became wageworkers for giant consolidated mining companies. By the end of the nineteenth century, the Amalgamated Copper Company and the American Smelting and Refining Company dominated the industry.

Mining towns that survived, like Butte, became only slightly less rowdy places, but they did settle into more complex patterns of urban living. Though the population remained predominantly young and male, the young men were increasingly likely to get married and raise families. Residents lived in neighborhoods divided by class and ethnicity. For example, in Butte the west side of town became home to the middle and upper classes. Mine workers lived on the east side in homes subdivided into apartments and in boardinghouses. "The houses were almost skin to skin," one resident described the area, "and boy, there were kids all over in the neighborhood." The Irish lived in one section; Finns, Swedes, Serbs, Croatians, and Slovenes in other sections. Each group formed its own social, fraternal, and religious organizations to relieve the harsh conditions of overcrowding, poor sanitation, and discrimination. Residents of the east side relied on one another for support and frowned on those who deviated from their code of solidarity. "They didn't try to outdo the other one," one neighborhood woman remarked. "If you did, you got into trouble. . . . If they thought you were a little richer than they were, they wouldn't associate with you." Although western mining towns retained distinctive qualities, in their social and ethnic divisions they came to resemble older cities east of the Mississippi River.

### REVIEW & RELATE

How and why did the nature of mining in the West change during the second half of the nineteenth century?

How did miners and residents of mining towns reshape the frontier landscape?

**LEARNINGCurve** bedfordstmartins.com/hewittlawson/LC

## Ranching and Farming Frontiers

Ranchers and farmers heading west also faced harsh realities. Cowboys worked long hours in tough but boring conditions on the open range. Farmers endured great hardships in trying to raise crops in an often inhospitable climate. Women played a critical role as pioneers, often setting out to acquire their own land or helping to run the family farm. Falling crop prices, however, led to soaring debt and forced many farmers into bankruptcy and off their land. Despite difficult physical and economic conditions, many of these women and men showed grit and determination not only in surviving but in improving their lives as well.

### The Life of the Cowboy

There is no greater symbol of the frontier West than the cowboy. As portrayed in novels and film, the cowboy hero was the essence of manhood, an independent figure who fought for justice and defended the honor and virtue of women. Never the aggressor, he fought to protect law-abiding residents of frontier communities. Having helped tame some wild western town, the cowboy rode off into the sunset in search of new frontiers to challenge him.

This romantic image excited generations of American readers and later movie and television audiences. In reality, cowboys' lives were much more mundane. Cowpunchers worked for paltry monthly wages, put in long days herding cattle, and spent part of the night guarding them on the open range. Their major task was to make the 1,500-mile **Long Drive** along the Chisholm Trail. Beginning in the late 1860s, cowboys moved cattle from ranches in Texas through Oklahoma to rail depots in Kansas towns such as Abilene and Dodge City; from there, cattle were shipped by train eastward to slaughterhouses in Chicago. Life along the trail was monotonous, and riders had to contend with bad weather, dangerous work, and disease.

Numbering around forty thousand and averaging twenty-four years of age, the cowboys who rode through the Great Plains from Texas to Kansas came from diverse backgrounds. The majority, about 66 percent, were white, predominantly southerners who had fought for the South during the Civil War. Most of the rest were divided evenly between Mexicans, who had first tended cattle during Spanish rule in the Southwest, and African Americans, some of whom were former slaves and others Union veterans of the Civil War.

**Explore**

See Documents 15.2 and 15.3 for two depictions of cowboy life.

Besides experiencing rugged life on the range, black and Mexican cowboys faced racial discrimination. Jim Perry, an African American who rode for the three-million-acre XIT

DOCUMENTS 15.2 AND 15.3

# Cowboy Myths and Realities: Two Views

William F. Cody, known as "Buffalo Bill," had been a real-life bison hunter in the American West and an army scout in the Indian wars of the 1860s and 1870s. Drawing on his authentic adventures and his heroism, Cody helped romanticize the figures that populated the American frontier, especially the cowboys, through his Wild West shows, a poster from which is shown here. The diary entries of George C. Duffield present a more mundane description of cowboy life. Duffield drove cattle on the open range in 1866 from Texas, where they were bred, to Iowa, where they went to market.

**Explore**

**15.2
Buffalo Bill's Wild
West Show, 1893**

**Explore**

### 15.3 George C. Duffield | Diary of a Real Cowboy, 1866

*12th*

Hard Rain & Wind. Big stampede & here we are among the Indians with 150 head of Cattle gone. Hunted all day & the Rain pouring down with but poor success. Dark days are these to me. Nothing but Bread & Coffee. Hands all Growling & Swearing—everything wet & cold. Beeves [steers] gone. Rode all day & gathered all but 35 mixed with 8 other Herds. Last Night 5000 Beeves stampeded at this place & a general mix up was the result.

*13th*

finished separating our Cattle & Moved up 4 miles. Very warm day—

*14th*

Last night there was a terrible storm. Rain poured in torrents *all* night & up to 12 AM today. Our Beeves left us in the night but for *once* on the whole trip we found them *all* together near camp at day break. *All* the other droves as far as I can hear are scattered to the four winds. Our Other Herd was all gone. We are now 25 Miles from Ark River & it is Very High. We are water bound by two creeks & but Beef & Flour to eat, am not Homesick but Heart sick. . . .

*16th*

Last night was a dark Gloomey night but we made it all right. Today it is raining & we have crossed Honey creek & am informed that there is another creek 6 miles ahead swimming. Twelve o clock today it rained one Hour so hard that a creek close by rose 20 ft in the afternoon. All wet.

Source: George C. Duffield, "Driving Cattle from Texas to Iowa, 1866," *Annals of Iowa* 14, no. 4 (1924): 253–54.

**Interpret the Evidence**

- What does the placement of Cody's portrait in the poster suggest about the role of white men in the West?
- How does Duffield's experience of the West differ from that conveyed in the poster?

**Put It in Context**

Why do you think Americans remember Buffalo Bill's version of the West rather than Duffield's?

Ranch in Texas for more than twenty years, complained: "If it weren't for my damned old black face I'd have been boss of one of these divisions long ago." Mexican *vaqueros*, or cowboys, earned one-third to one-half the wages of whites, whereas blacks were usually paid on a par with whites. Because the cattle kingdoms first flourished during Reconstruction, racial discrimination and segregation carried over into the Southwest. On one drive along the route to Kansas, a white boss insisted that a black cowboy eat and sleep separately from whites and shot at him when he refused to heed this order. Another white trail driver admitted that blacks "were usually called on to do the hardest work around the outfit." Nevertheless, the close proximity in which cowboys worked and the need for cooperation to overcome the pitfalls of the long drive made it difficult to enforce rigid racial divisions on the open range.

Large ranchers benefited the most from the cowboys' grueling work. Spaniards had originally imported cattle into the Southwest, and by the late nineteenth century some 5 million Texas longhorn steers grazed in the area. Cattle that could be purchased in Texas for $3 to $7 fetched a price of $30 to $40 in Kansas. The extension of railroads across the West opened up a quickly growing market for beef in the East. The development of refrigerated railroad cars guaranteed that slaughtered meat could reach eastern consumers without spoiling. With money to be made, the cattle industry rose to meet the demand. Fewer than 40 ranchers owned more than 20 million acres of land. One ranch in Texas spanned 200 miles and stocked 150,000 steers annually. Easterners and Europeans joined the boom and invested money in giant ranches. By the mid-1880s, approximately 7.5 million head of cattle roamed the western ranges, and large cattle ranchers became rich. Cattle ranching had become fully integrated into the national commercial economy.

Then the bubble burst. Ranchers who were already raising more cattle than the market could handle increasingly faced competition from cattle producers in Canada and Argentina. Prices spiraled downward. Another source of competition came from homesteaders who moved into the plains and fenced in their farms with barbed wire, thereby reducing the size of the open range. Yet the greatest disaster occurred from 1885 to 1887. Two frigid winters, together with a torrid summer drought, destroyed 90 percent of the cattle on the northern plains of the Dakotas, Montana, Colorado, and Wyoming. Under these conditions, outside capital to support ranching diminished, and many of the great cattle barons went into bankruptcy. This economic collapse consolidated the remaining cattle industry into even fewer hands. Some of those forced out of business turned to raising sheep, which require less water and grass than cattle to survive. The cowboy, never more than a hired hand, became a laborer for large corporations.

## Farmers Head West

The federal government played a major role in opening up the Great Plains to the farmers who eventually clashed with cattlemen. The Republican Party of Abraham Lincoln had opposed the expansion of slavery in order to promote the virtues of free soil and free labor for white men and their families. During the Civil War, preoccupation with battlefield losses did not stop the Republican-controlled Congress from passing the **Homestead Act**. As an incentive for western migration, the act established procedures for distributing 160-acre lots to western settlers, on condition that they develop and farm their land. What most would-be settlers did not know, however, was that lots of 160 acres were not suitable to conditions on the Great Plains. As geologist John Wesley Powell would demonstrate, the intensive techniques needed to farm 160-acre plots simply would not work in the harsh, dry climate of the Great Plains.

Reality did not deter pioneers and adventurers. In fact, weather conditions in the region temporarily fooled them. The decade after 1878 witnessed an exceptional amount of rainfall west of the Mississippi. Though not precisely predictable, this cycle of abundance and drought had been going on for millennia. One settler, convinced that Providence was smiling on Americans, remarked about the sudden burst of rain: "The Lord knowed we needed more land an' He's gone and changed the climate." In addition, innovation and technology bolstered dreams of success. Farmers planted heartier strains of wheat imported from Russia that survived the fluctuations of dry and wet and hot and cold weather. Machines produced by industrial laborers in northern factories to the east allowed farmers to plow tough land and harvest its yield. Steel-tipped plows, threshers, combines, and harvesters expanded production greatly, and windmills and pumping equipment provided sources of power and access to scarce water.

The people who accepted the challenge of carving out a new life were a diverse lot. The Great Plains attracted a large number of immigrants from Europe, some two million by 1900. Minnesota and the Dakotas welcomed communities of settlers from Sweden and Norway. Nebraska housed a considerable population of Germans, Swedes, Danes, and Czechs. About one-third of the people who migrated to the northern plains came directly from a foreign country. Many of the rest, both native-born and foreign-born, had lived in towns and villages along the Mississippi River before they decided to seek new opportunities farther west.

Railroads and land companies lured settlers to the plains with tales of the fabulous possibilities that awaited their arrival. The federal government had given railroads generous grants of public land on which to build their tracks as well as parcels surrounding the tracks that they could sell off to raise revenue for construction. Western railroads advertised in both the United States and Europe, proclaiming that migrants to the plains would find "the garden spot of the world." The land "will grow anything that any other country will grow, and with less work," the Rock Island Railroad announced, "because it rains here more than any other place, and at just the right time."

Having lured prospective settlers with exaggerated claims, railroads offered bargain rates to transport them to their new homes. Families and friends often journeyed together and rented an entire car on the train, known as "the immigrant car," in which they loaded their possessions, supplies, and even livestock. Often migrants came to the end of the rail line before reaching their destination. They completed the trip by wagon or stagecoach.

Commercial advertising alone did not account for the desire to journey westward. Settlers who had made the trip successfully wrote to relatives and neighbors back east and in the old country about the chance to start fresh. Linda Slaughter, the wife of an army doctor in the Dakotas, gushed: "The farms which have been opened in the vicinity of Bismarck have proven highly productive, the soil being kept moist by frequent rains. Vegetables of all kinds are grown with but little trouble." Descriptions of abundance, combined with a spirit of adventure, inspired Lucy Goldthorpe to claim a homestead near Epping in the Dakota Territory. "Even if you hadn't inherited a bit of restlessness and a pioneering spirit from your ancestors," she asserted, "it would have been difficult to ward off the excitement of the boom which, like the atmosphere, involved every conversation."

Those who took the chance shared a faith in the future and a willingness to work hard and endure misfortune. They found their optimism and spirits sorely tested. Despite the company of family members and friends, settlers faced a lonely existence on the vast expanse of the plains. Homesteads were spread out, and a feeling of isolation became a routine part of daily life.

With few trees around, early settlers constructed sod houses. These structures let in little light but a good deal of moisture, keeping them gloomy and damp. A Nebraskan who lived in this type of house jokingly remarked: "There was running water in our sod house. It ran through the

**Women Homesteaders in Nebraska**

The Chrisman sisters—Lizzie, Lutie, Jennie Ruth, and Hattie—are shown outside their sod house in 1886. They are among the thousands of homesteaders who moved west in the late nineteenth century and built homes from the only natural resource the Great Plains had in abundance: sod.   AP Photo

roof." Bugs, insects, and rodents, like the rain, often found their way inside to make living in such shelters even more uncomfortable.

If these dwellings were bleak, the climate posed even greater challenges. The plains did experience an unusual amount of rainfall in the late 1870s and early 1880s, but severe drought quickly followed. A plague of grasshoppers ravaged the northern plains in the late 1870s, destroying fruit trees and plants. Intense heat in the summer alternated with frigid temperatures in the winter. The Norwegian American writer O. E. Rolvaag, in *Giants in the Earth* (1927), his epic novel about Norwegian settlement in the Great Plains, described the extreme hardships that accompanied the fierce weather: "Blizzards from out of the northwest raged, swooped down and stirred up a greyish-white fury, impenetrable to human eyes. As soon as these monsters tired, storms from the northeast were sure to come, bringing more snow."

## Women Homesteaders

The women of the family were responsible for making these houses more bearable. Mothers and daughters were in charge of household duties, cooking the meals, canning fruits and vegetables, and washing and ironing clothing. Despite the drudgery of this work, women contributed significantly to the economic well-being of the family by occasionally taking in boarders and selling milk, butter, and eggs.

In addition, a surprisingly large number of single women staked out homestead claims by themselves. Some were young, unmarried women seeking, like their male counterparts, economic opportunity. Others were widows attempting to take care of their children after their husband's death. One such widow, Anne Furnberg, settled a homestead in the Dakota Territory in 1871. Born in Norway, she had lived with her husband and son in Minnesota. After her husband's death, the thirty-four-year-old Furnberg moved with her son near Fargo and eventually settled on eighty acres of land. She farmed, raised chickens and a cow, and sold butter and eggs in town. The majority of women who settled in the Dakotas were between the ages of twenty-one and twenty-five, most had never been married, and a majority were native-born children of immigrant parents. A sample of nine counties in the Dakotas shows that more than 4,400 women became landowners. Nora Pfundheler, a single woman, explained her motivation: "Well I was 21 and had no prospects of doing anything. The land was there, so I took it."

**Explore**

See Document 15.4 for a description of one Norwegian homesteader's experience.

Once families settled in and towns began to develop, women, married and single, directed some of their energies to moral reform and extending democracy on the frontier. Because of loneliness and grueling work, some men turned to alcohol for relief. Law enforcement in newly established communities was often no match for the saloons that catered to a raucous and drunken crowd. In their roles as wives, mothers, and sisters, many women tried to remove the source of alcohol-induced violence that disrupted both family relationships and public decorum. In Kansas in the late 1870s, women flocked to the state's Woman's Christian Temperance Union, founded by Amanda M. Way. Although they did not yet have the vote, in 1880 these women vigorously campaigned for a constitutional amendment that banned the sale of liquor.

Temperance women also threw their weight behind the issue of women's suffrage. In 1884 Kansas women established the statewide Equal Suffrage Association, which delivered to the state legislature a petition with seven thousand signatures in support of women's suffrage. Their attempt failed, but in 1887 women won the right to vote and run for office in all Kansas municipal elections. By the end of the nineteenth century, fifteen women had held city offices throughout the state. Julia Robinson, who campaigned for women's suffrage in Kansas, recalled the positive role that some men played: "My father had always said his family of girls had just as much right to help the government as if we were boys, and mother and he had always taught us to expect Woman Suffrage in our day." Kansas did not grant equal voting rights in state and national elections until 1912, but women obtained full suffrage before then in many western states.

## Farming on the Great Plains

Surviving loneliness, drudgery, and the weather still did not guarantee financial success for homesteaders. In fact, the economic realities of farming on the plains proved formidable. Despite the image of yeomen farmers—individuals engaged in subsistence farming with the aid of wives and children—most agriculture was geared to commercial transactions. Few farmers were independent or self-reliant. Farmers depended on barter and short-term credit. They borrowed from banks to purchase the additional land necessary to make agriculture economically feasible in the semiarid climate. They also needed loans to buy machinery to help increase production and to sustain their families while they waited for the harvest.

Instead of raising crops solely for their own use, farmers concentrated on the cash crops of corn and wheat.

DOCUMENT 15.4

# Gro Svendsen | Letter from a Homesteader, 1863

Many of the settlers who moved to Minnesota and the Dakotas migrated from northern Europe. Most did not speak English, left behind family members, and experienced geographical and emotional isolation. Women played a significant role in running farms, as shown in the following letter that Gro Svendsen wrote to her family in Norway about her life as a homesteader in Minnesota in 1863. Svendsen offers a typical account of the challenges many settlers faced.

**Explore**

*What emotions does Svendsen express about her life in America?*

*What differences between life in Norway and life on the Great Plains does this letter indicate?*

*Why would Svendsen's relatives think she might be exaggerating?*

Dear Parents, Sisters, and Brothers (always in my thoughts):

I have often thought that I ought to tell you about life here in the New World. Everything is so totally different from what it was in our beloved Norway. You never will really know what it's like, although you no doubt try to imagine what it might be. Your pictures would be all wrong, just as mine were.

I only wish that I could be with you to tell you all about it. Even if I were to write you countless pages, I still could not tell you everything.

I remember I used to wonder when I heard that it would be impossible to keep the milk here as we did at home. Now I have learned that it is indeed impossible because of the heat here in the summertime. One can't make cheese out of the milk because of flies, bugs, and other insects. I don't know the names of all these insects, but this I do know: If one were to make cheese here in the summertime, the cheese itself would be alive with bugs. Toward late autumn it should be possible to keep the milk. The people who have more milk than they need simply feed it to the hogs.

It's difficult, too, to preserve the butter. One must pour brine over it or salt it; otherwise it gets full of maggots. Therefore it is best, if one is not too far from town, to sell the butter at once. This summer we have been getting from eight to ten cents a pound. Not a great profit. For this reason people around here do not have many cows—just enough to supply the milk needed for the household. It's not wise to have more than enough milk, because the flies are everywhere. Even the bacon must be preserved in brine, and so there are different ways of doing everything. . . .

I could tell you even more, but possibly many who read this letter may think I am exaggerating. I assure you that all that I have told you I have experienced myself. If they do not believe me, they should come over and find out for themselves.

Source: Gro Svendsen, *Frontier Mother: The Letters of Gro Svendsen*, ed. Pauline Farseth and Theodore Blegen (Northfield, MN: Norwegian-American Historical Association, 1950), 39–40.

**Put It in Context**

What particular challenges did homesteaders who emigrated from other countries face?

The price of these commodities depended on the impersonal economic forces of an international market that connected American farmers to growers and consumers throughout the world. When supply expanded and demand remained relatively stable during the 1880s and 1890s, prices fell. This deflation made it more difficult for farmers to pay back their loans, and banks moved to foreclose. Corn growers had a hedge against falling prices. By withholding some of their corn from market, they could feed it to their hogs, fatten them up, and sell them at higher prices. The reduction in the supply of corn caused prices to rise until it was worth selling corn again.

This "corn-hog cycle," however, did not benefit wheat growers. When prices plummeted, they had little choice but to raise more wheat in the hope that increased volume would yield more income. Instead, the expansion in supply, coming as it did from so many farmers, merely depressed prices further, leaving wheat farmers with debts they could not repay. Under these circumstances, almost half of the homesteaders in the Great Plains picked up and moved either to another farm or to a nearby city. Large operators bought up the farms they left behind and ran them like big businesses. As had been the case in mining and ranching, western agriculture was increasingly commercialized and consolidated over the course of the second half of the nineteenth century.

The federal government unwittingly aided this process of commercialization and consolidation, to the benefit of large companies. The government sought to make bigger plots of land available in regions where small farming had proven impractical. The Desert Land Act (1877) offered 640 acres to settlers who would irrigate the land, but it brought small relief for farmers because the land was too dry. These properties soon fell out of the hands of homesteaders and into those of cattle ranchers. The Timber and Stone Act (1878) allowed homesteaders to buy 160 acres of forestland at $2.50 an acre. Lumber companies hired "dummy entrymen" to file claims and then quickly transferred the titles and added the parcels to their growing tracts of woodland.

#### REVIEW & RELATE

- How did market forces contribute to the boom and bust of the cattle ranching industry?
- How did women homesteaders on the Great Plains in the late nineteenth century respond to frontier challenges?

**LEARNINGCurve** bedfordstmartins.com/hewittlawson/LC

# Pushing Farther West

Some pioneers settled on the Great Plains or moved west for reasons beyond purely economic motives. The Mormons, for example, settled in Utah to find a religious home. The West Coast states of Washington, Oregon, and especially California, with their abundant resources and favorable climates, beckoned adventurers to travel beyond the Rockies and settle along the Pacific Ocean. The far West attracted many white settlers and foreign immigrants—especially Chinese—who encountered Spaniards and Mexicans already inhabiting the region. This encounter among diverse cultural groups sparked clashes that produced more oppression than opportunity for nonwhites.

## Mormons Head West

Unlike miners, cowboys, and farmers, **Mormons** sought refuge in the West for religious reasons. By 1870 the migration of Mormons (members of the Church of Jesus Christ of Latter-Day Saints) into the Utah Territory had attracted more than 85,000 settlers, most notably in Salt Lake City. Originally traveling to Utah under the leadership of Brigham Young in the late 1840s, Mormons had come under attack from opponents of their religion and the federal government for several reasons. Most important, Mormons believed in polygamy (the practice of having more than one wife at a time), which violated traditional Christian standards of morality. Far from seeing the practice as immoral, Mormon doctrine held polygamy as a blessing that would guarantee both husbands and wives an exalted place in the afterlife. Non-Mormons denounced polygamy as a form of involuntary servitude, similar to African American slavery. In reality, only a small minority of Mormon men had multiple wives, and most of these polygamists had only two wives.

Mormons also departed from the mainstream American belief in private property. The church considered farming a communal enterprise. To this end, church elders divided land among their followers, so that, as Brigham Young explained, "each person perform[ed] his several duties for the good of the whole more than for individual aggrandizement." Mormon communities also displayed a tolerant attitude toward the Native American tribes they encountered, learning their languages in order to convert rather than destroy them.

In the 1870s, the federal government took increased measures to control Mormon practices. In *Reynolds v. United States* (1879), the Supreme Court upheld the criminal conviction of a polygamist Mormon man. Previously in 1862 and 1874, Congress had banned plural marriages in the Utah Territory, and the justices ruled that despite their religious convictions, Mormons possessed no constitutional right to violate federal law. Congress went further in 1882 by passing the Edmunds Act, which disfranchised men engaging in polygamy. In 1887 Congress aimed to slash the economic power of the church by limiting Mormon assets to $50,000 and seizing the rest for the federal Treasury. A few years later, under this considerable pressure, the Mormons officially abandoned polygamy.

Related to the attack on polygamy was the question of women's suffrage. In 1870 voters in Utah endorsed a referendum granting women the right to vote, which enfranchised more than seventeen thousand women. Emmeline B. Wells, a Mormon woman who defended both women's rights and polygamy, argued that women "should be recognized as . . . responsible being[s]," capable of choosing plural marriage of their own free will. Opponents of enfranchisement contended that as long as polygamy existed, extending the vote to "enslaved" Mormon women would only perpetuate the practice because they would vote the way their husbands did. This point of view prevailed, and the Edmunds-Tucker Act (1887) rescinded the right to vote for women in the territory. Only with the rejection of polygamy did Congress accept statehood for Utah in 1896. The following year, the state extended the ballot to women.

## Californios

As with the nation's other frontiers, migrants to the West Coast did not find uninhabited territory. Besides Indians, the largest group that lived in California consisted of Spaniards and Mexicans. Since the eighteenth century, these *Californios* had established themselves as farmers and ranchers. The 1848 Treaty of Guadalupe Hidalgo, which ended the Mexican-American War, supposedly guaranteed the property rights of Californios and granted them U.S. citizenship, but reality proved different. Mexican American miners had to pay a "foreign miners tax," and Californio landowners lost their holdings to squatters, settlers, and local officials. Anglo politicians argued that the descendants of the original owners of Spanish land grants did not use them efficiently, and clever lawyers used the courts to deprive Californios of much of their property. By the end of the nineteenth century, about two-thirds of all land originally owned by Spanish-speaking residents had fallen into the hands of Euro-American settlers. By this time, many of these once proud and wealthy Californios had been forced into poverty and the low-wage labor force. The loss of land was matched by a diminished role in the region's government, as economic decline, ethnic bias, and the continuing

influx of white migrants combined to greatly reduce the political influence of the Californio population.

Spaniards and Mexicans living in the Southwest met the same fate as the Californios. Although they battled to keep their landholdings, they did not receive the first-class citizenship promised by the Treaty of Guadalupe-Hidalgo. When Anglo cattle ranchers began forcing Mexican Americans off their land near Las Vegas, New Mexico, a rancher named Juan Jose Herrera assembled a band of masked night riders known as *Las Gorras Blancas* (The White Caps). In 1889 and 1890, as many as seven hundred White Caps burned Anglo fences, haystacks, barns, and homes. They also set fire to thousands of railroad ties when the Atchison, Topeka, and Santa Fe Railroad refused to increase wages for Hispanic workers. In the end, however, Spanish-speaking inhabitants could not prevent the growing number of whites from pouring onto their lands and isolating them politically, economically, and culturally.

**Explore**

See Document 15.5 for a list of demands from the White Caps.

## The Chinese in the Far West

California and the far West also attracted a large number of Chinese immigrants. Migration to California and the West Coast was part of a larger movement in the nineteenth century out of Asia that brought impoverished Chinese to Australia, Hawaii, Latin America, and the United States. The Chinese migrated for several reasons in the decades after 1840. Internal conflicts in China sent them in search of refuge. Economic dislocation related to the British Opium Wars (1839–1842 and 1856–1860), along with bloody family feuds and a decade of peasant rebellion from 1854 to 1864, propelled migration. Faced with unemployment and starvation, the Chinese sought economic opportunity overseas. One man recounted the hardships that drove him to emigrate: "Sometimes we went hungry for days. My mother and [I] would go over the harvested rice fields of the peasants to pick the grains they dropped. . . . We had only salt and water to eat with the rice."

Chinese immigrants were attracted first by the 1848 gold rush and then by jobs building the transcontinental railroad. By 1880 the Chinese population had grown to 200,000, most of whom lived in the West. San Francisco became the center of the transplanted Chinese population, which congregated in the city's Chinatown. Under the leadership of a handful of businessmen, Chinese residents found jobs, lodging, meals, and social, cultural, and recreational outlets. Most of those who came were young unmarried men who intended to earn

# White Caps Flier, 1890

Before the United States acquired California and the territories of Arizona and New Mexico in 1848, most of the people living in the area were of Spanish heritage. In New Mexico, Hispanic villagers farmed on communal land. In the 1880s, Anglo authorities enclosed the communal land with barbed wire to promote individual farming. In response, a group of frustrated residents known as *Las Gorras Blancas*, or "White Caps," burned barns and destroyed the fences of ranchers who enclosed common lands. In 1890 the White Caps posted fliers in the town of Las Vegas, New Mexico, in which they described a range of grievances.

**Explore**

NUESTRA PLATFORMA— [Our Platform]

Our purpose is to protect the rights and interests of the people in general and especially those of the helpless classes.

We want the Las Vegas Grant settled to the benefit of all concerned, and this we hold is the entire community within the Grant.

We want no "land grabbers" or obstructionists of any sort to interfere. We will watch them.

We are not down on lawyers as a class, but the usual knavery and unfair treatment of the people must be stopped.

Our judiciary hereafter must understand that we will sustain it only when "Justice" is its watchword.

We are down on race issues, and will watch race agitators.

We favor irrigation enterprises, but will fight any scheme that tends to monopolize the supply of water sources to the detriment of residents living on lands watered by the same streams.

The people are suffering from the effects of partisan "bossism" and these bosses had better quietly hold their peace. The people have been persecuted and hauled about in every which way to satisfy their caprices.

We must have a free ballot and fair court and the will of the Majority shall be respected.

We have no grudge against any person in particular, but we are the enemies of bulldozers and tyrants.

If the old system should continue, death would be a relief to our suffering. And for our rights our lives are the least we can pledge.

If the fact that we are law-abiding citizens is questioned, come out to our houses and see the hunger and desolation we are suffering; and "this" is the result of the deceitful and corrupt methods of "bossism."

The White Caps 1,500 Strong and Gaining Daily

Source: *Las Vegas Daily Optic*, March 12, 1890, reprinted in *Foreigners in Their Native Land: Historical Roots of the Mexican Americans*, ed. David J. Weber (Albuquerque: University of New Mexico Press, 1973), 235–36.

## Interpret the Evidence

- Whom do the White Caps claim to represent, and what are their grievances?
- How did the White Caps support their claim to be law-abiding citizens? How might Anglo authorities have responded to their claims?

## Put It in Context

What kinds of difficulties did nonwhites face as white Americans moved westward during the nineteenth century?

enough money to return to China and start anew. The relatively few women who immigrated came as servants or prostitutes.

For many Chinese, the West proved unwelcoming. When California's economy slumped in the mid-1870s, many whites looked to the Chinese as scapegoats. White workingmen believed that the plentiful supply of Chinese laborers in the mines and railroads undercut their demands for higher wages. They contended that Chinese would work for less because they were racially inferior people who lived degraded lives. Anti-Chinese clubs mushroomed in California during the 1870s, and they soon became a substantial political force in the state. The Workingmen's Party advocated laws that restricted Chinese labor, and it initiated boycotts of goods made by Chinese people. Vigilantes attacked Chinese in the streets and set fire to factories that employed Asians. The Workingmen's Party and the

Democratic Party joined forces in 1879 to craft a new state constitution that blatantly discriminated against Chinese residents. In many ways, these laws resembled the Jim Crow laws passed in the South that deprived African Americans of their freedom following Reconstruction (discussed in chapter 16).

Pressured by anti-Chinese sentiment on the West Coast, the U.S. government enacted drastic legislation to prevent any further influx of Chinese. The **Chinese Exclusion Act** of 1882 banned Chinese immigration into the United States and prohibited those Chinese already in the country from becoming naturalized American citizens. As a result, the Chinese remained a predominantly male, aging, and isolated population until World War II. The exclusion act, however, did not stop anti-Chinese assaults. In the mid-1880s, white mobs drove Chinese out of Eureka, California; Seattle and Tacoma, Washington; and Rock Springs, Wyoming.

**Rock Springs Massacre**
This engraving depicts the Rock Springs massacre in Wyoming. On September 3, 1885, a mob of white coal miners killed at least 28 Chinese miners, injured 15, and burned 75 homes of Chinese residents. The violence came after years of anti-Chinese sentiment in the western United States. White miners blamed the Chinese for working for lower wages and taking their jobs.   The Granger Collection, New York

**REVIEW & RELATE**

What migrant groups were attracted to the far West? What drew them there?

Explain the rising hostility to the Chinese and other minority groups in the late-nineteenth-century far West.

**LEARNINGCurve** bedfordstmartins.com/hewittlawson/LC

## Conclusion: The Ambiguous Legacy of the Frontier

The legacy of the pioneering generation of Americans has proven mixed. Men and women pioneers left their old lives behind and boldly pushed into uncharted territory to reinvent themselves. They encountered numerous obstacles posed by difficult terrain, forbidding climate, and unfamiliar inhabitants of the land they sought to harness. They built their homes, tilled the soil to raise crops, and mined the earth to remove the metals it contained. They developed cities that would one day rival those back east: San Francisco, Los Angeles, Seattle, and Denver. These pioneers served as the advance guard of America's expanding national and international commercial markets. As producers of staple crops and livestock and consumers of manufactured goods, they contributed to the expansion of America's factories, railroads, and telegraph communication system. The nation would memorialize their spirit as a model of individualism and self-reliance.

In fact, settlement of the West required more than individual initiative and self-determination. Without the direct involvement of the federal government, settlers would not have received free or inexpensive homesteads and military protection to clear native inhabitants out of their way. Without territorial governors and judges appointed by Washington to preside over new settlements,

there would have been even less law, order, and justice than appeared in the rough-and-tumble environment that attracted outlaws, con artists, and speculators. Railroads, mining, and cattle ventures all relied heavily on foreign investors. Moreover, all the individualism and self-reliance that pioneers brought would not have saved them from the harsh conditions and disasters they faced without banding together as a community and pitching in to create institutions that helped them collectively. Despite their desire to achieve success, various pioneers—farmers, prospectors, cowboys—mostly found it difficult to make it on their own and began working for larger farming, mining, and ranching enterprises, with many of them becoming wageworkers. And for an experience that has been portrayed as a predominantly male phenomenon, settlement of the West depended largely on women.

Pioneers did not fully understand the land and people they encountered. More from ignorance than design, settlers engaged in agricultural, mining, and ranching practices that depleted fragile grasses, eroded hillsides, and polluted rivers and streams with runoff wastes. The settlement of the West nearly wiped out the bison and left Native Americans psychologically demoralized, culturally endangered, and economically impoverished. Some Indians willingly adopted white ways, but most of them fiercely resisted acculturation. Other nonwhite minorities in the West, such as Mexicans and Chinese, experienced less extreme treatment, but they suffered nonetheless.

Panoramic landscape paintings often depicted glorious scenes of the Wild West, but the truth was more nuanced. Annie Oakley pleased audiences with daring exploits that glorified a West she had not experienced. Geronimo surrendered and spent the rest of his life exiled from his native lands. He, too, tried to follow the path of Oakley, but his public appearances could not hide the devastation that he and other Native Americans had experienced. The western frontier represented both opportunity and loss.

LEARNINGCurve
Check what you know.
bedfordstmartins.com/hewittlawson/LC

# Chapter Review

Online Study Guide ▶ bedfordstmartins.com/hewittlawson

## KEY TERMS

Great Plains  (p. 461)
transcontinental railroad  (p. 462)
Treaty of Fort Laramie  (p. 465)
Battle of the Little Big Horn  (p. 466)
buffalo soldiers  (p. 466)
Dawes Act  (p. 467)
Ghost Dance  (p. 468)
Comstock Lode  (p. 469)
Long Drive  (p. 471)
Homestead Act  (p. 474)
Mormons  (p. 478)
*Californios*  (p. 479)
Chinese Exclusion Act  (p. 481)

## REVIEW & RELATE

1. What role did the federal government play in opening the West to settlement and economic exploitation?

2. Explain the determination of Americans to settle in land west of the Mississippi River despite the challenges the region presented.

3. How and why did federal Indian policy change during the nineteenth century?

4. Describe some of the ways that Indian peoples responded to federal policies. Which response do you think offered their greatest chance for survival?

5. How and why did the nature of mining in the West change during the second half of the nineteenth century?

6. How did miners and residents of mining towns reshape the frontier landscape?

7. How did market forces contribute to the boom and bust of the cattle ranching industry?

8. How did women homesteaders on the Great Plains in the late nineteenth century respond to frontier challenges?

9. What migrant groups were attracted to the far West? What drew them there?

10. Explain the rising hostility to the Chinese and other minority groups in the late-nineteenth-century far West.

## TIMELINE OF EVENTS

| | |
|---|---|
| **1848** | Gold discovered in California |
| **1851** | First Treaty of Fort Laramie |
| **1862** | Homestead Act passed |
| **1864** | Sand Creek massacre |
| **1865–1868** | Lakota Sioux lead Indian resistance |
| **Late 1860s** | Large-scale cattle drives begin |
| **1868** | Second Treaty of Fort Laramie |
| **1869** | Transcontinental railroad completed |
| **1870s** | Gold discovered in Black Hills of North Dakota |
| **1876** | Battle of the Little Big Horn |
| **1877** | Desert Land Act |
| **1878** | John Wesley Powell questions suitability of Great Plains for small-scale farming |
| | Timber and Stone Act |
| **1881** | Helen Hunt Jackson publishes *Century of Dishonor* |
| **1882** | Edmunds Act passed |
| | Chinese Exclusion Act passed |
| **1884** | Annie Oakley joins William Cody's Wild West show |
| **1885–1887** | Cattle industry collapses |
| **1886** | Geronimo captured |
| **1887** | Dawes Act passed |
| | Kansas women win right to vote and run for office in municipal elections |
| **1889–1890** | Mexican American White Caps attack Anglo property |
| **1890** | Massacre at Wounded Knee |
| **1893** | Western Federation of Miners formed |

# American Indians and Whites on the Frontier

Views on the relationship between whites and American Indians varied widely in the late-nineteenth-century West. Some white Americans advocated exterminating the Indians, whereas others sought to assimilate them. These attitudes differed significantly by region. Whites who were most likely to encounter Indians were generally the least sympathetic. Government officials were also divided. The most notable differences were between civilians in the Interior Department who favored peaceful solutions and those in the War Department who were inclined to use military force to resolve conflicts. However, even white reformers did not always understand Indian culture; as a result, they developed policies that led to the decline of Indian tribal societies. On the other side, Indian attitudes ranged from fierce resistance to accommodation and, in rare cases, assimilation. Even those who eventually adapted to white society and gained a measure of fame within it, like Zitkala-Ša (Document 15.9), never fully abandoned their pride in Indian traditions.

The following documents speak to important recurring questions in American history: How do white Americans and their leaders deal with differences among people rooted in race and nationality? How do those considered minorities forge strategies to gain political and economic access while maintaining their own identities and heritage? And how well did the U.S. government in the late nineteenth century balance its commitment to the competing values of continental expansion and equal justice under the law?

**DOCUMENT 15.6**

# James Michael Cavanaugh | Support for Indian Extermination, 1868

James Michael Cavanaugh was originally from Springfield, Massachusetts, but moved to Minnesota in 1854, where he served in Congress for one term. He subsequently moved to Colorado and then Montana and served in the House of Representatives as a Democrat from 1867 to 1871. In the following congressional speech, Cavanaugh explains his attitude toward Indians in a discussion about Indian appropriations with Republican representative Benjamin Butler of Massachusetts.

WILL SAY THAT I like an Indian better dead than living. I have never in my life seen a good Indian (and I have seen thousands) except when I have seen a dead Indian. I believe in the Indian policy pursued by New England in years long gone. I believe in the Indian policy which was taught by the great chieftain of Massachusetts, Miles Standish. I believe in the policy that exterminates the Indians, drives them outside the boundaries of civilization, because you cannot civilize them. Gentlemen may call this very harsh language; but perhaps they would not think so if they had had my experience in Minnesota and Colorado. In Minnesota the almost living babe has been torn from its mother's womb; and I have seen the child, with its young heart palpitating, nailed to the window-sill. I have seen women who were scalped, disfigured, outraged. In Denver, Colorado Territory, I have seen women and children brought in scalped. Scalped why? Simply because the Indian was "upon the war-path," to satisfy his devilish and barbarous propensities. You have made your treaties with the Indians, but they have not been observed. General [William Tecumseh] Sherman went out a year ago to Colorado Territory. He made a treaty; and in less than twenty-four hours after the treaty was made the Indians were again "upon the war-path." The Indian will make a treaty in the fall, and in the spring he is

again "upon the war-path." The torch, the scalping-knife, plunder, and desolation follow wherever the Indian goes.

But, Mr. Chairman, I will answer the gentleman's question more directly. My friend from Massachusetts [Mr. Butler] has never passed the barrier of the frontier. All he knows about Indians (the gentleman will pardon me for saying it) may have been gathered, I presume, from the brilliant pages of the author of "The Last of the Mohicans," or from the lines of the poet Longfellow in "Hiawatha." The gentleman has never yet seen the Indian upon the war-path. He has never been chased, as I have been, by these red devils—who seem to be the pets of the eastern philanthropists.

Mr. Chairman, I regret that I have not prepared myself with statistics as to Indian atrocities. I desire to answer the gentleman from Massachusetts fairly. I repeat that the Indian policy of the Government from beginning to end is wrong. If the management of the Indians is to continue as a part of the civil service, then there ought to be a bureau of Indian affairs, under the charge of a Cabinet officer, who should be responsible for all matters connected with the management of the Indians.

Source: United States Congress, *The Congressional Globe: Containing the Debates and Proceedings of the Second Session of the Fortieth Congress,* May 28, 1868, 2638.

# Thomas Nast | "Patience until the Indian Is Civilized—So to Speak," 1878

Through his cartoons, artist Thomas Nast crusaded against political corruption and mistreatment of freedpeople in the South. Although generally sympathetic to the rights of American Indians, in this illustration he raises questions about what the federal government should do regarding conflicts between white settlers and Indians in the West. Nast depicts Secretary of the Interior Carl Schurz (left), an Indian reformer, counseling patience to western settlers.

Library of Congress

**DOCUMENT 15.8**

# Helen Hunt Jackson | Challenges to Indian Policy, 1881

Helen Hunt Jackson's book *A Century of Dishonor* severely criticized U.S. policy toward Indians. Jackson sent a copy of her book to every member of Congress. Her handwritten inscription, intended to move lawmakers to action, contained the words of Benjamin Franklin: "Look upon your hands! They are stained with the blood of your relations." Despite her attack on the government's treatment of Indians and her advocacy of reform, Jackson believed that American Indians could not become citizens until they received proper training from enlightened white teachers.

There is not among these three hundred bands of Indians one which has not suffered cruelly at the hands either of the Government or of white settlers. The poorer, the more insignificant, the more helpless the band, the more certain the cruelty and outrage to which they have been subjected. This is especially true of the bands on the Pacific slope. These Indians found themselves of a sudden surrounded by and caught up in the great influx of gold-seeking settlers, as helpless creatures on a shore are caught up in a tidal wave. There was not time for the Government to make treaties; not even time for communities to make laws. The tale of the wrongs, the oppressions, the murders of the Pacific-slope Indians in the last thirty years would be a volume by itself, and is too monstrous to be believed.

It makes little difference, however, where one opens the record of the history of the Indians; every page and every year has its dark stain. The story of one tribe is the story of all, varied only by differences of time and place; but neither time nor place makes any difference in the main facts. Colorado is as greedy and unjust in 1880 as was Georgia in 1830, and Ohio in 1795; and the United States Government breaks promises now as deftly as then, and with an added ingenuity from long practice.

One of its strongest supports in so doing is the wide-spread sentiment among the people of dislike to the Indian, of impatience with his presence as a "barrier to civilization," and distrust of it as a possible danger. The old tales of the frontier life, with its horrors of Indian warfare, have gradually, by two or three generations' telling, produced in the average mind something like an hereditary instinct of unquestioning and unreasoning aversion which it is almost impossible to dislodge or soften. . . .

To assume that it would be easy, or by any one sudden stroke of legislative policy possible, to undo the mischief and hurt of the long past, set the Indian policy of the country right for the future, and make the Indians at once safe and happy, is the blunder of a hasty and uninformed judgment. The notion which seems to be growing more prevalent, that simply to make all Indians at once citizens of the United States would be a sovereign and instantaneous panacea for all their ills and all the Government's perplexities, is a very inconsiderate one. To administer complete citizenship of a sudden, all round, to all Indians, barbarous and civilized alike, would be as grotesque a blunder as to dose them all round with any one medicine, irrespective of the symptoms and needs of their diseases. It would kill more than it would cure. Nevertheless, it is true, as was well stated by one of the superintendents of Indian Affairs in 1857, that, "so long as they are not citizens of the United States, their rights of property must remain insecure against invasion. The doors of the federal tribunals being barred against them while wards and dependents, they can only partially exercise the rights of free government, or give to those who make, execute, and construe the few laws they are allowed to enact, dignity sufficient to make them respectable. While they continue individually to gather the crumbs that fall from the table of the United States, idleness, improvidence, and indebtedness will be the rule, and industry, thrift, and freedom from debt the exception. The utter absence of individual title to particular lands deprives every one among them of the chief incentive to labor and exertion—the very mainspring on which the prosperity of a people depends."

*(continued on page 488)*

All judicious plans and measures for their safety and salvation must embody provisions for their becoming citizens as fast as they are fit, and must protect them till then in every right and particular in which our laws protect other "persons" who are not citizens. . . .

Cheating, robbing, breaking promises—these three are clearly things which must cease to be done. One more thing, also, and that is the refusal of the protection of the law to the Indian's rights of property, "of life, liberty, and the pursuit of happiness."

When these four things have ceased to be done, time, statesmanship, philanthropy, and Christianity can slowly and surely do the rest. Till these four things have ceased to be done, statesmanship and philanthropy alike must work in vain, and even Christianity can reap but small harvest.

Source: Helen Hunt Jackson, *A Century of Dishonor: A Sketch of the United States Government's Dealings with Some of the Indian Tribes* (New York: Harper and Brothers, 1881), 337–38, 340–42.

## DOCUMENT 15.9

# Zitkala-Ša | Life at an Indian Boarding School, 1921

Gertrude Simmons Bonnin, who later took the Indian name Zitkala-Ša, lived on the Yankton Reservation in South Dakota, with her mother and brother until 1884, when missionaries recruited her to attend school so that she would become assimilated into Anglo-American culture. After attending a Quaker school in Wabash, Indiana, Zitkala-Ša briefly attended Earlham College and then taught at the Carlisle Indian Industrial School in Pennsylvania for two years. During that time, she experienced a reawakening of her American Indian heritage and consciousness and began publishing autobiographical accounts criticizing the educational practices of the schools she attended and at which she taught. In 1921 she recounted her own experiences in these Indian schools, including the incident she describes in the following selection.

THE FIRST DAY IN THE LAND of apples was a bitter-cold one; for the snow still covered the ground, and the trees were bare. A large bell rang for breakfast, its loud metallic voice crashing through the belfry overhead and into our sensitive ears. The annoying clatter of shoes on bare floors gave us no peace. The constant clash of harsh noises, with an undercurrent of many voices murmuring an unknown tongue, made a bedlam within which I was securely tied. And though my spirit tore itself in struggling for its lost freedom, all was useless.

A paleface woman, with white hair, came up after us. We were placed in a line of girls who were marching into the dining room. These were Indian girls, in stiff shoes and closely clinging dresses. The small girls wore sleeved aprons and shingled hair [haircut with the hair cut short from the back of the head to the nape of the neck]. As I walked noiselessly in my soft moccasins, I felt like sinking to the floor, for my blanket had been stripped from my shoulders. I looked hard at the Indian girls, who seemed not to care that they were even more immodestly dressed than I, in their tightly fitting clothes. While we marched in, the boys entered at an opposite door. I watched for the three young braves who came in our party. I spied them in the rear ranks, looking as uncomfortable as I felt.

A small bell was tapped, and each of the pupils drew a chair from under the table. Supposing this act meant they were to be seated, I pulled out mine and at once slipped into it from one side. But when I turned my head, I saw that I was the only one seated, and all the rest at our table remained standing. Just as I began to rise, looking shyly around to see how chairs were to be used, a second bell was sounded. All were seated at last, and I had to crawl back into my chair again. I heard a man's voice at one end of the hall, and I looked around to see him. But all the others hung their heads over their plates. As I glanced at the long chain of tables, I caught the eyes of a paleface woman upon me. Immediately I dropped my eyes, wondering why I was so keenly watched by the strange woman. The man ceased his mutterings, and then a third bell was tapped. Every one picked up his knife and fork and began eating. I began crying instead, for by this time I was afraid to venture anything more.

But this eating by formula was not the hardest trial in that first day. Late in the morning, my friend Judéwin gave me a terrible warning. Judéwin knew a few words of English; and she had overheard the paleface woman talk about cutting our long, heavy hair. Our mothers had taught us that only unskilled warriors who were captured had their hair shingled by the enemy. Among our people, short hair was worn by mourners, and shingled hair by cowards!

We discussed our fate some moments, and when Judéwin said, "We have to submit, because they are strong," I rebelled.

"No, I will not submit! I will struggle first!" I answered.

I watched my chance, and when no one noticed I disappeared. I crept up the stairs as quietly as I could in my squeaking shoes—my moccasins had been exchanged for shoes. Along the hall I passed, without knowing whither I was going. Turning aside to an open door, I found a large room with three white beds in it. The windows were covered with dark green curtains, which made the room very dim. Thankful that no one was there, I directed my steps toward the corner farthest from the door. On my hands and knees I crawled under the bed, and cuddled myself in the dark corner.

From my hiding place I peered out, shuddering with fear whenever I heard footsteps near by. Though in the hall loud voices were calling my name, and I knew that even Judéwin was searching for me, I did not open my mouth to answer. Then the steps were quickened and the voices became excited. The sounds came nearer and nearer. Women and girls entered the room. I held my breath and watched them open closet doors and peep behind large trunks. Some one threw up the curtains, and the room was filled with sudden light. What caused them to stoop and look under the bed I do not know. I remember being dragged out, though I resisted by kicking and scratching wildly. In spite of myself, I was carried downstairs and tied fast in a chair.

I cried aloud, shaking my head all the while until I felt the cold blades of the scissors against my neck, and heard them gnaw off one of my thick braids. Then I lost my spirit. Since the day I was taken from my mother I had suffered extreme indignities. People had stared at me. I had been tossed about in the air like a wooden puppet. And now my long hair was shingled like a coward's! In my anguish I moaned for my mother, but no one came to comfort me. Not a soul reasoned quietly with me, as my own mother used to do; for now I was only one of many little animals driven by a herder.

Source: Zitkala-Ša (Gertrude Bonnin), *American Indian Stories* (Washington, D.C.: Hayworth, 1921), 52–56.

**DOCUMENT 15.10**

## Chief Joseph | Views on Indian Affairs, 1879

In 1877, following a string of treaties broken by the U.S. government, Chief Joseph led the Nez Percé on a 1,300-mile march from their tribal land in Oregon to Canada, in search of a home. Thirty miles from the Canadian border, they were surrounded by U.S. troops. Explaining "I am tired of fighting. . . . I will fight no more forever," Joseph was forced into negotiations with U.S. army general Nelson Miles. After his capture, Chief Joseph was taken to Washington, D.C., where he addressed a gathering of cabinet members and congress-men and tried to convince them to return tribal lands to the Nez Percé.

AT LAST I WAS GRANTED permission to come to Washington and bring my friend Yellow Bull and our interpreter with me. I am glad we came. I have shaken hands with a great many friends, but there are some things I want to know which no one seems able to explain. I can not understand how the Government sends a man out to fight us, as it did General Miles, and then breaks his word. Such a government has something wrong about it. I can not understand why so many chiefs are allowed to talk so many different ways, and promise so many different things. I have seen the Great Father Chief [President Rutherford B. Hayes], the next Great Chief [Secretary of the Interior], the Commissioner Chief [E. A. Hayt, Commissioner of Indian Affairs], the Law Chief [Congressman Benjamin Butler], and many other law chiefs [congressmen], and they all say they are my friends, and that I shall have justice, but while their mouths all talk right I do not understand why nothing is done for my people. I have heard talk and talk, but nothing is done. Good words do not last long unless they amount to something. Words do not pay for my dead people. They do not pay for my country, now overrun by white men. They do not protect my father's grave. They do not pay for all my horses and cattle. Good words will not give me back my children. Good words will not make good the promise of your War Chief General Miles. Good words will not give my people good health and stop them from dying. Good words will not get my people a home where they can live in peace and take care of themselves. I am tired of talk that comes to nothing. It makes my heart sick when I remember all the good words and all the broken promises. There has been too much talking by men who had no right to talk. Too many misrepresentations have been made, too many misunderstandings have come up between the white men about the Indians. If the white man wants to live in peace with the Indian he can live in peace. There need be no trouble. Treat all men alike. Give them all the same law. Give them all an even chance to live and grow. All men were made by the same Great Spirit Chief. They are all brothers. The earth is the mother of all people, and all people should have equal rights upon it. You might as well expect the rivers to run backward as that any man who was born a free man should be contented when penned up and denied liberty to go where he pleases. If you tie a horse to a stake, do you expect he will grow fat? If you pen an Indian up on a small spot of earth, and compel him to stay there, he will not be contented, nor will he grow and prosper. I have asked some of the great white chiefs where they get their authority to say to the Indian that he shall stay in one place, while he sees white men going where they please. They can not tell me.

I only ask of the Government to be treated as all other men are treated. If I can not go to my own home, let me have a home in some country where my people will not die so fast. I would like to go to Bitter Root Valley. There my people would be healthy; where they are now they are dying. Three have died since I left my camp to come to Washington.

When I think of our condition, my heart is heavy. I see men of my race treated as outlaws and driven from country to country, or shot down like animals.

I know that my race must change. We can not hold our own with the white men as we are. We only ask an even chance to live as other men live. We ask to be recognized as men. We ask that the same law shall work alike on all men. If the Indian breaks the law, punish him by the law. If the white man breaks the law, punish him also.

Let me be a free man—free to travel, free to stop, free to work, free to trade where I choose, free to choose my own teachers, free to follow the religion of my fathers, free to think and talk and act for myself—and I will obey every law, or submit to the penalty.

Whenever the white man treats the Indian as they treat each other, then we shall have no more wars. We shall all be alike—brothers of one father and one mother, with one sky above us and one country around us, and one government for all. Then the Great Spirit Chief who rules above will smile upon this land, and send rain to wash out the bloody spots made by brothers' hands from the face of the earth. For this time the Indian race are waiting and praying. I hope that no more groans of wounded men and women will ever go to the ear of the Great Spirit Chief above, and that all people may be one people.

Source: "An Indian's View of Indian Affairs," *North American Review*, April 1879, 431–33.

## Interpret the Evidence

1. On what basis does James Michael Cavanaugh (Document 15.6) claim to be in a better position than Benjamin Butler to judge the best way to deal with Indians?
2. How does Thomas Nast's illustration (Document 15.7) compare with the arguments made by Congressman Cavanaugh?
3. What assumptions about Indians and their culture underlay the policy of assimilation advocated by reformers such as Helen Hunt Jackson (Document 15.8)?
4. What options did Indians have when confronted with white determination to eradicate their culture? What choice did Zitkala-Ša (Document 15.9) make? Why?
5. How did Chief Joseph's experience (Document 15.10) reflect the fundamental contradiction of federal policy toward Indians?

## Put It in Context

• Imagine that you are an American president in the second half of the nineteenth century and can design Indian policy. Based on what you have read, what would you do, and why? What challenges might you face as you attempted to implement your policy?

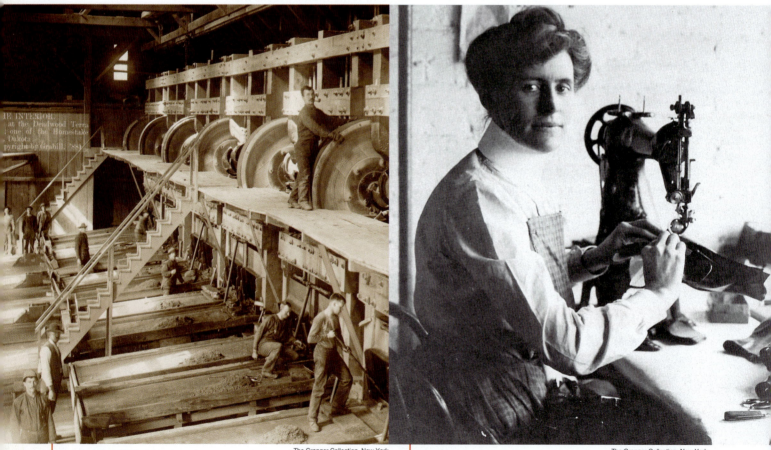

The Granger Collection, New York

The Granger Collection, New York

Sawmill in Terraville, South Dakota, 1888.

Shoe-factory worker in Lynn, Massachusetts, 1895.

# 16

# American Industry in the Age of Organization

## 1877–1900

The Granger Collection, New York

Duryea's Glen Cove Starch Works Factory, Glen Cove, New York.

In 1848 Will and Margaret Carnegie left Scotland and sailed to America, hoping to find a better life for themselves and their two children. Once settled in Pittsburgh, Pennsylvania, the family went to work, including thirteen-year-old Andrew, who found a job in a textile mill. For $1.25 per week, he dipped spools into an oil bath and fired the factory furnace—tasks that left him nauseated by the smell of oil and frightened by the boiler. Nevertheless, like the hero of the rags-to-riches stories that were so popular in his era, Andrew Carnegie persevered, rising from poverty to great wealth through a series of jobs and clever investments. As a teenager, he worked as a messenger in a telegraph office and was soon promoted to telegraph operator. A superintendent of the Pennsylvania Railroad Company noticed Andrew's aptitude and made him his personal assistant and telegrapher. While in this position, Carnegie learned about the fast-developing railroad industry and purchased stock in a sleeping car company; the returns from that investment tripled his annual salary. Carnegie then became a railroad superintendent in western Pennsylvania, and by the time he was thirty-five, he had earned handsome returns on his investments in various industrial companies, as well as from oil investments he made just as that industry was emerging.

Andrew Carnegie eventually founded the greatest steel company in the world and became one of the wealthiest men of his time. In an era before personal and corporate income taxes, Carnegie earned hundreds of millions of dollars. He also became one of the era's greatest philanthropists, fulfilling his sense of community obligation by giving away a great deal of his fortune.

John Sherman also believed in public service, but for him it would come through politics. Sherman was born in Lancaster, Ohio, in 1823, a quarter of a century before the Carnegies set sail for the United States. Sherman became a lawyer like his father, an Ohio Supreme Court judge, and in 1844 he set up a practice with his older brother, William Tecumseh Sherman, the future Civil War general and Indian fighter (see chapter 15). Like Carnegie, Sherman made shrewd investments that made him a wealthy man, although not on the same scale as Carnegie.

Sherman decided to enter politics and in 1854 won election from Ohio to the House of Representatives as a member of the newly created Republican Party. He rose up the leadership ranks as Republicans came to national power with the election of Abraham Lincoln to the presidency in 1860. From 1861 to 1896, Sherman held a variety of major political positions, including U.S. senator from Ohio and secretary of the treasury under President Rutherford B. Hayes. After his term as treasury secretary ended, he returned to the Senate and wielded power as one of the top Republican Party leaders. Sherman, who had joined the Radical Republicans during Reconstruction (see chapter 14), did not hesitate to move with the Republican Party as its interests shifted from racial equality to promoting business and industry. With his background as chair of the Senate Finance Committee and as secretary of the treasury, Sherman was the most respected Republican of his time in dealing with monetary and financial affairs. Marcus Alonzo Hanna, a wealthy industrialist, considered the Ohio senator "our main dependence in the Senate for the protection of our business interests." Like Hanna, Sherman believed that government should serve business. His most famous accomplishment, the Sherman Antitrust Act, which authorized the government to break up organizations that restrained competition, embodied this belief. It enacted limited reforms without harming powerful business interests. •

both photos: Library of Congress

# WHILE THE AMERICAN HISTORIES

of Andrew Carnegie and John Sherman began very differently, both men played a prominent role in developing the government-business partnership that was crucial to the rapid industrialization of the United States. Carnegie's organization and management skills helped shape the formation of large-scale business. At the same time, Sherman and his fellow lawmakers provided support for that enterprise, using the power of government to reduce risks for businessmen and to increase incentives for economic expansion. In the view of men like Carnegie and Sherman, government's primary purpose was, in fact, to advance the agenda and interests of the business community—an agenda they were certain was in the best interests of the country as a whole.

The emphasis Carnegie and Sherman placed on the government-business alliance was, in part, a reaction to the extreme economic volatility of the late nineteenth century. The economy experienced painful depressions in the 1870s, 1880s, and 1890s, each accompanied by business failures and mass unemployment. Though recovery came in every instance and industrial output continued to soar, these financial fluctuations left businessmen ever more intent on stabilizing profits, wages, and prices. When faced with harsh economic realities and swift change, businessmen chose organization, cooperation, and government support as strategies to deal with the challenges they confronted.

# America Industrializes

In this Age of Organization between 1870 and 1900, the United States grew into a global industrial power. Transcontinental railroads spurred this breathtaking transformation, linking regional markets into a national market for manufactured goods; at the same time, railroads themselves served as a massive new market for raw materials, new technologies, and, perhaps most important, steel. Building on advantages developed over the course of the nineteenth century, the Northeast and the Midwest led the way in the new economy, while efforts to industrialize the South met with uneven success. Men like Andrew Carnegie became both the heroes and the villains of their age. They engaged in ruthless practices that would lead some to label the new industrialists "robber barons," but they also created ingenious systems of industrial organization and corporate management that altered the economic landscape of the country and changed the place of the United States in the world.

## The New Industrial Economy

The industrial revolution of the late nineteenth century originated in Europe. Great Britain was the world's first industrial power, but by the 1870s Germany had emerged as a major challenger for industrial dominance, increasing its steel production at a rapid rate and leading the way in the chemical and electrical industries. The dynamic economic growth stimulated by industrial competition quickly crossed the Atlantic. Eager and ambitious American entrepreneurs and engineers soon began applying the latest industrial innovations to U.S. enterprises.

Industrialization transformed the American economy. As industrialization took hold, the U.S. gross domestic product, the output of all goods and services produced annually, quadrupled—from $9 billion in 1860 to $37 billion in 1890. During this same period, the number of Americans employed by industry doubled, as American workers moved from farms to factories and immigrants flooded in from overseas to fill newly created industrial jobs. Moreover, the nature of industry itself changed, as small factories catering to local markets were displaced by large-scale firms producing for national and international markets. The midwestern cities of Chicago, Cincinnati, and St. Louis joined Boston, New York, and Philadelphia as centers of factory production, while the exploitation of the natural resources in the West took on an increasingly industrial character. Trains, telegraphs, and telephones connected the country in ways never before possible. In 1889 the respected economist David A. Wells marveled at

what had occurred over the past two decades: "An almost total revolution has taken place, and is yet in progress, in every branch and in every relation of the world's industrial and commercial system."

Wells did not exaggerate. From 1870 to 1913, the United States experienced an extraordinary rate of growth in industrial output: In 1870 American industries turned out 23.3 percent of the world's manufacturing production; by 1913 this figure had jumped to 35.8 percent. In fact, U.S. output in 1913 almost equaled the combined total for Europe's three leading industrial powers: Germany, the United Kingdom, and France. Of these European countries, only Germany experienced a slight rise in output from 1870 to 1913 (2.5 percent), while Britain's output dropped a precipitous 17.8 percent and France's declined 3.9 percent. By the end of the nineteenth century, the United States was surging ahead of northern Europe as the manufacturing center of the world.

At the heart of the American industrial transformation was the railroad. Large-scale business enterprises would not have developed without a national market for raw materials and finished products. A consolidated system of railroads crisscrossing the nation facilitated the creation of such a market (Figure 16.1). In addition, railroads were direct consumers of industrial products, stimulating the growth of a number of industries through their consumption of steel, wood, coal, glass, rubber, brass, and iron. For example, late-nineteenth-century railroads purchased more than 90 percent of the steel produced in U.S. factories. Finally, railroads contributed to economic growth by increasing the speed and efficiency with which products and materials were transported. One observer guessed that in 1890 if the country had to rely only on roads and waterways instead of trains to ship agricultural and industrial goods, the nation would have lost approximately $560 million, or 5 percent, of its gross national product.

Before railroads could create a national market, they had to overcome several critical problems. In 1877 railroad lines dotted the country in haphazard fashion. They primarily served local markets and remained unconnected at key points. This lack of coordination stemmed mainly from the fact that each railroad had its own track gauge (the width between the tracks), making shared track use impossible and long-distance travel extremely difficult.

The consolidation of railroads solved many of these problems. In 1886 railroad companies finally agreed to adopt a standard gauge. Railroads also standardized time zones, thus eliminating confusion in train schedules. During the 1870s, towns and cities each set their own time zone, a practice that created discrepancies among them. In 1882 the time in New York City and in Boston varied by 11 minutes and 45 seconds. The following year, railroads

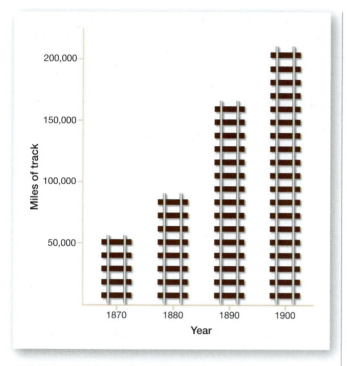

**FIGURE 16.1** **Expansion of the Railroad System, 1870–1900**

The great expansion of the railroads in the late nineteenth century fueled the industrial revolution and the growth of big business. Connecting the nation from East Coast to West Coast, transcontinental railroads created a national market for natural resources and manufactured goods. The biggest surge in railroad construction occurred west of the Mississippi River and in the South.

agreed to coordinate times and divided the country into four standard time zones. Most cities soon cooperated, but not until 1918 did the federal government legislate the standard time zones that the railroads had first adopted.

## Innovation and Inventions

As important as railroads were, they were not the only engine of industrialization. American technological innovation created new industries, while expanding the efficiency and productivity of old ones. Inventor Thomas Alva Edison began his career by devising ways to improve the telegraph and expand its uses. In 1866 a transatlantic telegraph cable connected the United States and Europe, allowing businessmen on both sides of the ocean to pursue profitable commercial ventures. New inventions also allowed business offices to run more smoothly: Typewriters were invented in 1868, carbon paper in 1872, adding machines in 1891, and mimeograph machines in 1892. As businesses grew, they needed more space for their operations. The construction of towering skyscrapers in the 1880s in cities such as Chicago and New York was made possible

by two innovations: structural steel, which had the strength to support tall buildings; and elevators, equipped with a safety device invented by Elisha Graves Otis in the 1850s.

Among the thousands of patents filed each year, Alexander Graham Bell's telephone revolutionized communications. By 1880 fifty-five cities offered local service and catered to a total of 50,000 subscribers, most of them business customers. A decade later, long-distance service connected New York, Boston, and Chicago, and by 1900 around 1.5 million telephones were in operation. Bell profited handsomely from his invention, created his own firm, and in 1885 established the giant American Telephone and Telegraph Company (AT&T).

Perhaps the greatest technological innovations that advanced industrial development in the late nineteenth century came in steel manufacturing. In 1859 Henry Bessemer, a British inventor, designed a furnace that burned the impurities out of melted iron and converted it into steel. The open-hearth process, devised by another Englishman, William Siemens, further improved the quality of steel by removing additional impurities from the iron. Railroads replaced iron rails with steel because it was lighter, stronger, and more durable than iron. Steel became the major building block of industry, furnishing girders and cables to construct manufacturing plants and office structures. As production became cheaper and more efficient, steel output soared from 13,000 tons in 1860 to 28 million tons in the first decade of the twentieth century.

Factory machinery needed constant lubrication, and the growing petroleum industry made this possible. A new drilling technique devised in 1859 tapped into pools of petroleum located deep below the earth's surface. In the post–Civil War era, new distilling techniques transformed this thick, smelly liquid into lubricating oil for factory machinery. This process of "cracking" crude oil also generated lucrative by-products for the home, such as kerosene and paraffin for heating and lighting. Robert A. Chesebrough discovered that a sticky oil residue could soothe cuts and burns, and in 1870 he began manufacturing a product he would soon trademark as Vaseline Petroleum Jelly. After 1900, the development of the gasoline-powered, internal combustion engine for automobiles opened up an even richer market for the oil industry.

Railroads also benefited from innovations in technology. Improvements included air brakes and automatic coupling devices to attach train cars to each other. Elijah McCoy, a trained engineer and the son of former slaves, was forced because of racial discrimination to work at menial railroad jobs shoveling coal and lubricating train parts every few miles to keep the gears from overheating. This grueling experience encouraged him to invent and patent an automatic lubricating device to improve efficiency.

Early innovations resulted from the genius of individual inventors, but by the late nineteenth century technological progress was increasingly an organized, collaborative effort. Thomas Edison and his team served as the model. In 1876 Edison set up a research laboratory in Menlo Park, New Jersey. Housed in a two-story, white frame building, Edison's "invention factory" was staffed by a team of inventors and craftsmen. Edison believed that "genius was 1 percent inspiration and 99 percent perspiration," and he devoted nearly every waking hour, often ignoring his family, to coordinating the invention process. In 1887 Edison opened another laboratory, ten times bigger than the one at Menlo Park, in nearby Orange, New Jersey. These facilities pioneered the research laboratories that would become a standard feature of American industrial development in the twentieth century.

Edison expected his research factories to produce "a minor invention every ten days and a big thing every six months or so." Edison and his crew largely succeeded. During his lifetime, Edison filed 1,093 U.S. patents; although he has received most of the credit, a good number of his inventions were the result of collaborative research. Out of his laboratory flowed inventions that revolutionized American business and culture. The phonograph and motion pictures changed the way people spent their leisure time. The electric lightbulb illuminated people's homes and made them safer by eliminating the need for candles and gas lamps, which were fire hazards. It also brightened city streets, making them available for outdoor evening activities, and lit up factories so that they could operate all night long.

Like his contemporaries who were building America's huge industrial empires, Edison cashed in on his workers' inventions. He joined forces with the Wall Street banker J. P. Morgan to finance the Edison Electric Illuminating Company, which in 1882 provided lighting to customers in New York City. Goods produced by electric equipment jumped in value from $1.9 million in 1879 to $21.8 million in 1890. In 1892, Morgan helped Edison merge his companies with several competitors and reorganized them as the General Electric Corporation, which became the industry leader.

## Building a New South

Although the largely rural South lagged behind the North and the Midwest in manufacturing, industrial expansion did not bypass the region. Well aware of global economic trends and eager for the South to achieve its economic potential, southern business leaders and newspaper editors, especially the *Atlanta Constitution*'s editor Henry Grady, saw industrial development as the key to the creation of a **New South**. Attributing the Confederate defeat in the Civil War to the North's superior manufacturing output and

railroad supply lines, New South proponents hoped to modernize their economy in a similar fashion. One of those boosters was Richard H. Edmonds, the Virginia-born editor of the *Manufacturers' Record*. He extolled the virtues of the "real South" of the 1880s, characterized by "the music of progress—the whirr of the spindle, the buzz of the saw, the roar of the furnace, the throb of the locomotive." The South of Edmonds's vision would move beyond the regional separatism of the past and become fully integrated into the national economy.

Railroads were the key to achieving such economic integration, so after the Civil War new railroad tracks were laid throughout the South. Not only did this expanded railroad system create direct connections between the North and the South, but it also facilitated the growth of the southern textile industry. Seeking to take advantage of plentiful cotton, cheap labor, and the improved transportation system, investors built textile mills throughout the South, especially in the Carolinas and Georgia. Victims of falling prices and saddled with debt, sharecroppers and tenant farmers moved into mill towns in search of better employment. Mill owners preferred to hire girls and young women, who worked for low wages, to spin cotton and weave it on the looms. To do so, however, owners had to employ their entire family, for mothers and fathers would not let their daughters relocate without their supervision. Whatever attraction the mills offered applied only to whites. The pattern of white supremacy emerging in the post-Reconstruction South kept African Americans out of all but the most menial jobs.

Blacks contributed greatly to the construction of railroads in the New South, but they did not do so as free men. Convicts, most of whom were African American, performed the exhausting work of laying tracks through hills and swamps. Southern states used the **convict lease** system, in which blacks, usually imprisoned for minor offenses, were hired out to private companies to serve their time or pay off their fine. The convict lease system brought additional income to the state and supplied cheap labor to the railroads and planters, but it left African American convict laborers impoverished and virtually enslaved.

The South attracted a number of industries besides textile manufacturing. In the 1880s, James B. Duke established a cigarette manufacturing empire in Durham, North Carolina. Nearby tobacco fields provided the raw material that black workers prepared for white workers, who then rolled the cigarettes by machine. Acres of timber pines in the Carolinas, Florida, and Alabama sustained a lucrative lumber industry, one of the few to employ whites and blacks equally. Rich supplies of coal and iron in Alabama fostered the growth of the steel industry in Birmingham, which produced more than a million tons of steel at the turn of the twentieth century (Map 16.1).

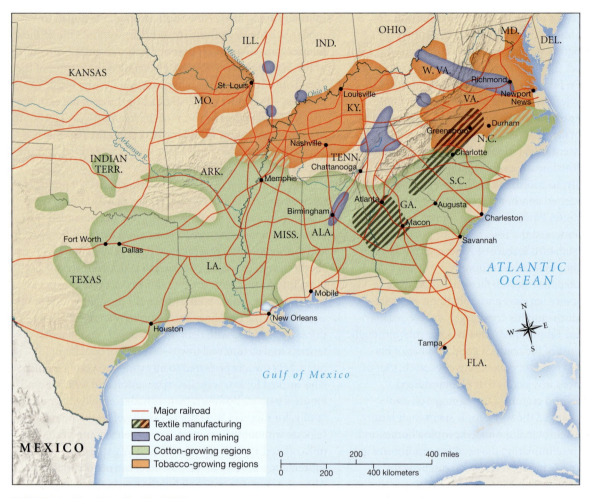

**MAP 16.1  The New South, 1900**
Although the South remained largely agricultural by 1900, it had made great strides toward building industries in the region. This so-called New South boasted an extensive railway network that
provided a national market for its raw materials and manufactured goods, including coal, iron, steel,
and textiles. Still, the southern economy in 1900 depended primarily on raising cotton and tobacco.

Despite this frenzy of industrial activity, the New
South in many ways resembled the Old South. Southern
entrepreneurs still depended on northern investors to
supply much of the capital for investment. Investors were
attracted by the low wages that prevailed in the South, but
low wages also meant that southern workers remained
poor and, in many cases, unable to buy the manufactured
goods produced by industry. Efforts to diversify agriculture beyond tobacco and cotton were constrained by a
sharecropping system based on small, inefficient plots. In
fact, even though industrialization did make considerable
headway in the South, the economy remained overwhelm-
ingly agricultural. This suited many white southerners
who wanted to hold on to the individualistic, agrarian
values they associated with the Old South. In this way,
they sought to remain distinct from what they considered
the acquisitive North. Yoked to old ideologies and a system of forced labor, modernization in the South could go
only so far.

## Industrial Consolidation

In both the North and the South, nineteenth-century
industrialists strove to minimize or eliminate competition. To gain competitive advantages and increase profits,
industrial entrepreneurs concentrated on reducing production costs, charging lower prices, and outselling the
competition. Successful firms could then acquire rival
companies that could no longer afford to compete, creating
an industrial empire in the process.

Building such industrial empires was not easy, however, and posed creative challenges for business ventures. Heavy investment in machinery resulted in very high fixed costs (or overhead) that did not change much over time. Because overhead costs remained stable, manufacturers could reduce the per-unit cost of production by increasing the output of a product—what economists call "economy of scale." Manufacturers thus aimed to raise the volume of production and find ways to cut variable costs—for labor and materials, for example. Shaving off even a few pennies from the cost of making each unit could save millions of dollars on the total cost of production. Through such savings, a factory owner could sell his product more cheaply than his competitors and gain a larger share of the market.

A major organizational technique for reducing costs and underselling the competition was **vertical integration**. "Captains of industry," as their admirers called them, did not just build a business; they created a system—a network of firms, each contributing to the final product. Men like Andrew Carnegie controlled the various phases of production from top to bottom (vertical), extracting the raw materials, transporting them to the factories, manufacturing the finished products, and shipping them to market. In 1881, when Carnegie combined his operations with those of Henry Clay Frick of Pennsylvania, he gained not only a talented factory manager but also access to Frick's coal business. By using vertical integration, Carnegie eliminated middlemen and guaranteed regular and cheap access to supplies. He also avoided duplications in machinery, lowered inventories, and gained increased flexibility by shifting segments of the labor force to areas where they were most needed. This integrated system demanded close and careful management of the overall operation, which Carnegie provided. He manufactured steel with improved efficiency and cut costs. His credo became "Watch the costs and the profits will take care of themselves."

Businessmen also employed another type of integration—**horizontal integration**. This approach focused on gaining greater control over the market by acquiring firms that sold the same products. John D. Rockefeller, the founder of the mammoth Standard Oil Company, specialized in this technique. In the mid-1870s, he brought a number of key oil refiners into an alliance with Standard Oil to control four-fifths of the industry. At the same time, the oil baron ruthlessly drove out or bought up marginal firms that could not afford to compete with him. One such competitor testified to a congressional committee in 1879 about how Standard Oil had squeezed him out: "[Rockefeller] said that he had facilities for freighting and that the coal-oil business belonged to them; and any concern that would start in that business, they had sufficient money to lay aside a fund and wipe them out."

Horizontal integration was also a major feature in the telegraph industry. By 1861 Western Union had strung 76,000 miles of telegraph line throughout the nation. Founded in 1851, the company had thrived during the Civil War by obtaining most of the federal government's telegraph business. The firm had 12,600 offices housed in railroad depots throughout the country and strung its lines adjacent to the railroads. In the eight years before Cornelius Vanderbilt bought Western Union in 1869, the value of its stock jumped from $3 million to $41 million. Seeing an opportunity to make money, Wall Street tycoon Jay Gould set out to acquire Western Union. In the mid-1870s, Gould, who had obtained control over the Union Pacific Railway, financed companies to compete with the giant telegraph outfit. Gould did not succeed until 1881, when he engineered a takeover of Western Union by combining it with his American Union Telegraph Company. Gould made a profit of $30 million on the deal. On February 15, the day after the agreement, the *New York Herald Tribune* reported: "The country finds itself this morning at the feet of a telegraphic monopoly," a business that controlled the market and destroyed competition.

Bankers played a huge role in engineering industrial consolidation. No one did it more skillfully than John Pierpont Morgan. In the 1850s, Morgan started his career working for a prominent American-owned banking firm in London, and in 1861 he created his own investment company in New York City. Unlike the United States, Great Britain had a surplus of capital that bankers sought to invest abroad. Morgan played the central role in channeling funds from Britain to support the construction of major American railroads. During the 1880s and 1890s, Morgan orchestrated the refinancing of several ailing railroads, including the Baltimore & Ohio and the Southern Railroad. To maintain control over these enterprises, the Wall Street financier placed his allies on their boards of directors and selected the companies' chief operating officers. Morgan then turned his talents for organization to the steel industry. In 1901 he was instrumental in merging Carnegie's company with several competitors in which he had a financial interest. United States Steel, Morgan's creation, became the world's largest industrial corporation, worth $1.4 billion. By the end of the first decade of the twentieth century, Morgan's investment house held more than 340 directorships in 112 corporations, amounting to more than $22 billion in assets, the equivalent of $608 billion in 2012, all at a time when there was no income tax.

## The Growth of Corporations

With economic consolidation came the expansion of **corporations**. Before the age of large-scale enterprise, the predominant form of business ownership was the partnership. Unlike partnerships, corporations provided investors with "limited liability." This meant that if the corporation went bankrupt, shareholders could not lose more than they had invested. Limited liability encouraged investment by keeping the shareholders' investment in the corporation separate from their other assets. In addition, corporations provided "perpetual life." Partnerships dissolved on the death of a partner, whereas corporations continued to function despite the death of any single owner. This form of ownership brought stability and order to financing, building, and perpetuating what was otherwise a highly volatile and complex business endeavor.

Capitalists devised new corporate structures to gain greater control over their industries. Rockefeller's Standard Oil Company led the way by creating the trust, a monopoly formed through consolidation. To evade state laws against monopolies, Rockefeller created a petroleum trust. He combined other oil firms across the country with Standard Oil and placed their owners on a nine-member board of trustees that ran the company. Subsequently, Rockefeller fashioned another method of bringing rival businesses together. Through a holding company, he obtained stock in a number of other oil companies and held them under his control.

The movement to create trusts, Rockefeller boasted, "was the origin of the whole system of modern economic administration." Statistics backed up his assessment. Between 1880 and 1905, more than three hundred mergers occurred in 80 percent of the nation's manufacturing firms. Great wealth became heavily concentrated in the hands of a relatively small number of businessmen. Around two thousand businesses, a tiny fraction of the total number, dominated 40 percent of the nation's economy.

**Explore**

See Document 16.1 for one cartoonist's interpretation of Rockefeller's power.

In their drive to consolidate economic power and shield themselves from risk, corporate titans generally had the courts on their side. In *Santa Clara County v. Southern Pacific Railroad Company* (1886), the Supreme Court decided that under the Fourteenth Amendment, which originally dealt with the issue of federal protection of African Americans' civil rights, a corporation was considered a "person." In effect, this ruling gave corporations the same right of due process that the framers of the amendment had meant to give to former slaves. In the 1890s, a majority of the Supreme Court embraced this interpretation. The right of due process shielded corporations from prohibitive government regulation of the workplace, including the passage of legislation reducing the number of hours in the workday.

Yet trusts did not go unopposed. In 1890 Congress passed Senator Sherman's Antitrust Act, which outlawed monopolies that prevented free competition in interstate commerce. The bill passed easily with bipartisan support because it merely codified legal principles that already existed. Sherman and his colleagues never intended to stifle large corporations, which through efficient business practices came to dominate the market. Rather, the lawmakers attempted to limit underhanded actions that destroyed competition. The judicial system further bailed out corporate leaders. In *United States v. E.C. Knight Company* (1895), a case against the "sugar trust," the Supreme Court rendered the Sherman Act virtually toothless by ruling that manufacturing was a local activity within a state and that, even if it was a monopoly, it was not subject to congressional regulation. This ruling left most trusts in the manufacturing sector beyond the jurisdiction of the **Sherman Antitrust Act**.

The introduction of managerial specialists, already present in European firms, proved the most critical innovation for integrating industry. With many operations controlled under one roof, large-scale businesses required a corps of experts to oversee and coordinate the various steps of production. Comptrollers and accountants pored over financial records to keep track of every penny spent and dollar earned. Traffic managers directed the movement of raw materials into plants and finished products out for distribution. Marketing executives were in charge of advertising goods and finding new markets. Efficiency experts sought to cut labor costs and make the production process operate more smoothly. Frederick W. Taylor, a Philadelphia engineer and businessman, developed the principles of scientific management. Based on his concept of reducing manual labor to its simplest components and eliminating independent action on the part of workers, managers introduced time-and-motion studies. Using a stopwatch, they calculated how to break down a job into simple tasks that could be performed in the least amount of time. From this perspective, workers were no different from the machines they operated.

Another vital factor in creating large-scale industry was the establishment of retail outlets that could sell the enormous volume of goods pouring out of factories. As consumer goods became less expensive, retail outlets sprang up to serve the growing market for household items, including watches, jewelry, sewing machines, cameras, and an assortment of rugs and furniture. Customers could shop at department stores—such as Macy's in New York City, Filene's in Boston, Marshall Field's in Chicago, Nordstrom's in Seattle, Gump's in San Francisco, Nieman Marcus in Dallas, Jacome's in Tucson, Rich's in Atlanta, and Burdine's in Miami—where they were waited on by a

**DOCUMENT 16.1**

## Horace Taylor | What a Funny Little Government, 1900

As large firms merged with competitors to form giant companies that dominated the marketplace, opponents of such trusts decried the power that these enterprises wielded over the economy and the political system. Responding to such concerns, Congress passed the Sherman Antitrust Act in 1890, but the law proved weak and was loosely enforced. In the following illustration, cartoonist Horace Taylor, a Democrat, sought to make trusts an issue in the 1900 election by attacking John D. Rockefeller, whose Standard Oil Company embodied the evils of trusts for many critics.

**Explore**

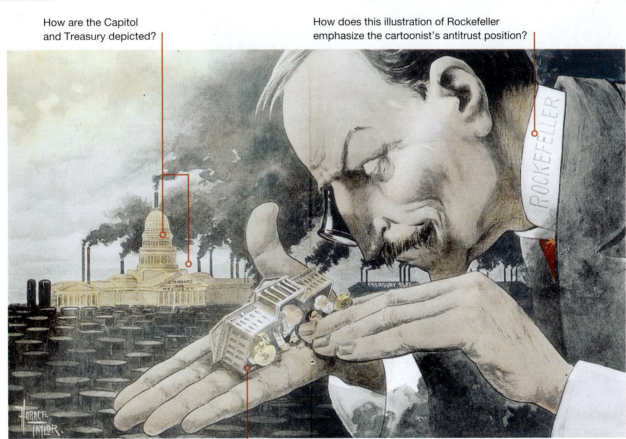

How are the Capitol and Treasury depicted?

How does this illustration of Rockefeller emphasize the cartoonist's antitrust position?

What is Rockefeller holding in his hand?

Collection of the New-York Historical Society

**Put It in Context**

What does this cartoon suggest about the relationship between big business and the federal government at the start of the twentieth century?

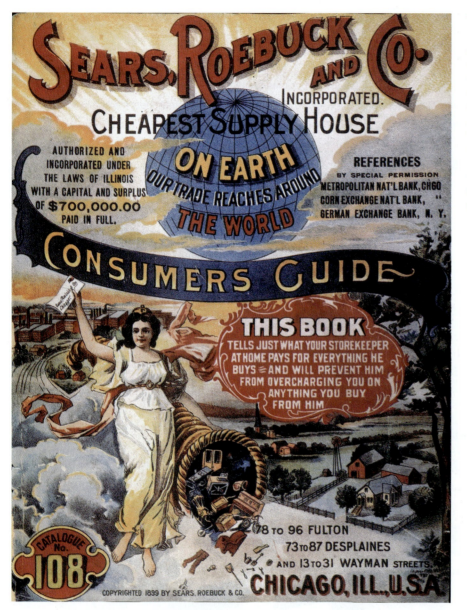

### 1899 Sears, Roebuck Catalog

The expansion of industrialization and completion of the transcontinental railroad created a national market for manufactured goods and led to the growth of consumer culture. The Chicago-based Sears, Roebuck used its mail-order catalog to attract customers throughout the United States and, as its cover suggests, the world. This colorful 1899 catalog offers the latest items in carpets, furniture, china, fashions, and photographic equipment and supplies.   The Granger Collection, New York

growing army of salesclerks. Or they could buy the cheaper items in Frank W. Woolworth's five and ten cent stores, which opened in towns and cities nationwide. Chain supermarkets—such as the Great Atlantic and Pacific Tea Company (A&P), founded in 1869—sold fruits and vegetables packed in tin cans. They also sold foods from the meatpacking firms of Gustavus Swift and Philip Armour, which shipped them on refrigerated railroad cars. Mail-order catalogs allowed Americans in all parts of the country to buy consumer goods without leaving their home. The catalogs of Montgomery Ward (established in 1872) and Sears, Roebuck (founded in 1886) offered tens of thousands of items. Rural free delivery (RFD), instituted by the U.S.

Post Office in 1891, made it even easier for farmers and others living in the countryside to obtain these catalogs and buy their merchandise without having to travel miles to the nearest post office. By the end of the nineteenth century, the industrial economy had left its mark on almost all aspects of life in almost every corner of America.

## REVIEW & RELATE

What were the key factors behind the acceleration of industrial development in late-nineteenth-century America?

How did industrialization change the way American businessmen thought about their companies and the people who worked for them?

## Free Markets and Rugged Individuals

American industrialization developed as rapidly as it did in large part because it was reinforced by traditional ideas and values. The notion that hard work and diligence would result in success meant that individuals felt justified, even duty-bound, to strive to achieve upward mobility and accumulate wealth. Churches, schools, intellectuals, and popular writers combined to buttress this doctrine of success. Those who succeeded believed that they had done so because they were more talented, industrious, and resourceful than others. Thus prosperous businessmen regarded competition and the free market as essential to the health of an economic world they saw based on merit. Yet these same businessmen also created trusts that destroyed competition, and they depended on the government for resources and protection. This obvious contradiction, along with the profoundly unequal distribution of wealth that characterized the late-nineteenth-century economy, generated a good deal of criticism of business tycoons and their beliefs.

### The Doctrine of Success

Those at the top of the new industrial order justified their great wealth in a manner that most Americans could understand. The ideas of the Scottish economist Adam Smith, in *The Wealth of Nations* (1776), had gained popularity during the American Revolution. Advocating **laissez-faire** ("let things alone"), Smith contended that an "Invisible Hand," guided by natural law, guaranteed the greatest economic success if the government let individuals pursue their own self-interest unhindered by outside and artificial influences. In the late nineteenth century, businessmen and their conservative allies on the Supreme Court used Smith's doctrines to argue against restrictive government regulation. They equated their right to own and manage property with the personal liberty protected by the Fourteenth Amendment. Thus the Declaration of Independence, with its defense of "life, liberty, and the pursuit of happiness," and the Constitution, which enshrined citizens' political freedom, became instruments to guarantee unfettered economic opportunity and safeguard private property.

The view that success depended on individual initiative was reinforced in schools and churches. The McGuffey Readers, widely used to educate children, taught moral lessons of hard work, individual initiative, reliability, and thrift. The popular dime novels of Horatio Alger portrayed the story of young men, such as Ragged Dick, who rose through pluck and luck from "rags to riches." Americans could also hear success stories in houses of worship. Russell Conwell,

pastor of the Grace Baptist Church in Philadelphia, delivered a widely printed sermon entitled "Acres of Diamonds," which equated godliness with riches and argued that ordinary people had an obligation to strive for material wealth. "I say that you ought to get rich, and it is your duty to get rich," Conwell declared, "because to make money honestly is to preach the gospel." Conwell followed his own advice and became wealthy from the fees he earned delivering his popular sermon.

If economic success was a matter of personal merit, it followed that economic failure was as well. The British philosopher Herbert Spencer proposed a theory of social evolution based on this premise in his book *Social Statics* (1851). Imagining a future utopia, Spencer wrote, "Man was not created with an instinct for his own degradation, but from the lower he has risen to the higher forms. Nor is there any conceivable end to his march to perfection." In his view, those at the top of the economic ladder were closer

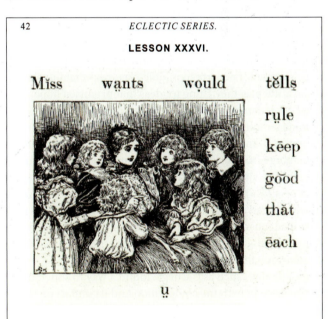

**McGuffey Reader**

Beginning in the mid-nineteenth century, McGuffey Readers became the most popular textbook for teaching elementary school pupils how to read. As this page from an edition first published in 1881 shows, the book included exercises that taught students moral lessons along with their readings. In emphasizing hard work and obedience, the readers instructed children in middle-class virtues.

to perfection than were those at the bottom. Any effort to aid the unfortunate would only slow the march of progress for society as a whole. Spencer's book proved extremely popular, selling nearly 400,000 copies in the United States by 1900. In recalling how Spencer's ideas influenced him, Carnegie wrote, "I remember that light came as in a flood and all was clear." Publication of Charles Darwin's landmark *On the Origin of Species* (1859) appeared to provide some scientific legitimacy for Spencer's view. The British naturalist argued that plants, animals, and humans progressed or declined because of their ability or inability to adapt favorably to the environment and transmit these characteristics to future generations. The connection between the two men's ideas has led some to label Spencer and his supporters "Social Darwinists." However, few defenders of laissez-faire principles in the late nineteenth century had actually read Darwin or referred to themselves as Social Darwinists, a term that came into widespread use only in the twentieth century.

Doctrines of success gained favor because they helped Americans explain the rapid economic changes that were disrupting their lives. Although most ordinary people would not climb out of poverty to middle-class respectability, let alone affluence, they clung to ideas that promised hope. After all, if a man like Carnegie could rise from poverty to become a multimillionaire, why not them? It mattered little that most of those who achieved extraordinary wealth did not emerge from the working class but rather came from the middle class. Ideas such as Spencer's that linked success with progress provided a way for those who did not do well to understand their failure and blame themselves for their own inadequacies. At the same time, the notion that economic success derived from personal merit legitimized the fabulous wealth of those who did rise to the top.

Capitalists such as Carnegie found a way to soften both the message of extreme competition and its impact on the American public. Denying that the government should help the poor, they proclaimed that men of wealth had a duty to furnish some assistance. In his famous essay **"The Gospel of Wealth"** (1889), Carnegie declared that "a man who died rich died disgraced." He argued that the rich should act as stewards of the wealth they earned. As trustees, they should administer their surplus income for the benefit of the community. Carnegie distinguished between charity (direct handouts to individuals), which he deplored, and philanthropy (building institutions that would raise educational and cultural standards), which he advocated. For example, Carnegie, Rockefeller, and railroad tycoons Leland Stanford and Cornelius Vanderbilt all gave endowments (and their names) to universities to provide education for those who worked hard to achieve it. Russell Conwell also gave away his fortune to various philanthropic enterprises, most

notably the founding of Temple University in Philadelphia, which opened its doors to poor men seeking a higher education. Carnegie was particularly generous in funding libraries (he provided the buildings but not the books) because they allowed people to gain knowledge through their own efforts.

Capitalists may have sung the praises of individualism and laissez-faire, but their actions contradicted their words. Successful industrialists in the late nineteenth century sought to destroy competition, not perpetuate it. Their efforts over the course of several decades produced giant corporations that measured the worth of individuals by calculating their value to the organization. As John D. Rockefeller, the master of consolidation, proclaimed, "The day of individual competition in large affairs is past and gone." **See Document Project 16: Debates about Laissez-Faire, page 517**.

Nor did capitalists strictly oppose government involvement. Although industrialists did not want the federal government to take any action that *retarded* their economic efforts, they did favor the use of the government's power to *promote* their enterprises and to stimulate entrepreneurial energies. Thus manufacturers pushed for congressional passage of high tariffs to protect goods from foreign competition and to foster development of the national marketplace. Industrialists demanded that federal and state governments dispatch troops when labor strikes threatened their businesses. They persuaded Washington to provide land grants for railroad construction and to send the army to clear Native Americans and bison from their tracks. They argued for state and federal courts to interpret constitutional and statutory law in a way that shielded property rights against attacks from workers. In large measure, capitalists succeeded not in spite of governmental support but because of it.

## Challenges to Laissez-Faire

Proponents of government restraint and unbridled individualism did not go unchallenged. Critics of laissez-faire created an alternative ideology for those who sought to organize workers and expand the role of government as ways of restricting capitalists' power over labor and ordinary citizens.

Lester Frank Ward attacked laissez-faire in his book *Dynamic Sociology* (1883). A largely self-taught man who worked as a civil servant for the federal government, Ward did not disparage individualism but viewed the main function of society as "the organization of happiness." Contradicting Herbert Spencer, Ward maintained that societies progressed when government directly intervened to help citizens—even the unfortunate. Indeed, society could initiate "the systematic realization of its own interests, in the same manner that an intelligent and keen-sighted individual pursues his life-purposes." Rejecting laissez-faire, Ward argued that what people "really need is more government in its primary sense, greater protection from the rapacity of the favored few."

Some academics supported Ward's ideas. Most notably, economist Richard T. Ely applied Christian ethics to his scholarly assessment of capital and labor. He condemned the railroads for dragging "their slimy length over our country, and every turn in their progress is marked by a progeny of evils." In his book *The Labor Movement* (1886), Ely suggested that the ultimate solution for social ills resulting from industrialization lay in "the union of capital and labor in the same hands, in grand, wide-reaching, co-operative enterprises."

Two popular writers, Henry George and Edward Bellamy, added to the critique of materialism and greed. In *Progress and Poverty* (1879), George lamented: "Amid the greatest accumulations of wealth, men die of starvation." He blamed the problem on rent, which he viewed as an unjustifiable payment on the increase in the value of land, what he called "unearned increment." His remedy was to have government confiscate rent earned on land by levying a single tax on landownership. Though he advocated government intervention, he did not envision an enduring role for the state once it had imposed the single tax. By contrast, Bellamy imagined a powerful central government. In his novel *Looking Backward, 2000–1887* (1888), Bellamy scorned the "imbecility of private enterprise" and attacked industrialists who "maim and slaughter workers by thousands." In his view, the federal government should take over large-scale firms, administer them as workers' collectives, and redistribute wealth equally among all citizens.

Neither Bellamy, George, Ward, nor Ely endorsed the militant socialism of Karl Marx. The German philosopher predicted that capitalism would be overthrown and replaced by a revolutionary movement of industrial workers that would control the means of economic production and establish an egalitarian society. Although his ideas gained popularity among European labor leaders, they were not widely accepted in the United States during this period. George referred to Marx as "the prince of muddleheads." George and other critics believed that the American political system could be reformed without resorting to the extreme solution of a socialist revolution. They favored a cooperative commonwealth of capital and labor, with the government acting as an umpire between the two.

## REVIEW & RELATE

- In the late nineteenth century, how did many Americans explain individual economic success and failure?

- How did the business community view the role of government in the economy at the end of the nineteenth century?

✓ *LEARNINGCurve* bedfordstmartins.com/hewittlawson/LC

# Society and Culture in the Gilded Age

Wealthy people in the late nineteenth century used their fortunes to support lavish, indulgent lifestyles. For many of them, especially those with recent wealth, opulence rather than good taste was the standard of adornment. This tendency inspired writer Mark Twain and his collaborator Charles Dudley Warner to describe this era of wealth creation and vast inequality as the **Gilded Age**.

Twain and Warner had the very wealthy in mind when they coined the phrase, but others further down the social ladder found ways to participate in the culture of consumption. The rapidly expanding middle class enjoyed modest homes furnished with mass-produced consumer goods. Women played the central role in running the household, as most wives remained at home to raise children. Women and men often spent their free time attending meetings and other events sponsored by the many social, cultural, and political organizations that flourished during this era. Such prosperity was, however, largely limited to whites. For the majority of African Americans still living in the South, life proved much harder. In response to black aspirations for social and economic advancement, white politicians imposed a rigid system of racial segregation on the South. Although whites championed the cause of individual upward mobility, they restricted opportunities to achieve success to whites only.

## Wealthy and Middle-Class Pleasures

In Chicago's Gold Coast, Boston's Back Bay, Philadelphia's Rittenhouse Square, San Francisco's Nob Hill, Denver's Quality Hill, and Cincinnati's Hilltop, urban elites lived lives of incredible material opulence. J. P. Morgan and John D. Rockefeller built lavish homes in New York City. William Vanderbilt constructed luxurious mansions along Fifth Avenue in Manhattan. High-rise apartment buildings also catered to the wealthy. Overlooking Central Park, the nine-story Dakota Apartments boasted fifty-eight suites, a banquet hall, and a wine cellar. Famous architects designed some of the finest of these stately homes, which their millionaire residents furnished with an eclectic mix of priceless art objects and furniture in a jumble of diverse styles. The rich and famous established private social clubs, sent their children to exclusive prep schools and colleges, and worshipped in the most fashionable churches.

Second homes, usually for use in the summer, were no less expensively constructed and decorated. Besides residences in Manhattan and Newport, Rhode Island, the Vanderbilts constructed a "home away from home" in the mountains of Asheville, North Carolina. The Biltmore, as they named it, contained 250 rooms, 40 master bedrooms, and an indoor swimming pool. Edward Julius Berwind of Philadelphia, who made his fortune in coal, constructed a magnificent summer residence in Newport. Modeled after a mid-eighteenth-century French chateau, The Elms cost $1.4 million (approximately $38.6 million in 2012) and was furnished with an assortment of Renaissance ceramics and French and Venetian paintings.

The wealthy also built and frequented opera houses, concert halls, museums, and historical societies as testimonies to their taste and sophistication. For example, the Vanderbilts, Rockefellers, Goulds, and Morgans financed the completion of the Metropolitan Opera House in New York City in 1883. When the facility opened, a local newspaper commented about the well-heeled audience: "The Goulds and the Vanderbilts and people of that ilk perfumed the air with the odor of crisp greenbacks." Upper-class women often traveled abroad to visit the great European cities and ancient Mediterranean sites.

Industrialization and the rise of corporate capitalism also brought an array of **white-collar workers** in managerial, clerical, and technical positions. These workers formed a new, expanded middle class and joined the businesspeople, doctors, lawyers, teachers, and clergy who constituted the old middle class. More than three million white-collar workers were employed in 1910, nearly three times as many as in 1870.

Middle-class families decorated their residences with comfortable, mass-produced furniture, musical instruments, family photographs, books, periodicals, and a variety of memorabilia collected in their leisure time. They could relax in their parlors and browse through mass-circulation magazines like *Ladies' Home Journal* and *The Delineator*, a fashion and arts journal. They might also read a wide variety of popular newspapers that competed with one another with sensationalist stories. Or they could read some of the era's outpouring of fiction, including romances, dime novels, westerns, humor, and social realism, an art form that depicted working-class life.

> **Explore**
>
> See Document 16.2 for the cover of a popular women's magazine from 1900.

In the face of rapid economic changes, middle-class women and men joined a variety of social and professional organizations that were arising to deal with the problems accompanying industrialization (Table 16.1). During the 1880s, charitable organizations such as the American Red Cross were established to provide disaster relief. In 1892 the General Federation of Women's Clubs was founded to improve women's educational and cultural lives. Four years later, the National Association of Colored Women organized to help relieve suffering among the black poor, defend black women, and promote the interests of the black race. Many scholarly organizations were formed during this decade, including the American Historical Association, the Modern Language Association, and the American Mathematical Society.

During these swiftly changing times, adults became increasingly concerned about the nation's youth and sought to create organizations that catered to young people. Formed before the Civil War in England and expanded to the United States, the Young Men's Christian Association (YMCA) grew briskly during the 1880s as it erected buildings where young men could socialize, build moral character, and engage in healthy physical exercise. The Young Women's Christian Association (YWCA) provided similar

**TABLE 16.1   An Age of Organizations, 1876–1896**

| Category | Year of Founding | Organization |
|---|---|---|
| **Charitable** | 1881 | American Red Cross |
| | 1887 | Charity Organization Society |
| | 1889 | Educational Alliance |
| | 1893 | National Council of Jewish Women |
| **Sports/Fraternal** | 1876 | National League of Baseball |
| | 1882 | Knights of Columbus |
| | 1888 | National Council of Women |
| | 1892 | General Federation of Women's Clubs |
| | 1896 | National Association of Colored Women |
| **Professional** | 1883 | Modern Language Association |
| | 1884 | American Historical Association |
| | 1885 | American Economic Association |
| | 1888 | American Mathematical Society |

DOCUMENT 16.2

## The Delineator, 1900

By 1900 *The Delineator* had become one of America's foremost women's magazines. On the surface, it appeared to cater to traditional gender norms, each month featuring stories on fashion, sewing, leisure, and home design. But the editors of *The Delineator* also called for women's rights and broader social reform. In 1907, for example, editor Theodore Dreiser organized a successful outreach program to find homes for abandoned and orphaned children.

**Explore**

© Sarah Fabian-Baddiel/Heritage-Images/The Image Works

### Interpret the Evidence

- What does this woman's clothing and activity suggest about her background?
- Who do you think was the target audience for this magazine?

### Put It in Context

What social and political trends during the late nineteenth century might account for the popularity of magazines like *The Delineator*?

opportunities for women. African Americans also participated in "Y" activities through the creation of racially separate branches.

## Changing Gender Roles

Middle-class wives generally remained at home, caring for the house and children, often with the aid of a servant. Whereas in the past farmers and artisans had worked from the home, now most men and women accepted as natural the separation of the workplace and the home caused by industrialization and urbanization. Although the birthrate and marriage rates among the middle class dropped during the late nineteenth century, wives were still expected to care for their husbands and family first to fulfill their feminine duties. Even though daughters increasingly attended colleges reserved for women, such as Smith, Radcliffe, Wellesley, and Mount Holyoke, their families viewed education as a means of providing refinement rather than a career. One physician aptly summed up the prevailing view that women could only use their brains "but little and in trivial matters" and should concentrate on serving as "the companion or ornamental appendage to man."

Middle-class women were now confronted with the new consumer culture. Department stores, chain stores, ready-made clothes, and packaged goods, from Jell-O and Kellogg's Corn Flakes to cake mixes, competed for the money and loyalty of female consumers. Hairdressers, cosmetic companies, and department stores offered a growing and ever-changing assortment of styles, even as they also provided new jobs to those unable to afford the latest fashions without a weekly paycheck. The expanding array of consumer goods did not, however, decrease women's domestic workload. They had more furniture to dust, fancier meals to prepare, changing fashions to keep up with, higher standards of cleanliness to maintain, and more time to devote to entertaining. Yet the availability of mass-produced goods to assist the housewife in her chores made her role as consumer highly visible, while making her role as worker nearly invisible.

For the more socially and economically independent young women—those who attended college or beauty and secretarial schools—new worlds of leisure opened up. Bicycling, tennis, and croquet became popular sports for women in the late nineteenth century. So, too, did playing basketball, both in colleges and through industrial leagues. Indeed, women's colleges made sports a requirement, to offset the stress of intellectual life and produce a more well-rounded woman. Young women who sought an air of sophistication dressed according to the image of the Gibson Girl, the creation of illustrator Charles Dana Gibson. In the 1890s, the Gibson Girl became the model for the energetic, athletic "new woman," with her upswept hair, fancy hats, long skirts, flowing blouses, and disposable income.

Middle-class men enjoyed their leisure by joining fraternal organizations. Writing in the *North American Review* in 1897, W. G. Harwood commented that the late nineteenth century was the "Golden Age of Fraternity." Five and a half million men (of some 19 million adult men in the United States) joined fraternal orders, such as the Odd Fellows, Masons, Knights of Pythias, and Elks. These groups offered middle-class men a network of business contacts and gave them a chance to enjoy a communal, masculine social environment otherwise lacking in their lives.

In fact, historians have referred to a "crisis of masculinity" afflicting a segment of middle- and upper-class men

**Shopping in a Department Store**
In cities around the country, department stores offered a variety of items appealing to middle-class consumers, especially women. In this photograph from 1893, shoppers interested in purchasing gloves receive personal attention from well-dressed salesclerks behind the counter of Rike's Department Store in Dayton, Ohio.    © Bettmann/CORBIS

in the late nineteenth and early twentieth centuries. Middle-class occupations whittled away the sense of autonomy that men had experienced in an earlier era when they worked for themselves. The emergence of corporate capitalism had swelled the ranks of the middle class with organization men, who held salaried jobs in managerial departments. At the same time, the push for women's rights, especially the right to vote, and women's increasing involvement in civic associations threatened to reduce absolute male control over the public sphere.

Responding to this gender crisis, middle-class men sought ways to exert their masculinity and keep from becoming frail and effeminate. Psychologists like G. Stanley Hall warned that unless men returned to a primitive state of manhood, they risked becoming feminized and spiritually paralyzed. To avoid this, they should build up their bodies and engage in strenuous activities to improve their physical fitness. Edgar Rice Burroughs's *Tarzan of the Apes* (1912) extolled primitive manhood and contrasted its natural virtues with the vices of becoming overcivilized.

Men turned to sports to cultivate their masculinity. Besides playing baseball and football, they could attend various sporting events. Baseball became the national pastime, and men could root for their home team and establish a community with the thousands of male spectators who filled up newly constructed ballparks. These fields of dirt and grass were situated amid urban businesses, apartment buildings, and traffic and served as a metaphor for the preservation of an older, pastoral life alongside the hubbub of modern technology. Baseball, which had started as a game played by elites in New York City in the 1840s, soon became a commercially popular sport. It spread across the country as baseball clubs in different cities competed with each other. The sport came into its own with the creation of the professional National League in 1876 and the introduction of the World Series in 1903 between the winners of the National League and the American League pennant races.

Boxing also became a popular spectator sport in the late nineteenth century. Bare-knuckle fighting—without the protection of gloves—epitomized the craze to display pure masculinity. A boxing match lasted until one of the fighters was knocked out, leaving both fighters bloody and battered.

During the late nineteenth century, middle-class women and men also had increased opportunities to engage in different forms of sociability and sexuality. Gay men and lesbians could find safe havens in New York City's Greenwich Village and Chicago's North Side for their own entertainment. Although treated by medical experts as sexual "inverts" who might be cured by an infusion of "normal" heterosocial contact, gays and lesbians began to emerge from the shadows of Victorian-era sexual constraints around the turn of the twentieth century. "Boston marriages" constituted another form of relationship between women. The term apparently came from Henry James's book *The Bostonians* (1886), which described a female couple living together in a monogamous, long-term relationship. This conjugal-style association appealed to financially independent women who did not want to get married. Many of these relationships were sexual, but some were not. In either case, they offered women of a certain class an alternative to traditional, heterosexual marriage.

## Black America and Jim Crow

While wealthy and middle-class whites experimented with new forms of social behavior, African Americans faced greater challenges to preserving their freedom and dignity. In the South, where the overwhelming majority of blacks lived, post-Reconstruction southern governments adopted various techniques to keep blacks from voting. To circumvent the Fifteenth Amendment, southern states devised suffrage qualifications that they claimed were racially neutral, and the Supreme Court ruled in their favor. They instituted the poll tax, a tax that each person had to pay in order to cast a ballot. Poll taxes fell hardest on the poor, a disproportionate number of whom were African American. Disfranchisement reached its peak in the 1890s, as white southern governments managed to deny the vote to most of the black electorate (Map 16.2). Literacy tests officially barred the uneducated of both races, but they were administered in a manner that discriminated against blacks while allowing illiterate whites to satisfy the requirement. Many literacy tests contained a loophole called a "grandfather clause." Under this exception, men whose father or grandfather had voted in 1860—a time when white men but not black men, most of whom were slaves, could vote in the South—were excused from taking the test.

In the 1890s, white southerners also imposed legally sanctioned racial segregation on the region's black citizens. Commonly known as **Jim Crow** laws (named for a character in a minstrel show, where whites performed in blackface), these new statutes denied African Americans equal access to public facilities and ensured that blacks lived apart from whites. In 1883, when the Supreme Court struck down the 1875 Civil Rights Act (see chapter 14), it gave southern states the freedom to adopt measures confining blacks to separate schools, public accommodations, seats on transportation, beds in hospitals, and sections of graveyards. In 1896 the Supreme Court sanctioned Jim Crow, constructing the constitutional rationale for legally keeping the races apart. In *Plessy v. Ferguson*, the high court ruled

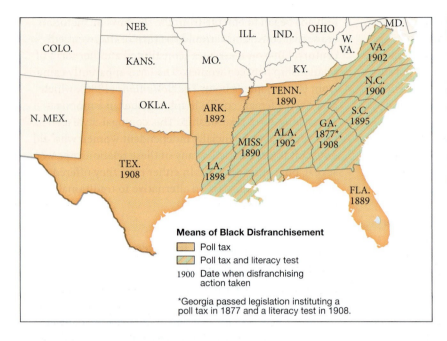

**MAP 16.2 Black Disfranchisement in the South, 1889–1908**

After Reconstruction, black voters posed a threat to the ruling Democrats by occasionally joining with third-party insurgents. To repel these challenges, Democratic Party leaders made racial appeals to divide poor whites and blacks. Chiefly in the 1890s and early twentieth century, white leaders succeeded in disfranchising black voters (and some poor whites), mainly by adopting poll tax and literacy requirements.

Means of Black Disfranchisement
- Poll tax
- Poll tax and literacy test
- 1900 Date when disfranchising action taken

*Georgia passed legislation instituting a poll tax in 1877 and a literacy test in 1908.

that a Louisiana law providing for "equal but separate" accommodations for "whites" and "coloreds" on railroad cars did not violate the equal protection clause of the Fourteenth Amendment. In its decision, the Court concluded that civil rights laws could not change racial destiny. "If one race be inferior to the other socially," the justices explained, "the Constitution of the United States cannot put them on the same plane." In practice, however, white southerners obeyed the "separate" part of the equation but never provided equal services. If blacks tried to overstep the bounds of Jim Crow in any way that whites found unacceptable, they risked their lives. Between 1884 and 1900, nearly 1,700 blacks were lynched in the South. Victims were often subjected to brutal forms of torture before they were hanged or shot.

In everyday life, African Americans carried on as best they could. Segregation provided many African Americans with opportunities to build their own businesses, control their own churches, develop their own schools staffed by black teachers, and form their own civic associations and fraternal organizations. Segregation, though harsh and unequal, did foster a sense of black community, promoted a rising middle class, and created social networks that enhanced racial pride. Founded in 1898, the North Carolina Life Insurance Company, one of the leading black-owned and black-operated businesses, employed many African Americans in managerial and sales positions. Burial societies ensured that their members received a proper funeral when they died. As with whites, black men joined lodges such as the Colored Masons and the Colored Odd Fellows, while women participated in the YWCA and the National Association of Colored Women. A small

percentage of southern blacks resisted Jim Crow by migrating to the North, where blacks still exercised the right to vote, more jobs were open to them, and segregation was less strictly enforced.

## REVIEW & RELATE

What role did consumption play in the society and culture of the Gilded Age?

How did industrialization contribute to heightened anxieties about gender roles and race?

*LEARNINGCurve* bedfordstmartins.com/hewittlawson/LC

# National Politics in the Era of Industrialization

Politicians such as John Sherman played an important role in the expanding industrial economy that provided new opportunities for the wealthy and the expanding middle class. For growing companies and corporations to succeed, they needed a favorable political climate that would support their interests. Businessmen frequently looked to Washington for assistance at a time when politicians were held in low repute. During this era, the office of the president was a weak and largely administrative post, and corporate leaders were unconcerned with the quality of the mind and character of presidents, legislators, and judges so long as these officials furthered their economic objectives. For much of this period, the two national political parties battled to a standoff, which resulted in congressional gridlock with little accomplished. Yet spurred by fierce partisan competition, political participation grew among the electorate.

## Why Great Men Did Not Become President

James Bryce, a British observer of American politics, devoted a chapter of his book *The American Commonwealth* (1888) to "why great men are not chosen presidents." He acknowledged that the office of president "is raised far above all other offices [and] offers too great a stimulation to ambition." Yet he believed that the White House attracted mediocre occupants because the president functioned mainly as an executor. The stature of the office had shrunk following the impeachment of Andrew Johnson and the reassertion of congressional power during Reconstruction (see chapter 14). Presidents considered themselves mainly as the nation's top administrator. They did not see their roles as formulating policy or intervening on behalf of legislative objectives. Presidents had only a small White House staff to assist them, which reflected the meager demands placed on their office, especially in times of peace, which prevailed until 1898. The Civil Service Act of 1883 had reduced even further the political patronage the president had at his disposal. With the office held in such low regard, Bryce asserted, "most of the ablest men for thought, planning, and execution in America, go into the business of developing the national resources of the country." During the Age of Organization, great men became corporate leaders, not presidents.

Perhaps aware that they could expect little in the way of assistance or imagination from national leaders, voters refused to give either Democrats or Republicans solid support. No president between Ulysses S. Grant and William McKinley won back-to-back elections or received a majority of the popular vote. The only two-time winner, the Democrat Grover Cleveland, lost his bid for reelection in 1888 before triumphing again in 1892. Republicans scored victories in four out of six presidential contests from 1876 to 1896, but the vote tallies were extremely close.

> **Explore**
>
> See Documents 16.3 and 16.4 for two views on presidential greatness.

Nevertheless, the presidency attracted accomplished individuals. Rutherford B. Hayes (1877–1881), James A. Garfield (1881), and Benjamin Harrison (1889–1893) all had served ably in the Union army as commanding officers during the Civil War and had prior political experience.

The nation greatly mourned Garfield following his assassination in 1881 by Charles Guiteau, a disgruntled applicant for federal patronage. Upon Garfield's death, Chester A. Arthur (1881–1885) became president. He had served as a quartermaster general during the Civil War, had a reputation as sympathetic to African American civil rights, and had run the New York City Customs House effectively. Grover Cleveland (1885–1889, 1893–1897) first served as mayor of Buffalo and then as governor of New York. All of these men, as even Bryce admitted, worked hard, possessed common sense, and were honest. However, they were uninspiring individuals who lacked qualities of leadership that would arouse others to action.

## Congressional Inaction

Character alone did not diminish the power of the president. More important was the structure of Congress, which prevented the president from providing vigorous leadership. Throughout most of this period, Congress remained narrowly divided. Majorities continually shifted from one party to the other. For all but two terms, Democrats controlled the House of Representatives, while Republicans held the majority in the Senate. Divided government meant that during his term in office no late-nineteenth-century president had a majority of his party in both houses of Congress. Turnover among congressmen in the House of Representatives, who were elected every two years, was quite high, and there was little power of incumbency. For example, of the twenty-one congressmen from Ohio elected in 1882, only ten had served in the previous session, and only four of the ten won reelection two years later. The Senate, however, provided more continuity and allowed senators, with six-year terms of office, to amass greater power than congressmen could, as evidenced by John Sherman serving six terms in the upper chamber.

For all the power that Congress wielded, it failed to govern effectively or efficiently. Contemporary observers lamented the dismal state of affairs in the nation's capital. A cabinet officer in 1869 complained: "You can't use tact with a Congressman! A Congressman is a hog! You must take a stick and hit him on the snout!"

Although both the House and the Senate contained men of great talent, fine speaking ability, and clever legislative minds, the rules of each body turned orderly procedure into chaos. In the House, measures did not receive adequate attention on the floor because the Speaker did not have the power to control the flow of systematic debate. Committee chairmen held a tight rein over the introduction and consideration of legislation and competed with one another for influence in the chamber. Congressmen showed little decorum as they conducted business on

# The Making of a Great President: Two Views

The British traveler James Bryce admired the United States and toured the country in the late 1880s. His book *The American Commonwealth* (1888), though flattering of U.S. traditions and accomplishments, found its political leaders lacking in greatness—an opinion that many subsequent historians have shared, although Bryce and more recent historians might differ in their definition of greatness. In the following passage from his book, Bryce comments on the ordinariness of most American presidents. Contrast Bryce's assessment with the excerpt from the obituary of President Grover Cleveland published in the *New York Times*.

**Explore**

### 16.3 James Bryce | Why Great Men Are Not Chosen Presidents, 1888

Europeans often ask, and Americans do not always explain, how it happens that this great office, the greatest in the world, unless we except the Papacy, to which any man can rise by his own merits, is not more frequently filled by great and striking men? In America, which is beyond all other countries the country of a "career open to talents," a country, moreover, in which political life is unusually keen and political ambition widely diffused, it might be expected that the highest place would always be won by a man of brilliant gifts. But since the heroes of the Revolution died out with Jefferson and Adams and Madison some sixty years ago, no person except General Grant has reached the chair whose name would have been remembered had he not been President, and no President except Abraham Lincoln has displayed rare or striking qualities in the chair. Who now knows or cares to know anything about the personality of James K. Polk or Franklin

Pierce? The only thing remarkable about them is that being so commonplace they should have climbed so high. . . .

. . . Besides, the ordinary American voter does not object to mediocrity. He has a lower conception of the qualities requisite to make a statesman than those who direct public opinion in Europe have. He likes his candidate to be sensible, vigorous, and, above all, what he calls "magnetic," and does not value, because he sees no need for, originality or profundity, a fine culture or a wide knowledge. Candidates are selected to be run for nomination by knots of persons who, however expert as party tacticians, are usually commonplace men; and the choice between those selected for nomination is made by a very large body, an assembly of over eight hundred delegates from the local party organizations over the country, who are certainly no better than ordinary citizens.

Source: James Bryce, *The American Commonwealth* (London: Macmillan, 1888), 1:100, 102–3.

the House floor. Representatives chatted with each other, their voices drowning out the speakers at the podium, or they ignored the business at hand and instead answered correspondence and read newspapers.

The Senate, though more manageable in size and more stable in membership (only one-third of its membership stood for reelection every two years), did not function much more smoothly. Despite party affiliations, senators thought very highly of their own judgments and very little of the value of party unity. The position of

majority leader, someone who could impose discipline on his colleagues and design a coherent legislative agenda, had not yet been created. An exasperated Woodrow Wilson, who favored the British system of parliamentary government, attributed the problem to the failure to place trust in somebody "to assume final responsibility and blame." Wilson, the author of *Congressional Government* (1885) and a future president, concluded: "Our government is defective as it parcels out power and confuses responsibility." Under these circumstances, neither the

**16.4** **Obituary of Grover Cleveland, 1908**

As a public man, considering the splendid record that he made, he will be put in the same class with Washington and Lincoln—one of the three great Presidents that this country has had. His greatness was justified by his exceptionally strong character and his many intellectual gifts. He was a man of great moral strength, and having the advantage of a fine intellect he thought seriously and deeply upon all subjects, and, having reached a conclusion, particularly as to a principle of morals or religion, or public weal [welfare], he was uncompromising. He agreed with David Crockett that the first thing was to determine what was right and then to do that thing.

What he was in public life he was equally in private life; strong in his views, tolerant in method, but uncompromising in principle. Most of his time was spent in promoting education and philanthropy—work which entailed sacrifices of his time and personal convenience, without fee or hope of reward beyond the desire to do that which was useful and good. These occupied, when not in public life, most of his time, so that when we look over his career, though he reached the proverbial three score and ten years, it is not to be measured by years alone, but by his splendid deeds and lofty ideals which affected all who came within the range of his influence.

Source: "All Washington Mourns, All Flags at Half Staff in Tribute to Dead Statesman," *New York Times*, June 25, 1908, 5.

**Interpret the Evidence**

- What qualities was Bryce surprised to find missing in American presidents? How might Bryce have characterized the values and beliefs of the typical American voter?
- What does the obituary of Grover Cleveland tell you about the qualities many Americans associated with "greatness"? What qualities do you think make a president "great"?

**Put It in Context**

What role did late-nineteenth-century presidents play in the great economic growth of the United States?

president nor Congress governed efficiently or responsibly.

## An Energized and Entertained Electorate

Despite all the difficulties of the legislative process, political candidates eagerly pursued office and conducted extremely heated campaigns. The electorate considered politics a form of entertainment. Political parties did not stand for clearly stated issues or offer innovative solutions; instead, campaigns took on the qualities of carefully staged performances. Candidates crafted their oratory to arouse the passions and prejudices of their audiences, and their managers handed out buttons, badges, and ceramic and glass plates stamped with the candidates' faces and slogans.

Partisanship helped fuel high political participation. During this period, voter turnout in presidential elections was much higher than at any time in the twentieth century. Region, as well as historical and cultural allegiances,

**1892 Presidential Campaign Plate**

Before radio, television, and the Internet, political parties advertised candidates in a variety of colorful ways, including banners, buttons, ribbons, and ceramic and glass plates. Voters, who turned out in record numbers during the late nineteenth century, coveted these items. This plate shows the 1892 Democratic presidential ticket of Grover Cleveland and Adlai Stevenson, who lost the election.    Collection of Steven F. Lawson

replaced ideology as the key to party affiliation. The wrenching experience of the Civil War had cemented voting loyalties for many Americans. After Reconstruction, white southerners tended to vote Democratic; northerners and newly enfranchised southern blacks generally voted Republican. However, geographic region alone did not shape political loyalties; a sizable contingent of Democratic voters remained in the North, and southern whites and blacks periodically abandoned both the Democratic and Republican parties to vote for third parties.

Religion played an important role in shaping party loyalties during this period of intense partisanship. The Democratic Party tended to attract Protestants of certain sects, such as German Lutherans and Episcopalians, as well as Catholics. These faiths emphasized religious ritual and the acceptance of personal sin. They believed that the government should not interfere in matters of morality, which should remain the province of Christian supervision on Earth and divine judgment in the hereafter. By contrast, other Protestant denominations, such as Baptists, Congregationalists, Methodists, and Presbyterians, highlighted the importance of individual will and believed that the law

could be shaped to eradicate ignorance and vice. These Protestants were more likely to cast their ballots for Republicans, except in the South, where regional loyalty to the Democratic Party trumped religious affiliation.

Some people went to the polls because they fiercely disliked members of the opposition party. Northern white workers in New York City or Cincinnati, Ohio, for example, might vote against the Republican Party because they viewed it as the party of African Americans. Other voters cast their ballots against Democrats because they identified them as the party of Irish Catholics, intemperance, and secession.

Although political parties commanded fierce loyalties, the parties remained divided internally. For example, the Republicans pitted "Stalwarts" against "Half Breeds." Led by Senators Roscoe Conkling and Chester Arthur of New York, Zachariah Chandler of Michigan, and John Logan of Illinois, the Stalwarts presented themselves as the "Old Guard" of the Republican Party, what they called the "Grand Old Party" (GOP). The Half Breeds, a snide name given to them by the Stalwarts, tended to be younger Republicans and were represented by Senators James G. Blaine, John Sherman, and James A. Garfield of Ohio and George Frisbie Hoar of Massachusetts. This faction claimed to be more open to new ideas and less wedded to the old causes that the Republican Party promoted, such as racial equality. In the end, however, the differences between the two groups had less to do with ideas than with which faction would have greater power within the Republican Party.

Overall, the continuing strength of party loyalties produced equilibrium as voters cast their ballots primarily along strict party lines. The outcome of presidential elections depended on key "undecided" districts in several states in the Midwest and in New York and nearby states, which swung the balance of power in the electoral college. Indeed, from 1876 to 1896 all winning candidates for president and vice president came from Ohio, Indiana, Illinois, New York, and New Jersey.

## REVIEW & RELATE

- What accounted for the inefficiency and ineffectiveness of the federal government in the late nineteenth century?

- How would you explain the high rates of voter turnout and political participation in an era of uninspiring politicians and governmental inaction?

## Conclusion: Industry in the Age of Organization

From 1877 to 1900, American businessmen demonstrated a zeal for organization. Prompted by new technology that opened up national markets of commerce and communication, business entrepreneurs created large-scale corporations that promoted industrial expansion. Borrowing from European investors and importing and improving on European technology, by 1900 U.S. industrialists had surpassed their overseas counterparts.

Capitalists made great fortunes and lived luxurious lifestyles, emulating the fashions of European elites. Most corporate leaders did not rise from poverty but instead came from the upper middle class and had access to education and connections. Those like Andrew Carnegie, who rose from rags to riches, were the exceptions. The wealthy explained their success as the result of individual effort and hard work. This idea was reinforced in schoolbooks such as the McGuffey Readers, the novels of Horatio Alger, and religious sermons, like those of Russell Conwell.

Although most working Americans did not achieve much wealth in the Age of Organization, they had faith in the possibility of improving their economic position. Members of the middle class lived less extravagantly than did the wealthy; nonetheless, they enjoyed the comforts of the growing consumer economy. Although Jim Crow restricted the black middle class and a heightened sense of masculinity inhibited opportunities available to white women, both groups managed to carve out ways to lift themselves economically and socially.

In gaining success, the wealthy exchanged individualism for organization, competition for consolidation, and laissez-faire for government support. Without pro-business policies from Washington lawmakers and favorable decisions from the Supreme Court, big business would not have developed as rapidly as it did in this era. To prosper, corporations needed sympathetic politicians—whether to furnish free land for railroad expansion, enact tariffs to protect manufacturers, or protect private property. Even when a public outcry led to the regulation of trusts, the pro-business senator John Sherman shaped the legislation so as to minimize damage to corporate interests. In general, national politicians avoided engaging in fierce ideological conflicts, but they, too, organized. The political parties they fashioned encouraged a high level of political participation among voters.

It remained for those who did not share in the glittering wealth of the Gilded Age to find ways to resist corporate domination. The next chapter explores the efforts of workers and farmers to remedy the economic, social, and political ills that accompanied industrialization.

# Chapter Review

Online Study Guide ▶ bedfordstmartins.com/hewittlawson

## KEY TERMS

## REVIEW & RELATE

1. What were the key factors behind the acceleration of industrial development in late-nineteenth-century America?

2. How did industrialization change the way American businessmen thought about their companies and the people who worked for them?

3. In the late nineteenth century, how did many Americans explain individual economic success and failure?

4. How did the business community view the role of government in the economy at the end of the nineteenth century?

5. What role did consumption play in the society and culture of the Gilded Age?

6. How did industrialization contribute to heightened anxieties about gender roles and race?

7. What accounted for the inefficiency and ineffectiveness of the federal government in the late nineteenth century?

8. How would you explain the high rates of voter turnout and political participation in an era of uninspiring politicians and governmental inaction?

## TIMELINE OF EVENTS

| | |
|---|---|
| 1859 | Charles Darwin publishes *On the Origin of Species* |
| | Henry Bessemer improves steel production process |
| 1860–1890 | U.S. gross domestic product quadruples |
| 1866 | Transatlantic telegraph cable completed |
| 1868 | Typewriter invented |
| 1870–1900 | U.S. becomes a global industrial power |
| 1870–1910 | Number of U.S. white-collar workers triples |
| 1870s | John D. Rockefeller takes control of oil refining business |
| 1872 | Montgomery Ward established |
| 1876 | Thomas Edison establishes research laboratory in Menlo Park, New Jersey |
| 1881 | James Garfield assassinated |
| 1883 | Civil Service Act passed |
| 1884–1900 | 1,700 blacks lynched in the South |
| 1885 | Alexander Graham Bell founds American Telephone and Telegraph |
| 1886 | U.S. railroads adopt standard gauge |
| | *Santa Clara County v. Southern Pacific Railroad Company* |
| 1889 | Andrew Carnegie publishes "The Gospel of Wealth" |
| 1890 | Sherman Antitrust Act passed |
| 1890s | African Americans disfranchised in the South |
| 1891 | Rural free delivery (RFD) begins |
| 1895 | *United States v. E.C. Knight Company* |
| 1896 | *Plessy v. Ferguson* |
| 1901 | United States Steel established |

## DOCUMENT PROJECT 16

# Debates about Laissez-Faire

From the nation's founding, the pursuit of individual opportunity has held a central place among American values. The Declaration of Independence extolled the "pursuit of happiness," which has increasingly been interpreted as the chance to accumulate material wealth. The Bill of Rights, adopted after the Constitution was ratified, protected personal liberties from interference by the federal government. Early Supreme Court decisions upheld the binding nature of contracts. The immigrants who came to the United States in the eighteenth and nineteenth centuries assumed that they would have the opportunity to achieve whatever success their talents and hard work would bring.

In the late nineteenth century, as big business consolidated and giant trusts came to dominate whole industries, defenders of unfettered big business argued that individual effort and initiative were still the central engine of the American economy. Championing Adam Smith's notion of laissez-faire—the idea that the marketplace should be left to regulate itself—they argued that government should do nothing to constrain the development of industry. Yet as poverty expanded while a small number of industrialists and financiers accumulated great wealth, reformers questioned whether individualism undermined community, and contended that the government should regulate the free market to promote the greater public welfare. With the gap between rich and poor growing, even industrialists realized that if they did not help the poor in some way, the working classes would rise up against them. Nevertheless, they continued to resist government interference.

Defenders of the status quo argued that individualism must be preserved as the natural order of society. Critics countered that cooperation rather than individual competition made social progress possible and that the government should protect ordinary people from the harm done by greedy capitalists. As you read the following documents, which provide contrasting views of the meaning of success, consider these questions: How does each author define success? How do these authors intend to promote success? And what can be done to relieve the plight of those who do not succeed?

**DOCUMENT 16.5**

# William Graham Sumner | A Defense of Laissez-Faire, 1883

Yale professor William Graham Sumner believed that millionaires deserved their wealth, a notion that appealed to successful industrialists. Men like Andrew Carnegie, he declared, "may fairly be regarded as the naturally selected agents of society." The poor, he argued, also justly deserved their fate. Sumner and other defenders of economic inequality maintained that if the government tried to help these unfortunate losers in the competitive struggle, progress would be halted and civilization would decay.

There is no possible definition of "a poor man." A pauper is a person who cannot earn his living; whose producing powers have fallen positively below his necessary consumption; who cannot, therefore, pay his way. A human society needs the active co-operation and productive energy of every person in it. A man who is present as a consumer, yet who does not contribute either by land, labor, or capital to the work of society, is a burden. On no sound political theory ought such a person to share in the political power of the State. He drops out of the ranks of workers and producers. Society must support him. It accepts the burden, but he must be cancelled from the ranks of the rulers likewise. So much for the pauper. About him no more need be said. But he is not the "poor man." The "poor man" is an elastic term, under which any number of social fallacies may be hidden.

Neither is there any possible definition of "the weak." Some are weak in one way, and some in another; and those who are weak in one sense are strong in another. In general, however, it may be said that those whom humanitarians and philanthropists call the weak are the ones through whom the productive and conservative forces of society are wasted. They constantly neutralize and destroy the finest efforts of the wise and industrious, and are a dead-weight on the society in all its struggles to realize any better things. Whether the people who mean no harm, but are weak in the essential powers necessary to the performance of one's duties in life, or those who are malicious and vicious, do the more mischief, is a question not easy to answer.

Under the names of the poor and the weak, the negligent, shiftless, inefficient, silly, and imprudent are fastened upon the industrious and prudent as a responsibility and a duty. On the one side, the terms are extended to cover the idle, intemperate, and vicious, who, by the combination, gain credit which they do not deserve, and which they could not get if they stood alone. On the other hand, the terms are extended to include wage-receivers of the humblest rank, who are degraded by the combination. The reader who desires to guard himself against fallacies should always scrutinize the terms "poor" and "weak" as used, so as to see which or how many of these classes they are made to cover.

The humanitarians, philanthropists, and reformers, looking at the facts of life as they present themselves, find enough which is sad and unpromising in the condition of many members of society. They see wealth and poverty side by side. They note great inequality of social position and social chances. They eagerly set about the attempt to account for what they see, and to devise schemes for remedying what they do not like. In their eagerness to recommend the less fortunate classes to pity and consideration they forget all about the rights of other classes; they gloss over all the faults of the classes in question, and they exaggerate their misfortunes and their virtues. They invent new theories of property, distorting rights and perpetrating injustice, as any one is sure to do who sets about the re-adjustment of social relations with the interests of one group distinctly before his mind, and the interests of all other groups thrown into the background. When I have read certain of these discussions I have thought that it must be quite disreputable to be respectable, quite dishonest to own property, quite unjust to go one's own way and earn one's own living, and that the only really admirable person was the good-for-nothing. The man who by his own effort raises himself above poverty appears, in these discussions, to be of no account. The man who has done nothing to raise himself above poverty finds that the social doctors flock about him, bringing the capital which they have collected from the other class, and promising him the aid of the State to give him what the other had to work for. In all these schemes and projects the organized intervention of society through the State is either planned or hoped for, and the State is thus made to become the protector and guardian of certain classes. The agents who are to direct the State action are, of course, the reformers and philanthropists. . . . Here it may suffice to observe that, on the theories of the social philosophers to whom I have referred, we should get a new maxim of judicious living: Poverty is the best policy. If you get wealth, you will have to support other people; if you do not get wealth, it will be the duty of other people to support you.

Source: William Graham Sumner, *What the Social Classes Owe Each Other* (New York: Harper and Brothers, 1883), 19–24.

**DOCUMENT 16.6**

## Edward Bellamy | *Looking Backward, 2000–1887*, 1888

Edward Bellamy's best-selling novel *Looking Backward, 2000–1887* offered utopian socialist solutions to the problems facing the rapidly industrializing United States. After falling into a medically induced sleep, Bellamy's narrator, Julian West, awakens in the year 2000 to find that many of the social inequities of the late nineteenth century have been resolved. In the following passage, Dr. Leete, who has revived West, attempts to explain the dramatic change in U.S. society. The passage begins with Leete asking West questions about his era.

"What should you name as the most prominent feature of the labor troubles of your day?"

"Why, the strikes, of course," I replied.

"Exactly; but what made the strikes so formidable?"

"The great labor organizations."

"And what was the motive of these great organizations?"

"The workmen claimed they had to organize to get their rights from the big corporations," I replied.

"That is just it," said Dr. Leete, "the organization of labor and the strikes were an effect, merely, of the concentration of capital in greater masses than had ever been known before. Before this concentration began, while as yet commerce and industry were conducted by innumerable petty concerns with small capital, instead of a small number of great concerns with vast capital, the individual workman was relatively important and independent in his relations to the employer. Moreover, when a little capital or a new idea was enough to start a man in business for himself, workingmen were constantly becoming employers and there was no hard and fast line between the two classes. Labor unions were needless then, and general strikes out of the question. But when the era of small concerns with small capital was succeeded by that of the great aggregations of capital, all this was changed. The individual laborer who had been relatively important to the small employer was reduced to insignificance and power-lessness over against the great corporation, while, at the same time, the way upward to the grade of employer was closed to him. Self-defence drove him to union with his fellows.

"The records of the period show that the outcry against the concentration of capital was furious. Men believed that it threatened society with a form of tyranny more abhorrent than it had ever endured. They believed that the great corporations were preparing for them the yoke of a baser servitude than had ever been imposed on the race, servitude not to men but to soulless machines incapable of any motive but insatiable greed. Looking back, we cannot wonder at their desperation, for certainly humanity was never confronted with a fate more sordid and hideous than would have been the era of corporate tyranny which they anticipated.

"Meanwhile, without being in the smallest degree checked by the clamor against it, the absorption of business by ever larger monopolies continued. In the United States, where this tendency was later in developing than in Europe, there was not, after the beginning of the last quarter of the century, any opportunity whatever for individual enterprise in any important field of industry, unless backed by a great capital. During the last decade of the century, such small businesses as still remained were fast failing survivals of a past epoch, or mere parasites on the great corporations, or else existed in fields too small to attract the great capitalists. Small businesses, as far as they still remained, were reduced to the condition of rats and mice, living in holes and corners, and counting on evading notice for the enjoyment of existence. The railroads had gone on combining till a few great syndicates controlled every rail in the land. In manufactories, every important staple was controlled by a syndicate. These syndicates, pools, trusts, or whatever their name, fixed prices and crushed all competition except when combinations as vast as themselves arose. Then a struggle, resulting in a still greater consolidation, ensued. The great city bazar crushed its country rivals with branch stores, and in the city itself absorbed its smaller rivals till the business of a whole quarter was concentrated under one roof with a hundred former proprietors of shops serving as clerks. Having no business of his own to put his money in, the small capitalist, at the same time that he took service under the corporation, found no other investment for his money but its stocks and bonds, thus becoming doubly dependent upon it.

"The fact that the desperate popular opposition to the consolidation of business in a few powerful hands had no effect to check it, proves that there must have been a strong economical reason for it. The small capitalists, with their innumerable petty concerns, had, in fact, yielded the field to the great aggregations of capital, because they belonged to a day of small things and were totally incompetent to the demands of an age of steam and telegraphs and the gigantic scale of its enterprises. To restore the former order of things, even if possible, would have involved returning to the day of stage-coaches. Oppressive and intolerable as was the regime of the great consolidations of capital, even its victims, while they cursed it, were forced to admit the prodigious increase of efficiency which had been imparted to the national industries, the vast economies effected by concentration of management and unity of organization, and to confess that since the new system had taken the place of the old, the wealth of the world had increased at a rate before undreamed of. To be sure this vast increase had gone chiefly to make the rich richer, increasing the gap between them and the poor; but the fact remained that, as a means merely of producing wealth, capital had been proved efficient in proportion to its consolidation. The restoration of the old system with the subdivision of capital, if it were possible, might indeed bring back a greater equality of conditions with more individual dignity and freedom, but it would be at the price of general poverty and the arrest of material progress. . . .

"Early in the last century the evolution was completed by the final consolidation of the entire capital of the nation. The industry and commerce of the country, ceasing to be conducted by a set of irresponsible corporations and syndicates of private persons at their caprice and for their profit, were intrusted to a single syndicate representing the people, to be conducted in the common interest for the common profit. The nation, that is to say, organized as the one great business corporation in which all other corporations were absorbed; it became the one capitalist in the place of all other capitalists, the sole employer, the final monopoly in which all previous and lesser monopolies were swallowed up, a monopoly in the profits and economies of which all citizens shared."

Source: Edward Bellamy, *Looking Backward, 2000–1887* (Boston: Ticknor, 1888), 71–78.

DOCUMENT 16.7

# Andrew Carnegie | The Gospel of Wealth, 1889

Andrew Carnegie, who immigrated to the United States and experienced poverty as a young boy, made his fortune in the steel industry and became one of the richest men in the United States. Recognizing the dangers of widespread poverty among the mass of American workers, Carnegie sought to use philanthropy to provide opportunities for individuals to help themselves, as he explains in the following essay, which is usually referred to as "The Gospel of Wealth." As you read, note the distinction that Carnegie makes between charity and philanthropy.

THE BEST USES to which surplus wealth can be put have already been indicated. Those who would administer wisely must, indeed, be wise; for one of the serious obstacles to the improvement of our race is indiscriminate charity. It were better for mankind that the millions of the rich were thrown into the sea than so spent as to encourage the slothful, the drunken, the unworthy. Of every thousand dollars spent in so-called charity today, it is probable that nine hundred and fifty dollars is unwisely spent—so spent, indeed, as to produce the very evils which it hopes to mitigate or cure. . . .

In bestowing charity, the main consideration should be to help those who will help themselves; to provide part of the means by which those who desire to improve may do so; to give those who desire to rise the aids by which they may rise; to assist, but rarely or never to do all. Neither the individual nor the race is improved by almsgiving. Those worthy of assistance, except in rare cases, seldom require assistance. The really valuable men of the race never do, except in case of accident or sudden change. Every one has, of course, cases of individuals brought to his own knowledge where temporary assistance can do genuine good, and these he will not overlook. But the amount which can be wisely given by the individual for individuals is necessarily limited by his lack of knowledge of the circumstances connected with each. He is the only true reformer who is as careful and as anxious not to aid the unworthy as he is to aid the worthy, and, perhaps, even more so, for in almsgiving more injury is probably done by rewarding vice than by relieving virtue.

The rich man is thus almost restricted to following the examples of Peter Cooper, Enoch Pratt of Baltimore, Mr. Pratt of Brooklyn, Senator Stanford [noted philanthropists], and others, who know that the best means of benefiting the community is to place within its reach the ladders upon which the aspiring can rise—free libraries, parks, and means of recreation, by which men are helped in body and mind; works of art, certain to give pleasure and improve the public taste; and public institutions of various kinds, which will improve the general condition of the people; in this manner returning their surplus wealth to the mass of their fellows in the forms best calculated to do them lasting good.

Thus is the problem of rich and poor to be solved. The laws of accumulation will be left free, the laws of distribution free. Individualism will continue, but the millionaire will be but a trustee for the poor, intrusted for a season with a great part of the increased wealth of the community, but administering it for the community far better than it could or would have done for itself. The best minds will thus have reached a stage in the development of the race in which it is clearly seen that there is no mode of disposing of surplus wealth creditable to thoughtful and earnest men into whose hands it flows, save by using it year by year for the general good. This day already dawns. Men may die without in-curring the pity of their fellows, still sharers in great business enterprises from which their capital cannot be or has not been withdrawn, and which is left chiefly at death for public uses; yet the day is not far distant when the man who dies leaving behind him millions of available wealth, which was free for him to administer during life, will pass away "unwept, unhonored, and unsung," no matter to what uses he leaves the dross which he cannot take with him. Of such as these the public verdict will then be: "The man who dies thus rich dies disgraced."

Such, in my opinion, is the true gospel concerning wealth, obedience to which is destined some day to solve the problem of the rich and the poor, and to bring "Peace on earth, among men good will."

Source: Andrew Carnegie, *The Gospel of Wealth and Other Timely Essays* (New York: Century, 1901), 16–19.

**DOCUMENT 16.8**

# Henry Demarest Lloyd | Critique of Wealth, 1894

Many academics and writers attacked industrial capitalists, claiming that their excessive wealth came at the expense of workers and the general public. Lawyer and journalist Henry Demarest Lloyd wrote numerous articles for the *Chicago Tribune* exposing corruption in business and politics. A reformer influenced by British socialists, Lloyd supported legislation to ban child labor and to allow women to vote. In his 1894 book *Wealth against Commonwealth*, he denounced ruthless and unsavory competitive practices by industrialists who created monopolies that exploited working people. In the following excerpt, Lloyd raises questions about the fundamental value of industrial capitalism and its threat to social progress.

IF OUR CIVILIZATION IS DESTROYED, . . . it will not be by . . . barbarians from below. Our barbarians come from above. Our great money-makers have sprung in one generation into seats of power kings do not know.

The forces and the wealth are new, and have been the opportunity of new men. Without restraints of culture, experience, the pride, or even the inherited caution of class or rank, these men, intoxicated, think they are the wave instead of the float, and that they have created the business which has created them. To them science is but a never-ending repertoire of investments stored up by nature for the syndicates, government but a fountain of franchises, the nations but customers in squads, and a million the unit of a new arithmetic of wealth written for them. They claim a power without control, exercised through forms which make it secret, anonymous, and perpetual. The possibilities of its gratification have been widening before them without interruption since they began, and even at a thousand millions they will feel no satiation and will see no place to stop. They are gluttons of luxury and power, rough, unsocialized, believing that mankind must be kept terrorized. Powers of pity die out of them, because they work through agents and die in their agents, because what they do is not for themselves. . . .

. . . In casting about for the cause of our industrial evils, public opinion has successively found it in "competition," "combination," the "corporations," "conspiracies," "trusts." But competition has ended in combination, and our new wealth takes as it chooses the form of corporation or trust, or corporation again, and with every change grows greater and worse. Under these kaleidoscopic masks we begin at last to see progressing to its terminus a steady consolidation, the end of which is one-man power. The conspiracy ends in one, and one cannot conspire with himself. When this solidification of many into one has been reached, we shall be at last face to face with the naked truth that it is not only the form but the fact of arbitrary power, of control without consent, of rule without representation that concerns us.

Business motived by the self-interest of the individual runs into monopoly at every point it touches the social life—land monopoly, transportation monopoly, trade monopoly, political monopoly in all its forms, from contraction of the currency to corruption in office. The society in which in half a lifetime a man without a penny can become a hundred times a millionaire is as over-ripe, industrially, as was, politically, the Rome in which the most popular bully could lift himself from the ranks of the legion on to the throne of the Caesars. Our rising issue is with business. Monopoly is business at the end of its journey. It has got there. The irrepressible conflict is now as distinctly with business as the issue so lately met was with slavery. Slavery went first only because it was the cruder form of business. . . .

Our system, so fair in its theory and so fertile in its happiness and prosperity in its first century, is now, following the fate of systems, becoming artificial, technical, corrupt; and, as always happens in human institutions, after noon, power is stealing from the many to the few. Believing wealth to be good, the people believed the wealthy to be good. But, again in history, power has intoxicated and hardened its possessors, and Pharaohs are bred in counting-rooms as they were in palaces. Their furniture must be banished to the world-garret [attic], where lie the out-worn trappings of the guilds and slavery and other old lumber of human institutions.

Source: Henry Demarest Lloyd, *Wealth against Commonwealth* (New York: Harper and Brothers, 1902), 510–12, 515.

## Interpret the Evidence

1. According to William Graham Sumner (Document 16.5), how are reformers mistaken in their attempts to help the poor?

2. Do Sumner (Document 16.5) and Andrew Carnegie (Document 16.7) agree on whether the wealthy have a responsibility to help the poor?

3. According to Edward Bellamy's *Looking Backward* (Document 16.6), why should the federal government intervene to halt the expansion of big business?

4. How do wealthy Americans maintain their power at the expense of everyone else, according to Henry Demarest Lloyd (Document 16.8)?

5. What might Bellamy and Lloyd see as the greatest obstacles to the realization of America's potential? What about Sumner and Carnegie? What changes in U.S. society and government might each man suggest to eliminate those obstacles?

## Put It in Context

- Despite their different philosophies, what do these men think about the growth of organizations during the late nineteenth century?

background photos: pages 518–19 and 522–23, Library of Congress

**LEARNINGCurve**
Check what you know.
bedfordstmartins.com/hewittlawson/LC

The Granger Collection, New York

The Granger Collection, New York

Striking coal miners' wives protest the arrival of Pinkerton detectives in Buchtel, Ohio, 1884.

Horse-drawn harvester and binder invented by Cyrus Hall McCormick.

their own communities, where family, neighbors, and local businesses were more likely to come to their aid.

## The Industrialization of Labor

The industrialization of the United States described in chapter 16 transformed the workplace, bringing together large numbers of laborers under difficult conditions. In 1870 few factories employed 500 or more workers. Thirty years later, more than 1,500 companies had workforces of this size, including General Electric, International Harvester, Pullman Palace Car Company, and U.S. Steel. Just after the Civil War, manufacturing employed 5.3 million workers; thirty years later, the figure soared to more than 15.1 million. Most of these new industrial workers came from two main sources. First, farmers like the Leases who could not make a decent living from the soil moved to nearby cities in search of factory jobs. Although mostly white, this group also included blacks who sought to escape the oppressive conditions of sharecropping. Between 1870 and 1890, some 80,000 African Americans journeyed from the rural South to cities in the South and the North to search for employment. Second, the economic opportunities in America drew millions of immigrants from Europe over the course of the nineteenth century. Immigrant workers initially came from northern Europe, mainly from England, Ireland, Germany, and Scandinavia. However, by the end of the nineteenth century, the number of immigrants from southern and eastern European countries, such as Austria-Hungary, Greece, Italy, and Russia, had surpassed those coming from northern Europe.

Inside factories, **unskilled workers**, those with no particular skill or expertise, encountered a system undergoing critical changes, as small-scale manufacturing gave way to larger and more mechanized operations. Immigrants, who made up the bulk of unskilled laborers, had to adjust both to a new country and to unfamiliar, unpleasant, and often dangerous industrial work. A traveler from Hungary who visited a steel mill in Pittsburgh that employed many Hungarian immigrants compared the factories to penitentiaries. "In making a tour of these prisons," he wrote, "wherever the heat is most insupportable, the flames most choking, there we are certain to find compatriots bent and wasted with toil." Nor were any government benefits—such as workers' compensation or unemployment insurance—available to industrial laborers who were hurt in accidents or laid off from their jobs.

**Skilled workers**, who had particular training or abilities and were more difficult to replace, were not immune to the changes brought about by industrialization and the creation of large-scale business enterprises. In the early days of manufacturing, skilled laborers operated as independent craftsmen. They provided their own tools, worked at their own pace, and controlled their production output. This approach to work enhanced their sense of personal dignity, reflected their notion of themselves as free citizens, and distinguished them from the mass of unskilled laborers. Mechanization, however, undercut their autonomy by dictating both the nature and the speed of production through practices of scientific management (see chapter 16). Instead of producing goods, skilled workers increasingly applied their craft to servicing machinery and keeping it running smoothly. One example of workers' resistance to this loss of independence on the shop floor occurred in Lowell, Massachusetts. Responding to a new regulation requiring all employees to report to their jobs in work clothes at the opening bell and to remain there with the door locked until the closing bell, a machinist promptly packed his tools, quit, and told his boss that he had not "been brought up under a system of slavery." While owners reaped the benefits of the mechanization and regimentation of the industrial workplace, many skilled workers saw such "improvements" as a threat to their freedom.

**Explore**

See Document 17.1 for one worker's opinion on mechanization.

Still, most workers did not oppose the technology that increased their productivity and resulted in higher wages. Compared to their mid-nineteenth-century counterparts, industrial laborers now made up a larger share of the general population, earned more money, and worked fewer hours. During the 1870s and 1880s, the average industrial worker's real wages (actual buying power) increased by 20 percent. At the same time, the average workday declined from ten and a half hours to ten hours. From 1870 to 1890, the general price index dropped 30 percent, allowing consumers to benefit from lower prices.

Yet workers were far from content, and the lives of industrial workers remained extremely difficult. Although workers as a group saw improvements in wages and hours, they did not earn enough income to support their families adequately. Also, there were widespread disparities based on job status, race, ethnicity, sex, and region. Skilled workers earned more than unskilled workers. Whites were paid more than African Americans, who were mainly shut out of better jobs. Immigrants from northern Europe, who had settled in the United States before southern Europeans, tended to hold higher-paying skilled positions. Southern factory workers, whether in textiles, steel, or armaments, earned less than their northern counterparts. And women, an increasingly important component of the industrial workforce, earned less than men. On average, women earned only 25 percent of what men did.

Between 1870 and 1900, the number of female wage-workers grew by 66 percent, accounting for about one-quarter

DOCUMENT 17.1

# John Morrison | Testimony on the Impact of Mechanization, 1883

Like other skilled laborers, New York City machinist John Morrison saw the introduction of machinery that accompanied industrialization as a threat to his identity as a craftsman. Though highly paid compared with unskilled workers, craftsmen led the way in organizing unions and engaging in strikes against big business. In the following excerpt from his testimony before a U.S. Senate committee investigating conflicts between capital and labor, Morrison discusses the source of many skilled workingmen's discontent.

**Explore**

Question: Is there any difference between the conditions under which machinery is made now and those which existed ten years ago?

Answer: A great deal of difference.

Question: State the differences as well as you can.

Answer: Well, the trade has been subdivided and those subdivisions have been again subdivided, so that a man never learns the machinist's trade now. Ten years ago he learned, not the whole of the trade, but a fair portion of it. Also, there is more machinery used in the business, which again makes machinery. In the case of making the sewing-machine, for instance, you find that the trade is so subdivided that a man is not considered a machinist at all. Hence it is merely laborers' work and it is laborers that work at that branch of our trade. The different branches of the trade are divided and subdivided so that one man may make just a particular part of a machine and may not know anything whatever about another part of the same machine. In that way machinery is produced a great deal cheaper than it used to be formerly, and in fact, through this system of work,

100 men are able to do now what it took 300 or 400 men to do fifteen years ago. By the use of machinery and the subdivision of the trade they so simplify the work that it is made a great deal easier and put together a great deal faster. There is no system of apprenticeship, I may say, in the business. You simply go in and learn whatever branch you are put at, and you stay at that unless you are changed to another. . . .

Question: Are the machinists here generally contented, or are they in a state of discontent and unrest?

Answer: There is mostly a general feeling of discontent, and you will find among the machinists the most radical workingmen, with the most revolutionary ideas. You will find that they don't so much give their thoughts simply to trade unions and other efforts of that kind, but they go far beyond that; they only look for relief through the ballot or through a revolution, a forcible revolution.

Source: *Report of the Committee of the Senate upon the Relations between Labor and Capital*, 48th Cong. (1885), 755–59.

**Interpret the Evidence**

- How does Morrison explain the subdivision of labor in the modern factory?
- How does Morrison characterize the mood of skilled laborers?

**Put It in Context**

How did the introduction of machinery affect skilled workers?

of all nonfarm laborers. The majority of employed women, including those working in factories, were single and between the ages of sixteen and twenty-four. Overall, only 5 percent of married women worked outside the home, although 30 percent of African American wives were employed. Women workers were concentrated in several areas. White and black women continued to serve as maids and domestics. Others took over jobs that were once occupied by men. They

became teachers, nurses, clerical workers, telephone operators, and department store salesclerks. Although these jobs were initially seen as opening up new opportunities for women, they soon became identified as "women's work," which meant lower pay and less potential for professional advancement. Other women toiled in manufacturing jobs requiring fine eye-hand coordination, such as cigar rolling and work in the needle trades and textile industry.

Women also turned their homes into workplaces. In crowded apartments, they sewed furs onto garments, made straw hats, prepared artificial flowers, and fashioned jewelry. Earnings from piecework (work that pays at a set rate per unit) were even lower than factory wages, but they allowed married women with young children to contribute to the family income. When sufficient space was available, families rented rooms to boarders, and women provided meals and house-keeping for the lodgers. Some female workers found other ways to balance work with the needs and constraints of family life. To gain greater autonomy in their work, black laundresses began cleaning clothes in their own homes, rather than their white employers' homes, so that they could control their own work hours. In 1881 black washerwomen in Atlanta conducted a two-week strike to secure higher fees from white customers.

Manufacturing also employed many child workers. By 1900 about 10 percent of girls and 20 percent of boys between the ages of ten and fifteen worked, and at least 1.7 million children under the age of sixteen held jobs. Employers often exposed children to dangerous and unsanitary conditions. Although some children got fresh air working as newsboys, shining shoes, and collecting junk, most worked long, hard hours breathing in dust and fumes as they labored in textile mills, tobacco plants, print shops, and coal mines. In Indiana, young boys worked the night shift in dark, windowless glass factories. One of the adults working in a Rhode Island textile mill lamented: "Poor, puny weak little children are kept at work the entire year without intermission or even a month for schooling." Children under the age of ten, known as "breaker boys," climbed onto filthy coal heaps and picked out unprocessed material. Working up to twelve-hour days, these children received less than a dollar a day.

Women and children worked because the average male head of household could not support his family on his own pay, despite the increase in real wages. As Carroll D. Wright, director of the Massachusetts Bureau of the Statistics of Labor, reported in 1882, "A family of workers can always live well, but the man with a family of small children to support, unless his wife works also, has a small chance of living properly." For example, in 1883 in Joliet, Illinois, a railroad brakeman tried to support his wife and eight children on $360 a year. They rented a three-room house for $5 per month and ate mainly bread and potatoes. A state investigator described the way they lived: "Clothes ragged, children half dressed and dirty. They all sleep in one room regardless of sex. The house is devoid of furniture, and the entire concern is as wretched as could be imagined." Although not all laborers lived in such squalor, many wageworkers barely lived at subsistence level.

Although the average number of working hours dropped during this era, many laborers put in more than 10 hours a day on the job. In 1890 bakers worked more than 65 hours a week, steelworkers more than 66, and canners 77. In the steel industry, blast-furnace operators toiled 12 hours a day, 7 days a week. They received a day off every 2 weeks, but only if they worked a 24-hour shift. Given the long hours and backbreaking work, it is not surprising that accidents were a regular feature of industrial life. Each year tens of thousands were injured on the job, and thousands died as a result of mine cave-ins, train wrecks, explosions in industrial plants, and fires at textile mills and garment factories. Railroad employment was especially unsafe—accidents ended the careers of one in six workers.

Agricultural refugees who flocked to cotton mills in the South also faced dangerous working conditions. Working twelve-hour days breathing the lint-filled air from the processed cotton posed health hazards, especially for the very young and the elderly. Textile workers also had to place their hands into heavy machinery to disentangle threads, making them extremely vulnerable to serious injury. Wages scarcely covered necessities, and on many occasions families did not know where their next meal was coming from. North Carolina textile worker J. W. Mehaffry complained that the mill owners "were slave drivers" who "work their employees, women, and children from 6 a.m. to 7 p.m. with a half hour for lunch." The company supplied houses, but the occupants had "very little furniture, just a couple of beds.

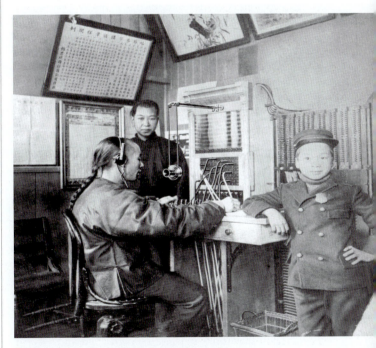

**Chinese American Telephone Operator**

The invention of the telephone brought jobs to many Americans, especially women. Yet not all operators were women, as this photograph shows. San Francisco's Chinatown employed workers from its own community, and in this photo a Chinese man works as a telephone operator while a child in a school uniform and an adult stand by him. © CORBIS

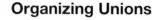

Just enough to get by on is about all we had." Their meals usually consisted of potatoes, cornbread, and dried beans cooked in fat. This diet, without dairy products and fresh meat, led to outbreaks of pellagra, a debilitating disease caused by niacin (vitamin B3) deficiency.

Although wages and working hours improved slightly for some workers, employers kept the largest share of the increased profits that resulted from industrialization. In 1877 John D. Rockefeller collected dividends at the rate of at least $720 an hour, roughly double what his average employee earned in a year. Despite some success stories, prospects for upward mobility for most American workers remained limited. Unskilled workers might climb up the economic ladder during their lifetime, but usually not more than one rung. A manual worker might rise into the ranks of the semiskilled but would not make it into the middle class. And to achieve even this small upward mobility required putting the entire family to work and engaging in rigorous economizing, what one historian called "ruthless underconsumption." The Horatio Alger "rags to riches" stories (see chapter 16) proved a myth for nearly all workers. Despite their best efforts, most Americans remained part of the working class.

## Organizing Unions

Faced with improving but inadequate wages and hazardous working conditions, industrial laborers sought to counter the concentrated power of corporate capitalists by joining forces. They attempted to organize **unions**—groups of workers seeking rights and benefits from their employers through their collective efforts. Union organizing was prompted by attitudes that were common among employers. Most employers were convinced that they and their employees shared identical interests, and they believed that they were morally and financially entitled to establish policies on their workers' behalf. They refused to engage in negotiations with labor unions (a process known as **collective bargaining**) and rejected unions as illegitimate organizations. Although owners appreciated the advantages of companies banding together to eliminate competition or to lobby for favorable regulations, similar collective efforts by workers struck them as unfair, even immoral. It was up to the men who supplied the money and the machines—rather than the workers—to determine what was a fair wage and what were satisfactory working conditions. In 1877 William H. Vanderbilt, the son of transportation tycoon Cornelius Vanderbilt, explained this way of thinking: "Our men feel that although I . . . may have my millions and they the rewards of their daily toil, still we are about equal in the end. If they suffer, I suffer, and if I suffer they cannot escape." Needless to say, many workers disagreed. One of labor's central demands was the institution of the eight-hour workday. The idea came from Great Britain, which had industrialized earlier in the nineteenth century. In 1817 the British socialist Robert Owen had summarized this demand as "Eight hours labor, Eight hours recreation, Eight hours rest." This goal had not yet been achieved in Britain or the rest of industrial Europe when American labor activists picked it up in the 1860s, spreading the message through parades and rallies sponsored by Eight-Hour Leagues.

A growing number of working people failed to see the relationship between employer and employee as mutually beneficial. Increasingly, they considered labor unions to be the best vehicle for communication and negotiation between workers and owners. Though not the first national workers' organization, the **Noble Order of the Knights of Labor**, founded by Uriah Stephens in 1869, initiated the most extensive and successful campaign after the Civil War to unite workers and

**Women in the Knights of Labor**

Under the leadership of Terence Powderly, the Knights of Labor admitted women in 1881. Four years later, the Knights established the Women's Work Department, directed by Leonora Barry, a married garment worker in Philadelphia. This photograph shows women delegates to the 1886 Knights of Labor convention, one of whom holds her infant child.    © Bettmann/CORBIS

challenge the power of corporate capitalists. "There is no mutuality of interests . . . [between] capital and labor," the Massachusetts chapter of the Knights proclaimed. "It is the iron heel of a soulless monopoly, crushing the manhood out of sovereign citizens." In fact, the essential premise of the Knights was that *all* workers shared common interests that were very different from those of owners. Thus the union excluded only those it believed preyed on citizens both economically and morally—lawyers, bankers, saloon-keepers, and professional gamblers.

The Knights did not enjoy immediate success. Their participation in the Great Railroad Strike of 1877 (see chapter 14) drew some attention to the union, but the Knights did not really begin to flourish until Terence V. Powderly replaced Stephens as Grand Master of the organization in 1879. Powderly advocated the eight-hour workday, the abolition of child labor, and equal pay for women. Under his leadership, the Knights accepted African Americans, immigrants, and women as members, though they excluded Chinese immigrant workers, as did other labor unions. As a result, the Knights experienced a surge in membership from 9,000 in 1879 to nearly a million in 1885 (including John McLuckie), about 10 percent of the industrial workforce.

Rapid growth proved to be a mixed blessing. As membership grew, Powderly and the national organization exercised less and less control over local chapters. In fact, local chapters often defied the central organization by engaging in strikes, a labor tactic Powderly had officially disavowed. Nonetheless, with Powderly standing mainly on the sidelines, members of the Knights struck successfully against the Union Pacific Railroad and the Missouri Pacific Railroad in 1885. The following year, on May 1, 1886, local assemblies of the Knights joined a nationwide strike to press for an eight-hour workday, again without Powderly's approval. However, this strike was soon overshadowed by events in Chicago that would prove to be the undoing of the Knights (Figure 17.1).

For months before the general strike, the McCormick Harvester plant in Chicago had been at the center of an often violent conflict over wages and work conditions. On May 3, 1886, police killed two strikers in a clash between union members and strikebreakers who tried to cross the picket lines. In response, a group of anarchists led by the German-born activist August Spies called for a rally in **Haymarket Square** to protest police violence. Consisting mainly of foreign-born radicals, anarchists believed that government represented the interests of capitalists and stifled freedom for workers. Anarchists differed among themselves, but they generally advocated tearing down government authority, restoring personal freedom, and forming worker

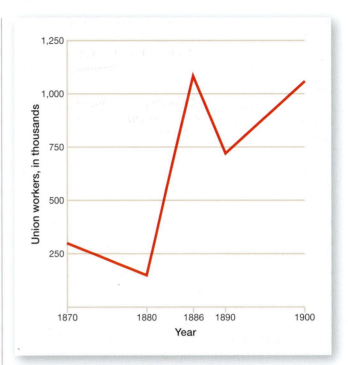

**FIGURE 17.1 Union Membership, 1870–1900**

Union membership fluctuated widely in the late nineteenth century. After reaching a low point in 1880, the number of union members rebounded after organizing by the Knights of Labor. Membership plummeted in the years after the Haymarket Square incident of 1886 but soared again in the 1890s through the efforts of the American Federation of Labor and western miners. Source: Data from Richard B. Freeman, "Spurts in Union Growth: Defining Moments and Social Processes" (working paper 6012, National Bureau of Economic Research, Cambridge, MA, 1997).

communes to replace capitalism. To achieve their goals, anarchists like Spies advocated the violent overthrow of government.

The Haymarket rally began at 8:30 in the evening of May 4 and attracted no more than 1,500 people, who listened to a series of speeches as rain fell. By 10:30 p.m., when the crowd had dwindled to some 300 people, 180 policemen decided to break it up. As police moved into the square, someone set off a bomb. The police fired back, and when the smoke cleared, seven policemen and four protesters lay dead. Most of the fatalities and injuries resulted not from the bomb but from the police crossfire after the explosion. A subsequent trial convicted eight anarchists of murder, though there was no evidence that any of them had planted a bomb or used weapons; four of them, including August Spies, were executed. Although Powderly and other union leaders denounced the anarchists and the bombing, the incident greatly tarnished the labor movement. Capitalists and their allies in the press attacked labor unionists as radicals prone to violence and denounced strikes as un-American. Following the Haymarket incident, the membership rolls of the Knights plunged to below 500,000. By the mid-1890s, the Knights had fewer than 20,000 members.

As the fortunes of the Knights of Labor faded, the **American Federation of Labor (AFL)** grew in prominence, offering an alternative vision of unionization. Instead of one giant industrial union that included all workers, skilled and unskilled, the AFL organized only skilled craftsmen—the labor elite—into trade unions. In 1886 Samuel Gompers, a British-born cigar maker, became president of the AFL. Gompers considered trade unions "the business organizations of the wage earners to attend to the business of the wage earners" and favored the use of strikes. No social reformer, the AFL president concentrated on obtaining better wages and hours for workers so that they could share in the prosperity generated by industrial capitalism. By 1900 the AFL had around a million members. It achieved these numbers by recruiting the most independent, highest-paid, and least replaceable segment of the labor force—white male skilled workers. Unlike the Knights, the AFL had little or no place for women and African Americans in its ranks.

As impressive as the AFL's achievement was, the union movement as a whole experienced only limited success in the late nineteenth century. Only about one in fifteen industrial workers belonged to a union in 1900. Union membership was low for a variety of reasons. First, the political and economic power of corporations and the prospects of retaliation made the decision to sign up for union membership a risky venture. Second, the diversity of workers made organizing a difficult task. Foreign-born laborers came from many countries and were divided by language, religion, ethnicity, and history. Moreover, European immigrants quickly adopted native-born whites' racial prejudices against African Americans. Third, despite severe limitations in social mobility, American workers generally retained their faith in the benefits of the capitalist system. The pervasive doctrine of success defined workers not as laborers locked into the lower class but as businessmen on the rise, each with the potential to become a Rockefeller or a Carnegie. Finally, the government used its legal and military authority to side with employers and suppress militant workers.

Southern workers were the most resistant to union organizing. The agricultural background of mill workers left them with a heightened sense of individualism and isolation. In addition, their continued connection to family and friends in the countryside offered a potential escape route from industrial labor. Finally, employers' willingness to use racial tensions to divide working-class blacks and whites prevented them from joining together to further their common economic interests.

## Clashes between Workers and Owners

Despite the difficulties of organizing workers, labor challenged some of the nation's largest industries in the late nineteenth century. Faced with owners' refusal to recognize or negotiate with unions, workers marshaled their greatest source of power: withholding their labor and going on strike. Employers in turn had powerful weapons at their command to break strikes. They could recruit strikebreakers and mobilize private and public security forces to protect their businesses. That workers went on strike against such odds testified to their desperation and courage.

Workers in the United States were not alone in their efforts to combat industrial exploitation. In England, laborers organized for better wages and working conditions. In 1888 in London, young women who worked as matchmakers staged a walkout to protest the exorbitant fines that employers imposed on them for arriving even one minute late to work. With community support, they won their demands. From 1888 to 1890, the number of strikes throughout Europe grew from 188 to 289. In 1890 thousands of workers in Budapest, Hungary, rose up to protest unsafe working conditions. European workers also campaigned for the right to vote, which unlike white male American workers, they were denied on economic grounds.

In the United States in the 1890s, labor mounted several highly publicized strikes. Perhaps the most famous was the 1892 **Homestead strike**. Steelworkers at Carnegie's Homestead, Pennsylvania, factory lived seven miles east of Pittsburgh and, like John McLuckie, played an active role in local politics and civic affairs. Residents generally believed that Andrew Carnegie's corporation paid decent wages that allowed them to support their families and buy their own homes. In 1892 craftsmen earned $180 a month, and they appeared to have Carnegie's respect. Others, like McLuckie, earned less than half that amount, and unskilled workers made even less.

In 1892, with steel prices falling, Carnegie decided to replace some of his skilled craftsmen with machinery, cut wages, save on labor costs, and bust McLuckie's union, the Amalgamated Association of Iron and Steel Workers, with which he had voluntarily negotiated in the past. Knowing that his actions would provoke a strike and seeking to avoid the negative publicity that would result, Carnegie left the country and went to Scotland, leaving his plant manager, Henry Clay Frick, in charge.

Fiercely anti-union, Frick prepared for the strike by building a three-mile, fifteen-foot-high fence, capped with barbed wire and equipped with searchlights, around three sides of the Homestead factory. A hated symbol of the manager's hostility, the fence became known as "Fort Frick." Along the fourth side of the factory flowed the Monongahela

River. Frick had no intention of negotiating seriously with the union on a new contract, and on July 1 he ordered a lockout. Only employees who rejected the union and accepted lower wages could return to work. The small town rallied around the workers, and the union members won a temporary victory. On July 6, barge-loads of armed Pinkerton detectives, hired by Frick to protect the plant, set sail toward the factory entrance alongside the Monongahela. McLuckie, the head of the Amalgamated, denounced the Pinkertons as "a band of cutthroats, thieves, and murderers in the employ of unscrupulous capital for the oppression of honest labor." From the shore, union men shot at the barges and set fire to a boat they pushed toward the Pinkertons. When the smoke cleared, the Pinkertons surrendered and hastily retreated onshore as women and men chased after them.

This triumph proved costly for the union. The battle left nine strikers and three Pinkerton detectives dead. Although community officials were on the workers' side, Frick convinced the governor of Pennsylvania to send in state troops to protect the factory and the strikebreakers. On July 23, Alexander Berkman, an anarchist who had no connection with the union, entered Frick's office and shot the steel executive in the neck, leaving him wounded but alive. The resulting unfavorable publicity, together with the state's prosecution of the union, broke the strike. Subsequently, steel companies blacklisted the union leaders for life, and McLuckie fled Pennsylvania and wound up nearly penniless in Arizona. Ever the philanthropist, when Carnegie heard of McLuckie's plight in 1900, he tried to give his former adversary some money anonymously. The proud and still defiant McLuckie declined the offer, but a friend of Carnegie's arranged for an Arizona railroad to hire him as a machinery-repair superintendent.

**Explore**

See Document 17.2 for an anarchist's account of the Homestead strike.

Like Andrew Carnegie, George Pullman considered himself an enlightened employer who took good care of the men who worked in his luxury sleeping railcar factory outside Chicago. However, also like the steel titan, Pullman placed profits over personnel. In 1893 a severe economic depression prompted Pullman to cut wages without correspondingly reducing the rents that his employees paid for living in company houses. This dual blow to worker income and purchasing power led to a fierce strike the following year. The Pullman workers belonged to the American Railway Union, headed by Eugene V. Debs, who believed that labor organizing was an integral part of a worker's rights of political and economic citizenship. After George Pullman refused to negotiate, the union voted to go on strike.

In the end, the **Pullman strike** was broken not by the Pullman company but by the federal government. The railroad managers association persuaded President Grover Cleveland's attorney general, Richard Olney, a former railroad lawyer, that strikers were interfering with delivery of the U.S. mail transported by train. Cleveland ordered federal troops to get the railroads operating, but the workers still refused to capitulate. Olney then obtained an injunction (a court order) from the federal courts to restrain Debs and other union leaders from continuing the strike. The government used the Sherman Antitrust Act to punish unions for conspiring to restrain trade, something it had rarely done with respect to large corporations. Refusing to comply, Debs and other union officials were charged with contempt, convicted under the Sherman Antitrust Act, and sent to jail. The strike collapsed. **See Document Project 17: The Pullman Strike of 1894, page 550.**

Debs remained unrepentant. After serving his jail sentence, he became even more radical. In 1901 he helped establish the Socialist Party of America. German exiles who came to the United States following revolutions in Europe in 1848 had brought with them the revolutionary ideas of the German philosopher Karl Marx. Marx argued that capital and labor were engaged in a class struggle that would end in a victory for the proletariat, the abolition of private property, and socialist rule. This revolution would come about through the violent overthrow of capitalist government and its replacement by communism. Marxist ideas attracted a small following in the United States, mainly among the foreign-born population. By contrast, other types of European socialists, including the German Social Democratic Party, which Marx denounced, appealed for working-class support by advocating the creation of a more just and humane economic system through the ballot box, not by violent revolution. Debs, born and raised in Terre Haute, Indiana, favored this nonviolent, democratic brand of socialism and managed to attract a broader base of supporters by articulating socialist doctrines in the language of cooperation and citizenship that many Americans shared. Debsian socialism appealed not only to industrial workers but also to dispossessed farmers and miners in the Southwest and Midwest.

Western miners had a history of labor activism, and by the 1890s they were ready to listen to radical ideas. Shortly after the Homestead strike ended in 1892, silver miners in Coeur d'Alene, Idaho, walked out after owners slashed their wages by 15 percent. Employers refused to recognize any union, obtained an injunction against the strike, imported strikebreakers to run the mines, and persuaded Idaho's governor to impose martial law, in which the military took over the normal operation of civilian affairs. The work stoppage lasted four months, resulting in the arrest of six hundred strikers, including their leader, Ed Boyce.

## Emma Goldman | Reflections on the Homestead Strike, 1931

Emma Goldman was one of the most prominent radicals of the late nineteenth and early twentieth centuries. Goldman argued for sexual freedom and women's liberation. In addition, as an anarchist, she initially advocated the overthrow of capitalism through violent attacks. To this end, during the Homestead strike Goldman's lover, Alexander Berkman, attempted unsuccessfully to assassinate Henry Clay Frick, the manager of Carnegie's steel plant. In this passage from her autobiography, Goldman describes the events that led to the assassination attempt.

**Explore**

A few days after our return to New York the news was flashed across the country of the slaughter of steel-workers by Pinkertons. Frick had fortified the Homestead mills, built a high fence around them. Then, in the dead of night, a barge packed with strike-breakers, under protection of heavily armed Pinkerton thugs, quietly stole up the Monongahela River. The steel-men had learned of Frick's move. They stationed themselves along the shore, determined to drive back Frick's hirelings. When the barge got within range, the Pinkertons had opened fire, without warning, killing a number of Homestead men on the shore, among them a little boy, and wounding scores of others.

The wanton murders aroused even the daily papers. Several came out in strong editorials, severely criticizing Frick. He had gone too far; he had added fuel to the fire in the labour ranks and would have himself to blame for any desperate acts that might come.

We were stunned. We saw at once that the time for our manifesto had passed. Words had lost their meaning in the face of the innocent blood spilled on the banks of the Monongahela. Intuitively each felt what was surging in the heart of the others. Sasha [Alexander Berkman] broke the silence. "Frick is the responsible factor in this crime," he said; "he must be made to stand the consequences." It was the psychological moment for an *Attentat* [political violence]; the whole country was aroused, everybody was considering Frick the perpetrator of a cold-blooded murder. A blow aimed at Frick would re-echo in the poorest hovel, would call the attention of the whole world to the real cause behind the Homestead struggle. It would also strike terror in the enemy's ranks and make them realize that the proletariat of America had its avengers.

Source: Emma Goldman, *Living My Life* (New York: Alfred Knopf, 1931), 86–87.

### Interpret the Evidence

- How does Goldman characterize the Pinkerton detectives?
- What did Goldman think the assassination of Frick would achieve?

### Put It in Context

Why do you think public perception turned against militant labor activism in the aftermath of Homestead and other strikes during the late nineteenth century?

Although the workers lost, the following year they succeeded in forming the Western Federation of Miners, a radical union that continued their fight.

The **Industrial Workers of the World (IWW)**, which emerged largely through the efforts of the Western Federation of Miners, sought to raise wages, improve working conditions, and gain union recognition for the most exploited segments of American labor. The IWW, or "Wobblies" as they were popularly known, offered an alternative to Samuel Gompers's American Federation of Labor by attempting to unite all skilled and unskilled workers in an effort to overthrow capitalism. The

Wobblies favored strikes and direct-action protests rather than collective bargaining or mediation. At their rallies and strikes, they often encountered government force and corporation-inspired mob violence. Nevertheless, the IWW had substantial appeal among lumberjacks in the Northwest, dockworkers in port cities, miners in the West, farmers in the Great Plains, and textile workers in the Northeast. Of their 150 strikes, the most successful ones involved miners in Goldfield, Nevada (1906–1907); textile workers in Lawrence, Massachusetts (1912); and silk workers in Paterson, New Jersey (1913).

Even though industrialists usually had state and federal governments as well as the media on their side, workers continued to press for their rights. Workers used strikes as a last resort when business owners refused to negotiate or recognize their demands to organize themselves into unions. Although most late-nineteenth-century strikes failed, striking unionists nonetheless called for collective bargaining, higher wages, shorter hours, and improved working conditions—an agenda that unions and their political allies would build on in the future.

## Working-Class Leisure in Industrial America

Despite the economic hardships and political repression that industrial laborers faced in the late nineteenth century, workers carved out recreational spaces over which they had control and that offered relief from their backbreaking toil. Time clocks, often viewed as an annoying part of scientific management, nevertheless clearly emphasized the difference between working and nonworking hours. For many, Sunday became a day of rest that took on a secular flavor.

Working-class leisure patterns varied by gender, race, and region. Women did not generally attend spectator sporting events, such as baseball and boxing matches, which catered to men. Nor did they find themselves comfortable in union halls and saloons, where men found solace in drink. Working-class wives preferred to gather to prepare for births, weddings, and funerals or to assist neighbors who lost their homes because of fire, death, or greedy landlords.

Once employed, working-class daughters found a greater measure of independence and free time by living in rooming houses on their own. Women's wages were only a small fraction of men's earnings, so working women rarely made enough money to support a regular social life along with paying for rent, food, and clothes. Still, they found ways to enjoy their free time. Some single women went out in groups, hoping to meet men who would pay for drinks, food, or a vaudeville show. Others dated so that they knew they would be taken care of for the evening. Some of the men who "treated" on a date assumed a right to sexual favors in return, and some of these women then expected men to provide them with housing and gifts in exchange for an ongoing sexual relationship. Thus emotional and economic relationships became intertwined in complicated ways.

Around the turn of the twentieth century, dance halls flourished as one of the mainstays of working-class communities throughout the nation. Huge dance palaces that held three thousand to five thousand people were built in the entertainment districts of most large cities. They made their money by offering music with lengthy intermissions for the sale of drinks and refreshments. Women and men also attended cabarets, some of which were racially integrated. In so-called red-light districts of the city, prostitutes earned money entertaining their clients with a variety of sexual pleasures.

Not all forms of leisure were strictly segregated along class lines. A number of forms of cheap entertainment appealed not only to working-class women and men but also to their middle-class counterparts. By the turn of the twentieth century, most large American cities featured amusement parks. Brooklyn's Coney Island stood out as the most spectacular of these sprawling playgrounds of fun and excitement. In 1884 the world's first roller coaster was built at Coney Island, providing thrills to those brave enough to ride it. Chicago residents could enjoy the Ferris wheel, which appeared at the 1893 World's Columbian Exposition. Designed by George Ferris, who operated a firm specializing in structural steel, the wheel rose 250 feet in the air, was propelled by two 1,000-horsepower steam engines, and accommodated 1,440 riders at a time.

Vaudeville houses—with their minstrel shows (whites in blackface) and comedians, singers, and dancers—brought howls of laughter to working-class audiences. Nickelodeons charged five cents to watch short films. Live theater generally attracted more wealthy patrons; however, the Yiddish theater, which flourished on New York's Lower East Side, and other immigrant-oriented stage productions appealed mainly to working-class audiences.

Southern workers also enjoyed music in their leisure time. Cheap banjoes and fiddles were mass-produced by the end of the nineteenth century. Pianos also became readily available, and one mountain boy, on hearing a piano for the first time, commented that it was the "beautifullest thing he had ever heard."

Itinerant musicians entertained audiences throughout the South. Lumber camps, which employed mainly

AT THE TROCADERO.
MICHIGAN AVE & MONROE ST

GREATEST SHOW IN TOWN

COMFORTS OF EUROPEAN MUSIC HALLS

DIMITRI IWANOFF'S IMPERIAL TROUPE OF RUSSIAN SINGERS AND DANCERS

EVERY EVENING AT 8 P.M — MATINEES — THURSDAYS, SATURDAYS & SUNDAYS AT 2:30 PM.
SPECIAL PROGRAMME SUNDAY AFTERNOONS AND EVENINGS.

**Trocadero Music Hall, 1893**

The Trocadero Music Hall in Chicago opened in 1893 to attract people attending the city's upcoming World's Fair. It provided a mix of classical music and exotic European variety acts, as shown above, but drew really huge audiences with the appearance of Eugene Sandow, a body builder who exhibited feats of great physical strength.   Library of Congress

African American men, offered a popular destination for these musicians. Each camp contained a "barrelhouse," also called a "honky tonk" or a "juke joint." Besides showcasing music, the barrelhouse also gave workers the opportunity to "shoot craps, dice, drink whiskey, dance, every modern devilment you can do," as one musician who played there recalled. From the Mississippi delta emerged a new form of music—the blues. W. C. Handy, "the father of the blues," discovered this music in his travels through the delta, where he observed that southern blacks "sang about everything. Trains, steamboats, steam whistles, sledge hammers, fast women, mean bosses, stubborn mules." They performed these songs of woe accompanying themselves with anything that would make a "musical sound or rhythmical effect, anything from a harmonica to a washboard." Meanwhile in New Orleans, an amalgam of black musical forms evolved into jazz. Musicians such as "Jelly Roll" Morton experimented

with a variety of sounds, putting together African and Caribbean rhythms with European music, mixing pianos with clarinets, trumpets, and drums. Blues and jazz spread throughout the South, appearing in juke joints in Atlanta and Memphis, where men and women danced the night away.

In mountain valley mill towns, southern white residents preferred "old time" music, but with a twist. Originally enjoyed by British settlers, traditional ballads and folk songs concerned the deeds of kings and princes; rural southerners modified the lyrics to extol the exploits of outlaws and adventurers. Country music, which combined romantic ballads and folk tunes to the accompaniment of guitars, banjoes, and organs, emerged as a distinct brand of music by the twentieth century. As with African Americans, in the late nineteenth century working-class and rural whites found new and exciting types of music to entertain them in their leisure. Religious music also appealed to both white and black audiences and drew crowds to evangelical revivals held in tents on acres of grass fields.

Mill workers also amused themselves by engaging in social, recreational, and religious activities. Women visited each other and exchanged confidences, gossip, advice on child rearing, and folk remedies. Men from various factories organized baseball teams that competed in leagues with one another. Managers of a mill in Charlotte, North Carolina, admitted that they "frequently hired men better known for their batting averages than their work records."

### REVIEW & RELATE

How did industrialization change the American workplace? What challenges did it create for American workers?

How did workers resist the concentrated power of industrial capitalists in the late nineteenth century, and why did such efforts have only limited success?

**LEARNINGCurve** bedfordstmartins.com/hewittlawson/LC

## Farmers Organize

Like industrial workers, farmers experienced severe economic hardships and a loss of political power in the face of rapid industrialization. The introduction of new machinery such as the combine harvester, introduced in 1878, led to substantial increases in the productivity of American farms. Soaring production, however, led to a decline in agricultural prices in the late nineteenth century, a trend that was accelerated by increased agricultural production around the world. Faced with an economic crisis caused by falling prices and escalating debt, farmers fought back, creating new organizations to champion their collective economic and political interests.

### Farmers Unite

From the end of the Civil War to the mid-1890s, increased production of wheat and cotton, two of the most important American crops, led to a precipitous drop in the price these crops fetched on the open market. Falling prices created a debt crisis for many farmers. Most American farmers were independent businessmen who borrowed money to pay for land, seed, and equipment. When their crops were harvested and sold, they repaid their debts with the proceeds. As prices fell, farmers increased production in an effort to cover their

debts. This tactic led to a greater supply of farm produce in the marketplace and even lower prices. Unable to pay back loans, many farmers lost their property in foreclosures to the banks that held their mortgages and furnished them credit.

To make matters worse, farmers lived isolated lives. Spread out across vast acres of rural territory, farmers had few social and cultural diversions to enliven the long, hard days they worked from sunup to sundown. As the farm economy declined, more and more of their children left the monotony of rural America behind and headed for cities in search of new opportunities and a better life.

Early efforts to organize farmers were motivated by a desire to counteract the isolation of rural life by creating new forms of social interaction and cultural engagement. In 1867, Oliver H. Kelly, who worked as a clerk in the Department of Agriculture, founded the Patrons of Husbandry to brighten the lonely existence of rural Americans through educational and social activities, including lectures, agricultural fairs, and picnics. Known as **Grangers** (from the French word for "granary"), the association grew rapidly in the early 1870s, especially in the Midwest and the South. Between 1872 and 1874, approximately fourteen thousand new Grange chapters were established.

In addition to helping to alleviate rural isolation, Grangers formed farm cooperatives to sell their crops at higher prices and pool their purchasing power to buy finished goods at wholesale prices. The Grangers' interest in promoting the collective economic interests of farmers led to their increasing involvement in politics. Rather than forming a separate political party, Grangers endorsed candidates who favored their cause. Perhaps their most important objective was the regulation of shipping and grain storage prices. In many areas, individual railroads had monopolies on both of these services and, as a result, were able to charge farmers higher-than-usual rates to store and ship their crops. By electing sympathetic state legislators, Grangers managed to obtain regulations that placed a ceiling on the prices railroads and grain elevators could charge. The Supreme Court temporarily upheld these victories in *Munn v. Illinois* (1877) by affirming the constitutionality of state regulation of private property that benefited the public interest. In 1886, however, in *Wabash v. Illinois* the Supreme Court reversed itself and struck down these state regulatory laws as hindering the free flow of interstate commerce.

Another apparent victory for regulation came in 1887 when Congress passed the Interstate Commerce Act, establishing the **Interstate Commerce Commission (ICC)** to regulate railroads. Although big businessmen could not prevent occasional government regulation, they

**Granger Movement, 1876**

As the farmer's central placement in this lithograph implies, farmers were the heart of the Granger move-ment. The title is a variation on the movement's motto, "I Pay for All." A farmer with a plough and two horses stands at the center of the scene providing food for all, while other occupational types positioned around him echo a similar refrain based on their profession. Note the attitude toward the broker implied by the label "I Fleece You All."   Library of Congress

managed to render it largely ineffective. Large railroad lines found it easier to influence decisions of the ICC than those of agencies at the state level, which were more inclined to support local farmers and other shippers. In time, railroad advocates came to dominate the ICC and enforced the law in favor of the railway lines rather than the shippers. Implementation of the Sherman Antitrust Act (see chapter 16) also favored big business. From the standpoint of most late-nineteenth-century capitalists, national regulations often turned out to be more of help than a hindrance.

By the late 1880s, the Grangers had abandoned electoral politics and once again devoted themselves strictly to social and cultural activities. A number of factors explain the Grangers' return to their original mission. First, prices began to rise for some crops, particularly corn, relieving the economic pressure on midwestern farmers. Second, the passage of regulatory

legislation in a number of states convinced some Grangers that their political goals had been achieved. Finally, a lack of marketing and business experience led to the collapse of many agricultural collectives.

The withdrawal of the Grangers from politics did not, however, signal the end of efforts by farmers to form organizations to advance their economic interests. While farmers in the midwestern corn belt experienced some political success and an economic upturn, farmers farther west in the Great Plains and in the Lower South fell more deeply into debt, as the price of wheat and cotton on the international market continued to drop. In both of these regions, farmers organized **Farmers' Alliances**. In the 1880s, Milton George formed the Northwestern Farmers' Alliance. At the same time, Dr. Charles W. Macune organized the much larger Southern Farmers' Alliance, which boasted more than 4 million members. Southern black farmers, excluded from the

Southern Farmers' Alliance by prevailing white supremacist sentiment, created a parallel Colored Farmers' Alliance, which attracted approximately a quarter of a million supporters. The Alliances formed a network of recruiters to sign up new members. No recruiter was more effective than Mary Elizabeth Lease, who excited farm audiences with her forceful and colorful rhetoric, delivering 160 speeches in the summer of 1890 alone. Not only did Lease urge farmers and workers to unite against capitalist exploitation, but she also agitated for women's rights and voiced her determination "to place the mothers of this nation on an equality with the fathers."

The Southern Farmers' Alliance advocated a sophisticated plan to solve the farmers' problem of mounting debt. Macune devised a proposal for a **subtreasury system**. Under this plan, the federal government would locate offices near warehouses in which farmers could store nonperishable commodities. In return, farmers would receive federal loans for 80 percent of the current market value of their produce. In theory, temporarily taking crops off the market would decrease supply and, assuming demand remained stable, lead to increased prices. Once prices rose, farmers would return to the warehouses, redeem their crops, sell them at the higher price, repay the government loan, and leave with a profit. Of the many recommendations proposed by the Alliances, the subtreasury system came closest to suggesting a realistic solution to the problem of chronic farm debt.

The first step toward creating a nationwide farmers' organization came in 1889, when the Northwestern and Southern Farmers' Alliances agreed to merge. Alliance leaders, including Lease, saw workers as fellow victims of industrialization, and they invited the Knights of Labor to join them. They also attempted to lower prevailing racial barriers by bringing the Colored Farmers' Alliance into the coalition. The following year, the National Farmers' Alliance and Industrial Union held its convention in Ocala, Florida. The group adopted resolutions endorsing the subtreasury system, as well as recommendations that would promote the economic welfare of farmers and extend political democracy to "the plain people." These proposals included tariff reduction, government ownership of banks and railroads, a constitutional amendment creating direct election of U.S. senators, adoption of the secret ballot, and provisions for state and local referenda to allow voters to initiate and decide public issues.

Finally, the Alliance pressed the government to increase the money supply by expanding the amount of silver coinage in circulation. In the Alliance's view, such a move would have two positive, and related, consequences. First, the resulting inflation would lead to higher prices for agricultural commodities, putting more money in farmers' pockets. Second, the real value of farmers' debts would decrease, since the debts were contracted in pre-inflation dollars and would be paid back with inflated currency. Naturally, the eastern bankers who supplied farmers with credit opposed such a policy. In fact, in 1873 Congress, under the leadership of Senator John Sherman, had halted the purchase of silver by the Treasury Department, a measure that helped reduce the money supply. Investment bankers, such as J. P. Morgan, opposed a bimetallic monetary standard that added silver to gold coinage. They believed that only the use of gold would preserve the faith that foreign investors had in U.S. currency. Under the Sherman Silver Purchase Act (1890), the government resumed buying silver, but the act placed limits on its purchase and did not guarantee the creation of silver coinage by the Treasury. In the past, some members of the Alliance, including Lease, had favored expanding the money supply with greenbacks (paper money). However, to attract support from western silver miners, Alliance delegates emphasized the free and unlimited coinage of silver. Alliance supporters met with bitter disappointment, though, as neither the Republican nor the Democratic Party embraced their demands. Rebuffed, farmers took an independent course and became more directly involved in national politics through the formation of the Populist Party.

## Populists Rise Up

In 1892 the National Farmers' Alliance moved into the electoral arena as a third political party. The People's Party of America, known as the **Populists**, held its first nominating convention in Omaha, Nebraska, in 1892. In addition to incorporating the Alliance's Ocala planks into their platform, they adopted recommendations to broaden the party's appeal to industrial workers. Populists endorsed a graduated income tax, which would impose higher tax rates on higher income levels. They also favored the eight-hour workday, a ban on using Pinkerton "mercenaries" in labor disputes, and immigration restriction, which stemmed from the unions' desire to keep unskilled workers from glutting the market and depressing wages. Reflecting the influence of women such as Mary Lease, the party endorsed women's suffrage. Although African Americans contributed to the founding of the Populists, the party did not offer specific proposals to prohibit racial discrimination or segregation. Rather, the party focused on remedies to relieve the economic plight of impoverished white and black farmers in general.

**Explore**

See Documents 17.3 and 17.4 to compare the central tenets of the Grange and the Populists.

In 1892 the Populists nominated for president former Union Civil War general James B. Weaver. Although Weaver came in third behind the Democratic victor, Grover Cleveland, and the Republican incumbent, Benjamin Harrison, he managed to win more than one million popular votes and 22 electoral votes. For a third

---

**DOCUMENTS 17.3 AND 17.4**

# Farmers and Workers Organize: Two Views

Farmers in the Midwest and the South organized to address the problems they faced as a result of industrialization and the growth of big business. The Patrons of Husbandry (the Grange) in the 1860s and 1870s and the Populists in the 1880s and 1890s both tried to deal with various social and economic issues. Compare the following pronouncement of the Grange with an excerpt from the Populist Party platform, adopted on July 4, 1892, in Omaha, Nebraska.

**Explore**

### 17.3   The Ten Commandments of the Grange, 1874

1. Thou shalt love the Grange with all thy heart and with all thy soul and thou shalt love thy brother granger as thyself.
2. Thou shalt not suffer the name of the Grange to be evil spoken of, but shall severely chastise the wretch who speaks of it with contempt.
3. Remember that Saturday is Grange day. On it thou shalt set aside thy hoe and rake, and sewing machine, and wash thyself, and appear before the Master in the Grange with smiles and songs, and hearty cheer. On the fourth week thou shalt not appear empty handed, but shalt thereby bring a pair of ducks, a turkey roasted by fire, a cake baked in the oven, and pies and fruits in abundance for the Harvest Feast. So shalt thou eat and be merry, and "frights and fears" shall be remembered no more.
4. Honor thy Master, and all who sit in authority over thee, that the days of the Granges may be long in the land which Uncle Sam hath given thee.
5. Thou shalt not go to law[yers].
6. Thou shalt do no business on tick [time]. Pay as thou goest, as much as in thee lieth.
7. Thou shalt not leave thy straw but shalt surely stack it for thy cattle in the winter.
8. Thou shalt support the Granger's store for thus it becometh thee to fulfill the laws of business.
9. Thou shalt by all means have thy life insured in the Grange Life Insurance Company, that thy wife and little ones may have friends when thou art cremated and gathered unto thy fathers.
10. Thou shalt . . . surely charter thine own ships, and sell thine own produce, and use thine own brains.

This is the last and best commandment. On this hang all the law, and profits, and if there be any others they are these.

Choke monopolies, break up rings, vote for honest men, fear God and make money. So shalt thou prosper and sorrow and hard times shall flee away.

Source: "The Ten Commandments of the Grange," *Oshkosh Weekly Times*, December 16, 1874, reprinted in *Rich Harvest: A History of the Grange, 1876–1900*, by D. Sven Nordin (Jackson: University Press of Mississippi, 1974), 240.

party competing for the presidency for the first time, this was a noteworthy accomplishment.

At the state level, Populists performed even better. They elected 10 congressional representatives, 5 U.S. senators, 3 governors, and 1,500 state legislators. Two years later, the party made even greater strides by increasing its total vote by 42 percent and achieving its greatest strength in the South. This electoral momentum positioned the Populists to make an even stronger run in the next presidential election. The economic depression that began in 1893 and the political discontent it generated further enhanced Populist chances for success.

**Explore**

### 17.4  Populist Party Platform, 1892

FINANCE—We demand a national currency, safe, sound, and flexible issued by the general government. . . .

1. We demand free and unlimited coinage of silver and gold at the present legal ratio of 16 to 1. . . .
3. We demand a graduated income tax.
4. We believe that the money of the country should be kept as much as possible in the hands of the people, and hence we demand that all State and national revenues shall be limited to the necessary expenses of the government, economically and honestly administered. . . .

TRANSPORTATION—Transportation being a means of exchange and a public necessity, the government should own and operate the railroads in the interest of the people. The telegraph and telephone . . . should be owned and operated by the government in the interest of the people.

LAND—The land, including all the natural sources of wealth, is the heritage of the people, and should not be monopolized for speculative purposes, and alien ownership of land should be prohibited. All land now held by railroads and other corporations in excess of their actual needs, and all lands now owned by aliens should be reclaimed by the government and held for actual settlers only.

EXPRESSION OF SENTIMENTS

1. Resolved, That we demand a free ballot, and a fair count in all elections . . . without Federal intervention, through the adoption by the States of the . . . secret ballot system.
2. Resolved, That the revenue derived from a graduated income tax should be applied to the reduction of the burden of taxation now levied upon the domestic industries of this country. . . .
4. Resolved, That we condemn the fallacy of protecting American labor under the present system, which opens our ports to [immigrants including] the pauper and the criminal classes of the world and crowds out our [American] wage-earners; and we . . . demand the further restriction of undesirable immigration.
5. Resolved, That we cordially sympathize with the efforts of organized workingmen to shorten the hours of labor. . . .
6. Resolved, That we regard the maintenance of a large standing army of mercenaries, known as the Pinkerton system, as a menace to our liberties, and we demand its abolition. . . .
9. Resolved, That we oppose any subsidy or national aid to any private corporation for any purpose.

Source: "People's Party Platform," *Omaha Morning World-Herald*, July 5, 1892.

### Interpret the Evidence

- What do the language and tone of these two documents tell you about the organizations that created them?
- What measures did the Populists propose that the Grangers did not? What issues did both address?

### Put It in Context

How did both the Grangers and the Populists respond to the shifts in economic and political power that occurred at the end of the nineteenth century?

**REVIEW & RELATE**

• Why was life so difficult for American farmers in the late nineteenth century?

• What were the similarities and differences between farmers' and industrial workers' efforts to organize in the late nineteenth century?

✓ **LEARNINGCurve** bedfordstmartins.com/hewittlawson/LC

## The Depression of the 1890s

When the Philadelphia and Reading Railroad went bankrupt in early 1893, it set off a chain reaction that pushed one-quarter of American railroads into insolvency. As a result, on May 5, 1893, "Black Friday," the stock market collapsed in a panic, triggering the **depression of 1893**. Making this situation worse, England and the rest of industrial Europe had experienced an economic downturn several years earlier. As a result, in the early 1890s foreign investors began selling off their American stocks, leading to a flow of gold coin out of the country and further damage to the banking system. Hundreds of banks failed, which hurt the business people and farmers who relied on a steady flow of bank credit to keep their enterprises afloat. By the end of 1894, some 3 million people, nearly 12 percent of the American workforce, remained unemployed. Tens of thousands of homeless people wandered the streets of major American cities. The depression became the chief political issue of the mid-1890s and resulted in a realignment of power between the two major parties. Rather than capitalizing on depression discontent, however, the Populist Party split apart and collapsed.

### Depression Politics

President Grover Cleveland's handling of the depression only made a bad situation worse. Railroad executive James J. Hill warned the president, "Business is at a standstill and the people are becoming thoroughly aroused. Their feeling is finding expression about as it did during the War of the Rebellion [Civil War]." With talk of civil war in the air, the Cleveland administration faced protest marches and labor strife. In the spring of 1894, Jacob Coxey, a wealthy businessman and Populist reformer from Ohio, and his associate, Carl Browne, led a march on Washington, D.C., demanding that Cleveland and Congress initiate a federal public works program to provide jobs for the unemployed. Coxey had previously supported the Greenback Party, which advocated inflating

the money supply with paper currency to stimulate the economy and help those in distress. Though highly critical of the favored few who dominated the federal government, Coxey had faith that if "the people . . . come in a body like this, peaceably to discuss their grievances and demanding immediate relief, Congress . . . will heed them and do it quickly." For him, "relief" meant both creating jobs and increasing the money supply. After traveling for a month from Ohio, Coxey led a parade of some five hundred unemployed people into the nation's capital. Attracting thousands of spectators, **Coxey's army** attempted to mount their protest on the grounds of the Capitol building. In response, police broke up the demonstration and arrested Coxey for trespassing. Cleveland turned a deaf ear to Coxey's demands for federal relief and also disregarded protesters participating in nearly twenty other marches on Washington.

In the coming months, Cleveland's political stock plummeted further. He responded to the Pullman strike in the summer of 1894 by obtaining a federal injunction against the strikers and dispatching federal troops to Illinois when the workers disobeyed it. The president's action won him high praise from the railroads and conservative business interests, but it showed millions of American workers that the Cleveland administration did not have a solution for ending the suffering caused by the depression. From the outset of his term, the president had made his intentions about government assistance clear: "While the people should patriotically and cheerfully support their Government, its functions do not include the support of the people." In normal times, these words reflected the prevailing philosophy of self-help that most Americans shared, but in the midst of a severe depression they sounded heartless.

Making matters worse, Cleveland convinced Congress to repeal the Sherman Silver Purchase Act. This angered western miners, who relied on strong silver prices, along with farmers in the South and Great Plains who were swamped by mounting debt. At the same time, the removal of silver as a backing for currency caused private investors to withdraw their gold deposits from the U.S. Treasury. To keep the government financially solvent, Cleveland worked out an agreement with a syndicate led by J. P. Morgan to help sell government bonds, a deal that netted the businessmen a huge profit. In the midst of economic suffering, this deal looked like a corrupt bargain between government and the rich designed to ensure that the rich got richer as the poor got poorer.

**Explore**

See Document 17.5 for one cartoonist's depiction of the debt crisis.

**DOCUMENT 17.5**

# Walter Huston | "Here Lies Prosperity," 1895

The "money question" became a focus of American politics in the first half of the 1890s and was exacerbated by the depression of 1893. Those who supported the gold standard believed that it provided the basis for a sound and stable economy. Proponents of the unlimited coinage of silver, especially Populists and Democrats such as William Jennings Bryan, asserted that expansion of the money supply would liberate farmers and workers from debt and bring prosperity to more Americans. The following cartoon illustrates the "free silver" point of view.

**Explore**

Why does the cartoonist use the phrases "enslaved," "stabbed in the back," "assassinated," and "traitors"? Whom does he accuse of these misdeeds?

According to this cartoon, what is the cause of poverty?

What burden keeps the working man in chains?

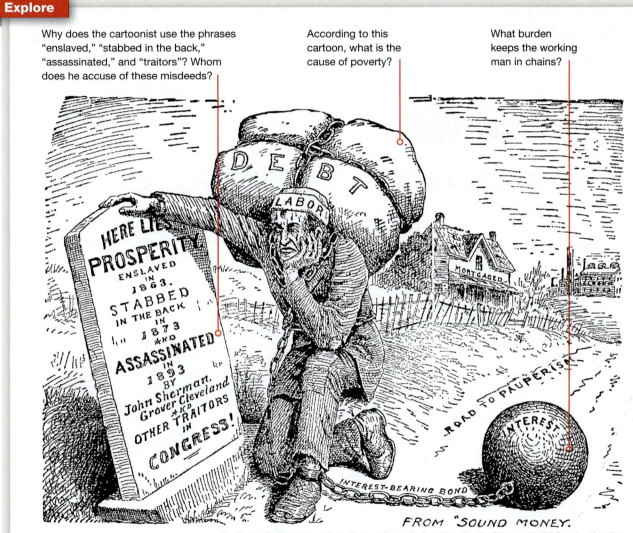

"The Situation: The Result of Interest Bearing Bonds and Sherman," in *Sound Money* (Massillon, OH), August 22, 1895. Reproduced from Worth Robert Miller, *Populist Cartoons: An Illustrated History of the Third Party Movement in the 1890s* (Kirksville, MO: Truman State University Press, 2011).

**Put It in Context**

How did the depression of 1893 affect the economic situation of farmers and working people? Whom did debt affect more?

In 1894 Congress also passed the Wilson-Gorman Act, which raised tariffs on imported goods. Intended to protect American businesses by keeping the price of imported goods high, it also deprived foreigners of the necessary income with which to buy American exports. This drop in exports did not help economic recovery. The Wilson-Gorman Act did include a provision that the Populists and other reformers endorsed: a progressive income tax of 2 percent on all annual earnings over $4,000. No federal income tax existed at this time, so even this mild levy elicited cries of "socialism" from conservative critics, who challenged the tax in the courts. They found a receptive audience in the Supreme Court. In *Pollack v. Farmers Loan and Trust* (1895), the justices, who had already struck down a number of attempts to regulate business, declared the income tax unconstitutional and denounced it as the opening wedge in "a war of the poor against the rich; a war constantly growing in intensity and bitterness."

With Cleveland's legislative program in shambles and his inability to solve the depression abundantly clear, the Democrats suffered a crushing blow at the polls. In the congressional elections of 1894, the party lost an astonishing 120 seats in the House. This defeat offered a preview of the political shakeup that loomed ahead.

## Political Realignment in the Election of 1896

The presidential election of 1896 marked a turning point in the political history of the nation, one that would shape national politics for the next thirty-six years. Democrats nominated William Jennings Bryan of Nebraska, a farmers' advocate who favored silver coinage. When he vowed that he would not see Republicans "crucify mankind on a cross of gold," the Populists endorsed him as well. Bryan was the first major party nominee for the White House since 1868 who did not come from Ohio, Indiana, or New York.

Republicans nominated William McKinley, the governor of Ohio and a supporter of the gold standard and high tariffs on manufactured and other goods. While Bryan barnstormed around the country, McKinley remained at his home in Canton, Ohio, to conduct his campaign from his front porch. His campaign manager, Marcus Alonzo Hanna, an ally of Ohio senator John Sherman, raised an unprecedented amount of money, about $16 million, mainly from wealthy industrialists who feared that the free and unlimited coinage of silver would debase the U.S. currency. Hanna saturated the country with pamphlets, leaflets, and posters, many of them written in the native languages of immigrant groups. He also hired a platoon of speakers to fan out across the country

denouncing Bryan's free silver cause as financial madness. Republican Theodore Roosevelt, who would later become president himself, remarked that Hanna advertised McKinley "as if he were patent medicine." By contrast, Bryan raised about $1 million and had to travel around the country making personal appearances, in part to compensate for his campaign's lack of funds.

The outcome of the election transformed the Republicans into the majority party in the United States. McKinley won 51 percent of the popular vote and 61 percent of the electoral vote, making him the first president since Grant in 1872 to win a majority of the popular vote. More important than this specific contest, however, was that the election proved critical in realigning the two parties. Voting patterns shifted with the 1896 election, giving Republicans the edge in party affiliation among the electorate not only in this contest but also in presidential elections over the next three decades (Map 17.1).

What happened to produce this critical realignment in electoral power? The main ingredient was Republicans' success in fashioning a coalition that included both corporate capitalists and their workers. Although Bryan made sincere appeals for the votes of urban dwellers and industrial workers along class lines, they generally fell on deaf ears. Many of these voters took out their anger on Cleveland's Democratic Party and Bryan as its standard-bearer for failing to end the depression. In addition, Bryan, who hailed from Nebraska and reflected

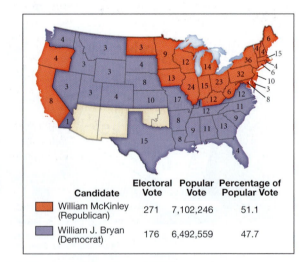

| Candidate | Electoral Vote | Popular Vote | Percentage of Popular Vote |
|---|---|---|---|
| William McKinley (Republican) | 271 | 7,102,246 | 51.1 |
| William J. Bryan (Democrat) | 176 | 6,492,559 | 47.7 |

**MAP 17.1    The Election of 1896**

William McKinley's election in 1896 resulted in a realignment of political power in the United States that lasted until 1932. Republicans became the nation's majority party by forging a coalition of big business and urban industrial workers from the Northeast and Midwest. Democratic strength was confined to the South and small towns and rural areas of the Great Plains and Mountain states.

small-town agricultural America and its values, could not win over the swelling numbers of urban immigrants who considered Bryan's world alien to their experience. A great orator, Bryan nevertheless sounded anti-urban, and his defeat signaled the decline of rural America in presidential politics. His campaign was the last serious effort to win the White House with mostly farm and small-town votes.

The election of 1896 broke the political stalemate in the Age of Organization. The core of Republican backing came from industrial cities of the Northeast and Midwest. Republicans won support from their traditional constituencies of Union veterans, businessmen, and African Americans and added to it the votes of a large number of urban wageworkers. The campaign persuaded voters that the Democratic Party represented the party of depression and that Republicans stood for prosperity and progress. Another factor helping the Republicans was that in 1897 the depression finally ended, largely as a result of gold discoveries in Alaska, which helped increase the money supply, and foreign crop failures, which raised American farm prices. Democrats managed to hold on to the South as their solitary political base.

## The Decline of the Populists

The year 1896 also marked the end of the Populists as a national force, as the party was torn apart by internal divisions over policy priorities and electoral strategy. Populist leaders such as Tom Watson of Georgia did not want the Populist Party to emphasize free silver above the rest of its reform program. Other northern Populists, who either had fought on the Union side during the Civil War or had close relatives who did, such as Mary Lease, could not bring themselves to join the Democrats, the party of the old Confederacy. Nevertheless, the Populist Party officially backed Bryan, but to retain its identity, the party nominated Watson for vice president on its own ticket. After McKinley's victory, the Populist Party collapsed.

Losing the presidential election alone did not account for the disintegration of the Populists. Several problems plagued the third party. The nation's recovery from the depression removed one of the Populists' prime sources of electoral attraction. Despite appealing to industrial workers, the Populists were unable to capture their support. The free silver plank attracted silver miners in Idaho and Colorado, but the majority of workers failed to identify with a party composed mainly of farmers. As consumers of agricultural products, industrial laborers did not see any benefit in raising farm prices. Populists also failed to create a stable, biracial coalition of dispossessed farmers. Most southern white Populists did not truly accept African Americans as equal partners, even though both groups had mutual economic interests. Southern white Populists framed their arguments around class as the central issue driving the exploitation of farmers and workers by wealthy planters and industrialists. However, in the end, they succumbed to racial prejudice.

To eliminate Populism's insurgent political threat, southern opponents found ways to disfranchise black and poor white voters. During the 1890s, southern states inserted into their constitutions voting requirements that virtually eliminated the black electorate and greatly diminished the white electorate. Seeking to circumvent the Fifteenth Amendment's prohibition against racial discrimination in the right to vote, conservative white lawmakers adopted regulations based on wealth and education because blacks were disproportionately poor and had lower literacy rates. They instituted poll taxes, which imposed a fee for voting, and literacy tests, which asked tricky questions designed to trip up would-be black voters (see chapter 16). In 1898 the Supreme Court upheld the constitutionality of these voter qualifications in *Williams v. Mississippi*. Recognizing the power of white supremacy, the Populists surrendered to its appeals.

Tom Watson provides a case in point. He started out by encouraging racial unity but then switched to divisive politics. In 1896 the Populist vice presidential candidate, who had assisted embattled black farmers in his home state of Georgia, called on citizens of both races to vote against the crushing power of corporations and railroads. By whipping up racial antagonism against blacks, his Democratic opponents appealed to the racial pride of poor whites to keep them from defecting to the Populists. Chastened by the outcome of the 1896 election and learning from the tactics of his political foes, Watson embarked on a vicious campaign to exclude blacks from voting. "What does civilization owe the Negro?" he bitterly asked. "Nothing! Nothing! NOTHING!!!" Only by disfranchising African Americans and maintaining white supremacy, Watson and other white reformers reasoned, would poor whites have the courage to vote against rich whites.

Nevertheless, even in defeat the Populists left an enduring legacy. Many of their political and economic reforms—direct election of senators, the graduated income tax, government regulation of business and banking, and a version of the subtreasury system (called the Commodity Credit Corporation, created in the 1930s)—became features of reform in the twentieth century. Populists also foreshadowed other attempts at

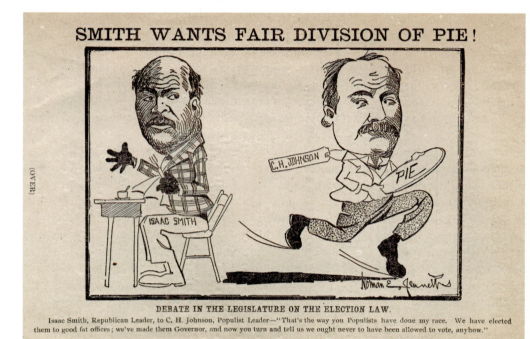

SMITH WANTS FAIR DIVISION OF PIE!

(OVER)

ISAAC SMITH

C. H. JOHNSON

PIE

DEBATE IN THE LEGISLATURE ON THE ELECTION LAW.

Isaac Smith, Republican Leader, to C. H. Johnson, Populist Leader—"That's the way you Populists have done my race. We have elected them to good fat offices; we've made them Governor, and now you turn and tell us we ought never to have been allowed to vote, anyhow."

### Populists and Race

The relationship between the Populists and African Americans was complex, but after 1896 the political connection between the two shattered. In this cartoon, Isaac Smith, a black Republican, chides C. H. Johnson, a Populist leader, for supporting a North Carolina election law that disfranchised blacks. Smith reminds Johnson that Populists had campaigned for African American votes in the past, and accuses him of walking off without sharing any of the pie.   North Carolina Collection, University of North Carolina Library at Chapel Hill

creating farmer-labor parties in the 1920s and 1930s. Perhaps their greatest contribution, however, came in showing farmers that their old individualist ways would not succeed in the modern industrial era. Rather than re-creating an independent political party, most farmers looked to organized interest groups, such as the Farm Bureau, to lobby on behalf of their interests. Whatever their approach, farmers both reflected and contributed to the Age of Organization.

### REVIEW & RELATE

How did the federal government respond to the depression of 1893?

What were the long-term political consequences of the depression of 1893?

✓ **LEARNING**Curve bedfordstmartins.com/hewittlawson/LC

## Conclusion: A Passion for Organization

From 1877 to 1900, industrial workers and farmers joined the march toward organization led by the likes of Carnegie, Rockefeller, and Morgan. These wealthy titans of industry and finance had created the large corporations that transformed the rhythms and meanings of factory labor and farm life. Working people such as John McLuckie met

the challenges of the new industrial order by organizing unions. Lacking the power of giant companies, which was reinforced by the federal government, labor unions nevertheless carved out sufficient space for workers to join together in their own defense to resist absolute corporate rule. At the same time, farmers, perhaps the most individualistic workers, and their advocates, such as Mary Elizabeth Lease, created organizations that proposed some of the most forward-looking solutions to remedy the ills accompanying industrialization. Though the political fortunes of the Grangers and Populists declined, their message persisted: Resourceful and determined workers and farmers could, and should, join together to ensure survival not just of the fittest but of the neediest as well.

Under the pressure of increased turmoil surrounding industrialization and a brutal economic depression, the political system reached a crisis in the 1890s. Despite the historic shift in party loyalties brought about by the election of William McKinley, it remained to be seen whether political party realignment could furnish the necessary leadership to address the problems of workers and farmers. Industrialization had proven painful and disorienting for millions of Americans. The events of the 1890s convinced many Americans, including many in the middle class, that the hands-off approach to social and economic problems that had prevailed in the past was no longer acceptable. In cities and states across the country, men and women took up the cause of reform. They had to wait for national leaders to catch up to them.

# Chapter Review

Online Study Guide ▶ bedfordstmartins.com/hewittlawson

## KEY TERMS

unskilled workers  (p. 529)
skilled workers  (p. 529)
unions  (p. 532)
collective bargaining  (p. 532)
Noble Order of the Knights of Labor  (p. 532)
Haymarket Square  (p. 533)
American Federation of Labor (AFL)  (p. 534)
Homestead strike  (p. 534)
Pullman strike  (p. 535)
Industrial Workers of the World (IWW)  (p. 536)
Grangers  (p. 539)
Interstate Commerce Commission (ICC)  (p. 539)
Farmers' Alliances  (p. 540)
subtreasury system  (p. 541)
Populists  (p. 541)
depression of 1893  (p. 544)
Coxey's army  (p. 544)

## REVIEW & RELATE

1. How did industrialization change the American workplace? What challenges did it create for American workers?

2. How did workers resist the concentrated power of industrial capitalists in the late nineteenth century, and why did such efforts have only limited success?

3. Why was life so difficult for American farmers in the late nineteenth century?

4. What were the similarities and differences between farmers' and industrial workers' efforts to organize in the late nineteenth century?

5. How did the federal government respond to the depression of 1893?

6. What were the long-term political consequences of the depression of 1893?

## TIMELINE OF EVENTS

| | |
|---|---|
| 1865–1895 | U.S. manufacturing jobs jump from 5.3 million to 15.1 million |
| 1867 | Patrons of Husbandry (Grange) founded |
| 1869 | Noble Order of the Knights of Labor founded |
| 1870–1900 | Number of female wageworkers increases by 66 percent |
| 1877 | Great Railroad Strike |
| 1879 | Terence Powderly becomes leader of Knights of Labor |
| 1880s | Northwestern, Southern, and Colored Farmers' Alliances formed |
| 1886 | Haymarket Square violence<br>American Federation of Labor founded |
| 1887 | Interstate Commerce Act passed |
| 1889 | Northwestern and Southern Farmers' Alliances merge |
| 1890 | Sherman Silver Purchase Act passed |
| 1890s | Southern states strip blacks of the right to vote |
| 1892 | Homestead steelworkers' strike<br>Populist Party established |
| 1893 | Depression triggered by stock market collapse |
| 1894 | Pullman strike<br>Coxey's army marches to Washington<br>Sherman Silver Purchase Act repealed |
| 1896 | Populists back William Jennings Bryan for president |
| 1897 | Depression ends<br>Populist Party declines |
| 1901 | Eugene Debs establishes Socialist Party of America |

# The Pullman Strike of 1894

Late-nineteenth-century industrialists exercised massive power over workers and the conditions of labor. Yet this power was not absolute. Workers organized into unions to secure higher wages, shorter hours, improved safety, and a fairer measure of control of the labor process. Even those corporate owners who were considered sympathetic to the needs of laborers and their families, such as railcar magnate George Pullman, assumed the right to manage their businesses as they saw fit. Though Pullman had constructed a model town with clean housing and parks for his employees, he refused to heed workers' economic complaints after the depression of 1893 began.

When the American Railway Union (ARU), headed by Eugene V. Debs, launched a nationwide strike against the Pullman company in May 1894 to improve economic conditions and gain recognition for the union, Pullman refused to negotiate. Rebuffed by Pullman, the union coordinated strike activities across the country from its headquarters in Chicago. Workers refused to operate trains with Pullman cars attached, and when the railroads hired strikebreakers, some 260,000 strikers brought rail traffic to a halt. In response, U.S. Attorney General Richard Olney, a member of many railroad boards, obtained a federal injunction ordering strikers back to work, but without success. At Olney's recommendation, President Grover Cleveland ordered federal troops into Chicago to enforce the injunction. Their clash with strikers resulted in thirteen deaths, more than fifty injuries, hundreds of thousands of dollars in property damages, and the spread of violence to twenty-six states. After the government arrested union leaders, including Debs, for disobeying the injunction, the strike collapsed in July 1894, and the Supreme Court upheld Debs's imprisonment.

The following documents reveal the points of view from four major combatants in the labor struggle. As you read these documents, consider the larger questions raised by this episode: Why have organizations been essential to advancing the rights of individuals in an industrialized society? Why was organized labor not more successful in gaining a larger share of power from capital? How did gender influence labor conflict and organizing? And what role should the government play in shaping the outcome of conflicts between labor and capital?

**DOCUMENT 17.6**

# George Pullman | Testimony before the U.S. Strike Commission, 1894

In July 1894, President Grover Cleveland appointed a Commission to Investigate the Chicago (Pullman) Strike. Although the Cleveland administration played a major role in ending the strike to the detriment of the American Railway Union, the president selected Carroll D. Wright, the U.S. commissioner of labor, to chair the commission. Wright had significant experience investigating labor conditions and collecting statistical data, and he was sympathetic to the plight of workers. George Pullman appeared before the commission to explain his position on the strike.

COMMISSIONER WRIGHT    . . . State generally what the idea was of establishing the town [of Pullman] in connection with your manufacturing plant. . . .

PULLMAN    [reading from a statement] The object in building Pullman was the establishment of a great manufacturing business on the most substantial basis possible, recognizing, as we did, and do now, that the working people are the most important element which enters into the successful operation of any manufacturing enterprise. We decided to build, in close proximity to the shops, homes for workingmen of such character and surroundings as would prove so attractive as to cause the best class of mechanics to seek that place for employment in preference to others. We also desired to establish the place on such a basis as would exclude all baneful [harmful] influences, believing that such a policy would result in the greatest measure of success, both from a commercial point of view, and also, what was equally important, or perhaps of greater importance, in a tendency toward continued elevation and improvement of the conditions not only of the working people themselves, but of their children growing up about them. . . .

If any lots had been sold in Pullman it would have permitted the introduction of the baneful elements which it was the chief purpose to exclude from the immediate neighborhood of the shops, and from the homes to be erected about them. The plan was to provide homes in the first place for all people who should desire to work in the shops, at reasonable rentals, with the expectation that as they became able and should desire to do so, they would purchase lots and erect homes for themselves within convenient distances, or avail themselves of the opportunity to rent homes from other people who should build in that vicinity. As a matter of fact, at the time of the strike 563 of the shop employees owned their homes, and 461 of that number are now employed in the shops; 560 others at the time of the strike lived outside; and, in addition, an estimated number from 200 to 300 others employed at Pullman were owners of their homes. . . .

Due attention was paid to the convenience and general well-being of the residents by the erection of stores and markets, a church, public schools, a library, and public halls for lectures and amusements; also a hotel and boarding houses. The basis on which rents were fixed was to make a return of 6 percent on the actual investment, which at that time, 1881, was a reasonable return to be expected from such an investment; and in calculating what, for such a purpose, was the actual investment in the dwellings on the one hand and the other buildings on the other, an allowance was made for the cost of the streets and other public improvements, just as it has to be considered in the valuation of any property for renting anywhere, all public improvements having to be paid for by the owner of a lot, either directly or by special assessment, and by him considered in the valuation. The actual operations have never shown a net return of 6 percent, the amount originally contemplated. The investment for several years returned a net revenue of about 4½ percent, but during the last two years additional taxes and heavier repairs have brought the net revenue down to 3.82 percent. . . .

*(continued on page 552)*

**COMMISSIONER NICOLAS WORTHINGTON**  I wanted to know what you had in mind at the time you made the statement that "it was very clear that no prudent man could submit to arbitration in this matter" when you were referring to your daily losses as a reason why any prudent man could not submit to arbitration?

**PULLMAN**  The amount of the losses would not cut any figure; it was the principle involved, not the amount that would affect my views as to arbitration.

**WORTHINGTON**  Then it was not the amount of losses that the company was then sustaining, but it was the fact that a continuance of the business at the rates that had been paid would entail loss upon the company?

**PULLMAN**  It was the principle that that should not be submitted to a third party. That was a matter that the company should decide for itself. . . .

**WORTHINGTON**  Now, let me ask you if, taking all the revenues of the Pullman company for the last year, so far as you are advised, if the company has lost money or made money during the last year?

**PULLMAN**  The company has made money during the last year.

Source: *Executive Documents of the Senate of the United States*, 53rd Cong. (1894–1895), 529–30, 553.

DOCUMENT 17.7

# Eugene V. Debs | On Radicalism, 1902

American Railway Union leader Eugene Debs served six months in jail after leading the Pullman strike. This experience moved him in more radical directions politically, and he established the Socialist Party. He ran as the party's presidential candidate five times, and in 1905 Debs helped form the Industrial Workers of the World, an organization interested in uniting all workers and challenging the capitalist system. In 1902 he described to the readers of the *Comrade*, a New York socialist newspaper, his thoughts on the Pullman strike and how he became a socialist.

In 1894 the American Railway Union was organized and a braver body of men never fought the battle of the working class.

Up to this time I had heard but little of Socialism, knew practically nothing about the movement, and what little I did know was not calculated to impress me in its favor. I was bent on thorough and complete organization of the railroad men and ultimately the whole working class, and all my time and energy were given to that end. My supreme conviction was that if they were only organized in every branch of the service and all acted together in concert they could redress their wrongs and regulate the conditions of their employment. The stockholders of the corporation acted as one, why not the men? It was such a plain proposition—simply to follow the example set before their eyes by their masters—surely they could not fail to see it, act as one, and solve the problem. . . .

Next followed the final shock—the Pullman strike—and the American Railway Union again won, clear and complete. The combined corporations were paralyzed and helpless. At this juncture there [was] delivered, from wholly unexpected quarters, a swift succession of blows that blinded me for an instant and then opened wide my eyes—and in the gleam of every bayonet and the flash of every rifle *the class struggle was revealed.* This was my first practical lesson in Socialism, though wholly unaware that it was called by that name.

An army of detectives, thugs, and murderers [was] equipped with badge and beer and bludgeon and turned loose; old hulks of cars were fired; the alarm bells tolled; the people were terrified; the most startling rumors were set afloat; the press volleyed and thundered, and over all the wires sped the news that Chicago's white throat was in the clutch of a red mob; injunctions flew thick and fast, arrests followed, and our office and headquarters, the heart of the strike, was sacked, torn out, and nailed up by the "lawful" authorities of the federal government; and when in company with my loyal comrades I found myself in Cook county jail at Chicago, with the whole press screaming conspiracy, treason, and murder. . . .

Acting upon the advice of friends we sought to employ John Harlan, son of the Supreme Justice, to assist in our defense—a defense memorable to me chiefly because of the skill and fidelity of our lawyers, among whom were the brilliant Clarence Darrow and the venerable Judge Lyman Trumbull, author of the thirteenth amendment to the Constitution, abolishing slavery in the United States.

Mr. Harlan wanted to think of the matter over night; and the next morning gravely informed us that he could not afford to be identified with the case, "for," said he, "you will be tried upon the same theory as were the anarchists, with probably the same result." That day, I remember, the jailer, by way of consolation, I suppose, showed us the blood-stained rope used at the last execution and explained in minutest detail, as he exhibited the gruesome relic, just how the monstrous crime of lawful murder is committed.

But the tempest gradually subsided and with it the blood-thirstiness of the press and "public sentiment." We were not sentenced to the gallows, nor even to the penitentiary—though put on trial for conspiracy—for reasons that will make another story.

The Chicago jail sentences were followed by six months at Woodstock [the Illinois jail where Debs was imprisoned] and it was here that Socialism gradually laid hold of me in its own irresistible fashion. Books and pamphlets and letters from socialists came by every mail and I began to read and think and dissect the anatomy of the system in which workingmen, however organized, could be shattered and battered and splintered at a single stroke. . . .

The American Railway Union was defeated but not conquered—overwhelmed but not destroyed. It lives and pulsates in the Socialist movement, and its defeat but blazed the way to economic freedom and hastened the dawn of human brotherhood.

Source: Eugene V. Debs, *Debs: His Life, Writings, and Speeches* (Chicago: Charles Kerr, 1908), 81–84.

**DOCUMENT 17.8**

# Jennie Curtis | Testimony before the U.S. Strike Commission, 1894

During the Pullman strike, seamstress Jennie Curtis was president of the American Railway Union Local 269, known as the "girls' union." Following a stirring speech by Curtis at an ARU convention, the union agreed to support workers striking against Pullman. In the following excerpt, Curtis explains to Carroll D. Wright, chairman of the congressional commission that later investigated the strike, the dire economic situation employees faced as the company cut back wages and raised rents.

**COMMISSIONER WRIGHT** State your name, residence, and occupation.

**CURTIS** Jennie Curtis; reside at Pullman; have been a seamstress for the Pullman company in the repair shops sewing room; worked for them five years.

**WRIGHT** Are you a member of any labor organization?

**CURTIS** Yes, sir; I am a member of the American Railway Union.

**WRIGHT** How long have you been a member of that union?

**CURTIS** Since about the 8th day of last May.

**WRIGHT** Do you hold any position in the union?

**CURTIS** I am president of the girls' union, local, No. 269, at Pullman.

**WRIGHT** Did you have anything to do with the strike at Pullman, which occurred on the 11th of May, 1894?

**CURTIS** No, sir.

**WRIGHT** Had you anything to do with any of the efforts to avoid the strike, or to settle the difficulties?

**CURTIS** I had not, further than being on a committee which called to see Mr. Pullman and Mr. Wickes, the general manager of the company, to ask for more wages, asking to arbitrate, and such as that.

**WRIGHT** Were you on those committees, or some of them?

**CURTIS** Yes, sir; I was.

**WRIGHT** State briefly what you did as a member serving upon those committees.

**CURTIS** I was on a committee that went from Pullman to speak for the girls in May before the strike, to ask for more wages. . . .

**WRIGHT** State what took place at the first interview.

**CURTIS** We went there and asked, as the men did, for more wages; we were cut lower than any of the men's departments throughout the works; in 1893 we were able to make 22 cents per hour, or $2.25 per day, in my department, and on the day of the strike we could only earn, on an average, working as hard as we possibly could, from 70 to 80 cents a day.

**COMMISSIONER JOHN D. KERNAN** Can you give us how the wages changed from month to month?

**CURTIS**    Whenever the men were cut in their wages the girls also received a cut. We were cut twice inside of a week in November, 1893, and in January our wages were cut again; that was the last cut we received, and we worked as hard as we possibly could and doing all we could, too. The most experienced of us could only make 80 cents per day, and a great many of the girls could only average 40 to 50 cents per day. . . .

**WRIGHT**    Do you pay rent in Pullman?

**CURTIS**    No, sir; not now.

**WRIGHT**    You pay board?

**CURTIS**    Yes, sir. My father worked for the Pullman company for thirteen years. He died last September, and I paid the rent to the Pullman company up to the time he died; I was boarding at the time of my father's death. He being laid off and sick for three months, owed the Pullman company $60 at the time of his death for back rent, and the company made me, out of my small earnings, pay that rent due from my father.

**KERNAN**    How did they make you do it?

**CURTIS**    The contract was that I should pay $3 on the back rent every pay day; out of my small earnings I could not give them $3 every pay day, and when I did not do so I was insulted and almost put out of the bank by the clerk for not being able to pay it to them. My wages were cut so low that I could not pay my board and give them $3 on the back rent, but if I had $2 or so over my board I would leave it at the bank on the rent. On the day of the strike I still owed them $15, which I am afraid they never will give me a chance to pay back.

Source: *Executive Documents of the Senate of the United States*, 53rd Cong. (1894–1895).

**DOCUMENT 17.9**

# Report from the Commission to Investigate the Chicago Strike, 1895

The commission appointed by President Grover Cleveland to investigate the Pullman strike concluded that strikes were wasteful, disruptive, and unlawful. Blaming both capital and labor for the strike, the commission believed that the Pullman trouble originated because neither the public nor the government had taken adequate measures to control monopolies and corporations and had failed "to reasonably protect the rights of labor and redress its wrongs."

**Committee Recommendations Following Investigation of the Chicago Strike**

**I.**

(1) That there be a permanent United States strike commission of three members, with duties and powers of investigation and recommendation as to disputes between railroads and their employees similar to those vested in the Interstate Commerce Commission as to rates, etc.

a. That, as in the interstate commerce act, power be given to the United States courts to compel railroads to obey the decisions of the commission, after summary hearing unattended by technicalities, and that no delays in obeying the decisions of the commission be allowed pending appeals.

b. That, whenever the parties to a controversy in a matter within the jurisdiction of the commission are one or more railroads upon one side and one or more national trade unions, incorporated under chapter 567 of the United States Statutes of 1885–86, or under State statutes, upon the other, each side shall have the right to select a representative, who shall be appointed by the President to serve as a temporary member of the commission in hearing, adjusting, and determining the particular controversy. . . .

c. That, during the pendency of a proceeding before the commission inaugurated by national trade unions, or by an incorporation of employees, it shall not be lawful for the railroads to discharge employees belonging thereto except for inefficiency, violation of law, or neglect of duty; nor for such unions or incorporation during such pendency to order, unite in, aid, or abet strikes or boycotts against the railroads complained of; nor, for a period of six months after a decision, for such railroads to discharge any such employees in whose places others shall be employed, except for the causes aforesaid; nor for any such employees, during a like period, to quit the service without giving thirty days' written notice of intention to do so, nor for any such union or incorporation to order, counsel, or advise otherwise. . . .

**II.**

(1) The commission would suggest the consideration by the States of the adoption of some system of conciliation and arbitration like that, for instance, in use in the Commonwealth of Massachusetts. That system might be reenforced by additional provisions giving the board of arbitration more power to investigate all strikes, whether requested so to do or not, and the question might be considered as to giving labor organizations a standing before the law, as heretofore suggested for national trade unions.

(2) Contracts requiring men to agree not to join labor organizations or to leave them, as conditions of employment, should be made illegal, as is already done in some of our States.

**III.**

(1) The commission urges employers to recognize labor organizations; that such organizations be dealt with through representatives, with special reference to conciliation and arbitration when difficulties are threatened or arise. It is satisfied that employers should come in closer touch with labor and should recognize that, while the interests of labor and capital are not identical, they are reciprocal.

(2) The commission is satisfied that if employers everywhere will endeavor to act in concert with labor; that if when wages can be raised under economic conditions they be raised voluntarily, and that if when there are reductions reasons be given for the reduction, much friction can be avoided. It is also satisfied that if employers will consider employees as thoroughly essential to industrial success as capital, and thus take labor into consultation at proper times, much of the severity of strikes can be tempered and their number reduced.

Source: *Report on the Chicago Strike of June–July, 1894 by the United States Strike Commission* (Washington, D.C.: Government Printing Office, 1895), LII–LIV.

**DOCUMENT 17.10**

# Grover Cleveland | Reflections on the Pullman Strike, 1904

After Grover Cleveland left the White House in 1897, he became a trustee of Princeton University. He delivered several addresses as part of a lecture series on public affairs that was established in his honor. In 1904, a decade after the Pullman strike, he discussed his administration's role in dealing with the strike in an article in the popular magazine *McClure's*.

IN THE LAST DAYS OF JUNE, 1894, a very determined and ugly labor disturbance broke out in the City of Chicago. Almost in a night it grew to full proportions of malevolence and danger. Rioting and violence were its early accompaniments; and it spread so swiftly that within a few days it had reached nearly the entire Western and Southwestern sections of our country. Railroad transportation was especially involved in its attacks. The carriage of United States mails was interrupted, interstate commerce was obstructed, and railroad property was riotously destroyed.

This disturbance is often called "The Chicago Strike." It is true that its beginning was in that city; and the headquarters of those who inaugurated it and directed its operations were located there; but the name thus given to it is an entire misnomer so far as it applies to the scope and reach of the trouble. Railroad operations were more or less affected in twenty-seven states and territories; and in all these the interposition of the General Government was to a greater or less extent invoked. . . .

The employees of the Pullman Palace Car Company could not on any reasonable and consistent theory be regarded as eligible to membership in an organization devoted to the interests of railway employees; and yet, during the months of March, April, and May, 1894, it appears that nearly 4,000 of these employees were enrolled in the American Railway Union. This, to say the least of it, was an exceedingly unfortunate proceeding, since it created a situation which implicated in a comparatively insignificant quarrel between the managers of an industrial establishment and their workmen, the large army of the Railway Union. It was the membership of these workmen in the Railway Union and the Union's consequent assumption of their quarrel, that gave it the proportions of a tremendous disturbance, paralyzing the most important business interests, obstructing the functions of the Government, and disturbing social peace and order. . . .

I shall not enter upon an enumeration of all the disorders and violence, the defiance of law and authority, and the obstructions of national functions and duties, which occurred in many localities as a consequence of this labor contention, thus tremendously reinforced and completely under way. It is my especial purpose to review the action taken by the Government for the maintenance of its own authority and the protection of the special interests intrusted to its keeping, so far as they were endangered by this disturbance; and I do not intend to especially deal with the incidents of the strike except in so far as a reference to them may be necessary to show conditions which not only justified but actually obliged the Government to resort to stern and unusual measures in the assertion of its prerogatives. . . .

Owing to the enforced relationship of Chicago to the strike which started within its borders, and because of its importance as a center of railway traffic, Government officials at Washington were not surprised by the early and persistent complaints of mail and interstate commerce obstructions which reached them from that city. It was from the first anticipated that this would be the seat of the most serious complications, and the place where the strong arm of the law would be most needed. In these circumstances it would have been a criminal neglect of duty if those charged with the protection of Governmental agencies and the enforcement of orderly obedience and submission to Federal authority, had been remiss in preparations for any emergency in that quarter.

. . . The Attorney-General, in making suggestions concerning legal proceedings, wrote: "It has seemed to me that if the rights of the United States were vigorously asserted in Chicago, the origin and center of the demonstration, the result would be to make it a failure everywhere else, and to prevent its spread over the entire country," and in that connection he indicated that it might be advisable, instead of relying entirely upon warrants issued under criminal statutes, against persons actually guilty of the offense of obstructing United States mails, that the courts should be asked to grant injunctions which would restrain and prevent any attempt to commit such offense.

Source: "The Government in the Chicago Strike of 1894," *McClure's Magazine*, July 1904, 227–29, 231–32.

## Interpret the Evidence

1. Why does George Pullman (Document 17.6) think he has treated his workers fairly? Why might workers have disagreed with him?

2. According to Eugene V. Debs (Document 17.7), what was the purpose of labor activism? How did the Pullman strike teach Debs about socialism?

3. How did being a woman affect Jennie Curtis's experiences as a Pullman worker (see Document 17.8)?

4. How do you think Pullman and Debs would have responded to the report on the Pullman strike issued by the Commission to Investigate the Chicago Strike (Document 17.9)?

5. What do you think of Grover Cleveland's belief that the Pullman employees had no business joining the American Railway Union (see Document 17.10)?

## Put It in Context

• What do these documents reveal about the complex relationship among labor, management, and government at the close of the nineteenth century?

background photos: pages 555 and 556–57, Library of Congress

The Granger Collection, New York

Private Collection/Peter Newark American Pictures/The Bridgeman Art Library

The Woolworth Building under construction, New York City, 1912.

An Italian family on the ferry from Ellis Island to New York City, 1905.

# 18

# Cities, Immigrants, and the Nation

## 1880–1914

Baseball team, Franklin, Virginia.

## AMERICAN HISTORIES

In the fall of 1905, Beryl Lassin faced a difficult choice. Living in the *shtetl* (a Jewish town) of Borrisnov in western Russia, Lassin had few if any opportunities as a young locksmith. Beryl and his wife, Lena, lived at a dangerous time in Russia. Jews were subject to periodic pogroms, state-sanctioned outbreaks of anti-Jewish violence carried out by local Christians. Beryl also faced a discriminatory military draft that required conscripted Jews to serve twenty-year terms in the army, far longer than their Christian countrymen. His wife's brother had already left Russia for the United States, and the couple decided that Beryl should follow his brother-in-law's example before the draft caught up with him. The couple couldn't afford two steamship tickets, so with the understanding that his wife would follow as soon as possible, Beryl set sail for America alone on the steamship *Zeeland*, which sailed from Antwerp, Belgium, on October 7, 1905. He was crammed into the steerage belowdecks with hundreds of other passengers, most of them fellow Jews. Ten days later, his ship chugged into New York harbor, where Beryl found a less than hospitable greeting. Disembarking at Ellis Island, the processing center for immigrants, he stood in long lines and underwent a strenuous medical examination, including a painful eye inspection, to ensure that he was fit to enter the country. He also had to prove that he had someplace to go, in his case the apartment of his brother-in-law on New York City's Lower East Side. With no money, Beryl boarded a ferry across the Hudson that took him to a new life in the United States.

Less than a year later, Lena joined her husband. Over the next decade, the couple had five children. Shortly after the youngest girl was born, Lena died of cancer. Her death threw the family into turmoil, as Beryl, now called Ben, had to place two of the three youngest children in the Hebrew Children's Home and the other in foster care. The children were reunited with their father when Ben remarried, but life was still difficult. Ben was injured at his job as a mechanic and did not work full-time again. To make ends meet, his three eldest boys dropped out of school and went to work. Still, like many other immigrants, Ben's family managed to leave the crowded Lower East Side, following a trail blazed by earlier Jewish immigrants to Harlem and then the Bronx. Ben preferred to speak in Yiddish and never learned to read English. Nor did he become an American citizen, and after World War I, as an alien, he had to register annually with the federal government. His children, however, were all citizens because they had been born in the United States.

On June 8, 1912, another immigrant followed a similar route that took her on a different journey. Seventeen years old and unmarried, Maria Vik decided to leave her home in the small village of Kiestyderocz, Hungary. As a Catholic, Maria did not experience the religious persecution that Beryl did. Like many other Hungarians who ventured to the United States at this time, Maria, the oldest daughter, left to help support her family back in the old country. She had an aunt living in the United States, and she came across with a Hungarian couple who escorted young women for domestic service in America. Her sea voyage began in Hamburg, Germany, aboard the ship *Amerika*, and unlike Beryl she had a cabin in second class.

Maria, too, landed at Ellis Island and passed the rigorous entry exams. Soon she boarded a train for Rochester in western New York. There she worked as a cook for a German physician, learned English, and led an active social life within the local Hungarian community. In Rochester, she met and fell in love with Karoly (Charles) Takacs, a cabinetmaker from Hungary, who,

**Beryl Lassin and
Maria Vik Takacs**

like Beryl Lassin, had come to avoid the military draft. Charles became a citizen in May 1916. By marrying him, Mary, as she was now called, became a citizen as well.

The couple moved forty-five miles west of Rochester to Middleport and purchased a small farm in a neighborhood filled with Hungarian immigrants. Because so many Hungarians lived in the area, Mary spoke mainly Hungarian and began to speak more English only when the oldest of her four children entered kindergarten.

The American histories of Beryl Lassin and Maria Vik Takacs took one to the urban bustle of New York City, the other to a quiet, rural village in western New York State. The Lassins, who rented walk-up apartments in five-story buildings and whose children had to drop out of school, did not fare as well economically as did the Takacses, who owned property and sent their three daughters to college. However, as different as their lives in America were, neither Beryl nor Maria regretted their choice to leave Europe for the United States. Like millions of other immigrants at the turn of the twentieth century, they had come to America to build better lives for themselves and their families, and both saw their children and grandchildren succeed in ways that they could have only dreamed of in their native countries. Indeed, Ben Lassin changed his surname to Lawson, and his son Murray married Ceil Puchowitzky (Parker), the daughter of another Russian-Jewish immigrant. Mary and Charles's daughter Irene married Robert Hewitt, whose family arrived from northern Europe in the nineteenth century. Murray's son, Steven F. Lawson, and Irene's daughter, Nancy A. Hewitt—the grandchildren of Beryl and Maria, respectively—became historians, got married, and wrote this textbook. The experiences of the Lawson and Hewitt families, like countless others, reflect the complicated ways that immigrants were transformed into Americans at the same time that the United States was forever changed by the new additions to its population. ●

photos: top photo courtesy of Steven F. Lawson; bottom photo courtesy of Irene Hewitt

THE LASSINS AND the Takacses were part of a flood of immigrants who entered the United States from 1880 to the outbreak of World War I in 1914. Unlike the majority of earlier immigrants, who had come from northern Europe, most of the more than 20 million people who arrived during this period came from southern and eastern Europe. They entered the United States mainly through seaports in the Northeast, but some came through ports in New Orleans, Louisiana, and Key West and Tampa, Florida, in the South; across the Texas and California borders from Mexico; and through ports in San Francisco and Seattle on the West Coast. Though many moved to small towns and rural villages, most remained in cities, which experienced enormous population growth as a result. In these large urban areas, impoverished immigrants entered the political mainstream of American life, welcomed by political bosses and their machines, who saw in them a chance to gain the allegiance of millions of new voters. At the same time, their coming upset many middle- and upper-class city dwellers who blamed these new arrivals for lowering the quality of urban life.

## A New Wave of Immigrants

For more than three hundred years following the settlement of the North American colonies, the majority of white immigrants to America were northern European Protestants. Black Americans were brought forcibly from Africa, mainly by way of the West Indies and the Caribbean. Although African Americans originally followed their own religious practices, most eventually converted to Protestantism. By the end of the nineteenth century, however, a new pattern of immigration had emerged, one that included much greater ethnic and religious diversity. These new immigrants often encountered hostility from those whose ancestors had arrived generations earlier, and faced the difficult challenge of retaining their cultural identities while becoming assimilated as Americans.

## Immigrants Arrive from Many Lands

Immigration to the United States was part of a worldwide phenomenon. In addition to the United States, European immigrants also journeyed to other countries in the Western Hemisphere, especially Canada, Argentina, Brazil, and Cuba. Others left China, Japan, and India and migrated to Southeast Asia and Hawaii. From England and Ireland, migrants ventured to other parts of the British empire, including Australia, New Zealand, and South Africa. As with those who came to the United States, these immigrants left their homelands to find new job opportunities or to obtain land to start their own farms. In countries like Australia, New Zealand, and South Africa, white settlers often pushed aside native peoples—Aborigines in Australia, Maori in New Zealand, and blacks in South Africa—to make communities for themselves. Whereas most immigrants chose to relocate voluntarily, some made the move bound by labor contracts that limited their movement during the terms of the agreement. Chinese, Mexican, and Italian workers made up a large portion of this group.

The late nineteenth century saw a shift in the country of origin of immigrants to the United States: Instead of coming from northern and western Europe, many now came from southern and eastern European countries, most notably Italy, Greece, Austria-Hungary, Poland, and Russia. In 1882 around 789,000 immigrants entered the United States, 87 percent of whom came from northern and western Europe. By contrast, twenty-five years later in 1907,

**SS Zeeland**

The SS *Zeeland* was a British and Belgian ocean liner first launched in 1901. Four years later, like thousands of other immigrants, Beryl Lassin made the journey from Russia to Antwerp, where he boarded this ship, and finally landed at Ellis Island. Traveling in steerage, the cheapest fare, he ate poor meals and suffered from overcrowding and poor sanitation. Photograph courtesy of the Peabody Essex Museum, image no. 204962

of the 1,285,000 newcomers who journeyed to America, 81 percent originated from southern and eastern Europe.

Most of those settling on American shores after 1880 were Catholic or Jewish and hardly knew a word of English. They tended to be even poorer than immigrants who had arrived before them, coming mainly from rural areas and lacking suitable skills for a rapidly expanding industrial society. In the words of one historian, who could easily have been describing Beryl Lassin's life: "Jewish poverty [in Russia] is a kind of marvel for . . . it has origins in fathers and grandfathers who have been wretchedly poor since time immemorial." Even after relocating to a new land and a new society, such immigrants struggled to break patterns of poverty that were, in many cases, centuries in the making.

Immigrants came from other parts of the world as well. From 1860 to 1924, some 450,000 Mexicans migrated to the U.S. Southwest. Many traveled to El Paso, Texas, near the Mexican border, and from there hopped aboard one of three railroad lines to jobs on farms and in mines, mills, and construction. Cubans, Spaniards, and Bahamians traveled to the Florida cities of Key West and Tampa, where they established and worked in cigar factories. Tampa grew from a tiny village of a few hundred people in 1880 to a city of 16,000 in 1900. Although Congress had excluded Chinese immigration after 1882, it did not close the door to migrants from Japan. Unlike the Chinese, the Japanese had not competed with white workers for jobs on railroad and other construction projects. Moreover, Japan had emerged as a major world power in the late nineteenth century and gained some grudging respect from American leaders by defeating Russia in the Russo-Japanese War of 1904–1905. Some 260,000 Japanese arrived in the United States during the first two decades of the twentieth century. Many of them first settled in Hawaii and then moved to the West Coast states of California, Oregon, and Washington, where they worked as farm laborers and gardeners and established

businesses catering to a Japanese clientele. Nevertheless, like the Chinese before them, Japanese immigrants were considered part of an inferior "yellow race" and encountered discrimination in their West Coast settlements.

This wave of immigration changed the composition of the American population. By 1910 one-third of the population was foreign-born or had at least one parent who came from abroad. Foreigners and their children made up more than three-quarters of the population of New York City, Detroit, Chicago, Milwaukee, Cleveland, Minneapolis, and San Francisco. Immigration, though not as extensive in the South as in the North, also altered the character of southern cities. About one-third of the population of Tampa, Miami, and New Orleans consisted of foreigners and their descendants. The borderland states of Texas, New Mexico, Arizona, and southern California contained similar percentages of immigrants, most of whom came from Mexico.

These immigrants came to the United States largely for economic, political, and religious reasons. Nearly all were poor and expected to find ways to make money in America. U.S. railroads and steamship companies advertised in Europe and recruited passengers by emphasizing economic opportunities in the United States. Early immigrants wrote to relatives back home extolling the virtues of what they had found, perhaps exaggerating their success. However, for people barely making a living, or for those subject to religious discrimination and political repression, what did it matter if they arrived in America and the streets were not paved in gold, as legend had it? In fact, if many of the streets were not paved at all, at least the immigrants could get jobs paving them!

The importance of economic incentives in luring immigrants is underscored by the fact that millions returned to their home countries after they had earned sufficient money to establish a more comfortable lifestyle. Of the more than 27 million immigrants from 1875 to 1919, 11 million returned home (Table 18.1). One immigrant from Canton, China, accumulated a small fortune as a merchant on Mott Street, in New York City's Chinatown. According to residents of his hometown in China, "[Having] made his wealth among the barbarians this man had faithfully returned to pour it out among his tribesmen, and he is living in our village now very happy." Jews, Mexicans, Czechs, and Japanese had the lowest rates of return. Immigrant groups facing religious or political persecution in their homeland were the least likely to return. It is highly doubtful that a poor Jewish immigrant like Beryl Lassin would have received a warm welcome home in his native Russia, if he had been allowed to return at all.

**TABLE 18.1   Percentage of Immigrant Departures versus Arrivals, 1875–1914**

| Year | Arrivals | Departures | Percentage of Departures to Arrivals |
|------|----------|------------|--------------------------------------|
| 1875–1879 | 956,000 | 431,000 | 45% |
| 1880–1884 | 3,210,000 | 327,000 | 10% |
| 1885–1889 | 2,341,000 | 638,000 | 27% |
| 1890–1894 | 2,590,000 | 838,000 | 32% |
| 1895–1899 | 1,493,000 | 766,000 | 51% |
| 1900–1904 | 3,575,000 | 1,454,000 | 41% |
| 1905–1909 | 5,533,000 | 2,653,000 | 48% |
| 1910–1914 | 6,075,000 | 2,759,000 | 45% |

## Creating Immigrant Communities

Immigrants were processed at their port of entry, and the government played no role in their relocation in America. New arrivals were left to search out transplanted relatives and other countrymen on their own. In cities such as New York, Boston, and Chicago, immigrants occupied neighborhoods that took on the distinct ethnic characteristics of the groups that inhabited them. A cacophony of different languages echoed in the streets as new residents continued to communicate in their mother tongues. The neighborhoods of immigrant groups often were clustered together, so residents were as likely to learn phrases in their neighbors' languages as they were to learn English.

The formation of **ghettos**—neighborhoods dominated by a single ethnic, racial, or class group—eased immigrants' transition into American society. Without government assistance or outside help, these communities assumed the burden of meeting some of the challenges that immigrants faced in adjusting to their new environment. Living within these ethnic enclaves made it easier for immigrants to find housing, hear about jobs, buy food, and seek help from those with whom they felt most comfortable. **Mutual aid societies** sprang up to provide social welfare benefits, including insurance payments and funeral rites. "A *landsman* died in the factory," a founder of one such Jewish association explained, and the worker was buried in an unmarked grave. When his Jewish neighbors heard about it, "his body [was] dug up, and the decision taken to start our organization with a cemetery." Group members established social centers where immigrants could play cards or dominoes, chat and gossip over tea or coffee, host dances and benefits, or just relax among people who shared a common heritage. In San Francisco's Chinatown, the largest Chinese community in California, such organizations usually consisted of people who had come from the same towns in China. These groups performed a variety of services, including finding jobs for their members, resolving disputes, campaigning against anti-Chinese discrimination, and sponsoring parades and other cultural activities. One society member explained: "We are strangers in a strange country. We must have an organization to control our country fellows and develop our friendship."

The same impulse to band together occurred in immigrant communities throughout the nation. On the West Coast, Japanese farmers joined *kenjinkai*, which not only provided social activities but also helped first-generation immigrants locate jobs and find housing. In Ybor City, Tampa's cigar-making section, mutual aid organizations rose to meet the needs of Spaniards, Cubans, Afro-Cubans, and Italians. El

**El Centro Español**

This 1912 postcard shows El Centro Español in Ybor City, the cigar-making district of Tampa, Florida. This facility served the Spanish community as a social club and mutual aid society. Immigrants attended dances, plays, and concerts and took English lessons, which eased their adaptation to a new homeland. Courtesy of the State Archives of Florida

Centro Español sponsored dances catering to Spaniards, only to be outdone by the rival El Centro Asturiano, which constructed a building that contained a 1,200-seat theater with a 27-by-80-foot stage, "$4,000 worth of modern lighting fixtures, a *cantina*, and a well stocked *biblioteca* (library)." Cubans constructed their own palatial $60,000 clubhouse, El Circulo Cubano, with lovely stained-glass windows, a pharmacy, a theater, and a ballroom. Less splendid and more economical, La Union Martí-Maceo became the home away from home for Tampa's Afro-Cubans. Besides the usual attractions, the club sponsored a baseball team that competed against other Latin teams. The establishment of such clubs and cultural centers speaks to the commitment of Tampa's immigrant groups to enhance their communities—a commitment backed up with significant financial expenditures.

Besides family and civic associations, churches and synagogues provided religious and social activities for ghetto dwellers. The number of Catholic churches nationwide more than tripled—from 3,000 in 1865 to 10,000 in 1900. Churches celebrated important landmarks in their parishioners' lives—births, baptisms, weddings, and deaths—in a far warmer and more personal manner than did clerks in city hall. Like mutual aid societies, churches offered food and clothing to those who were ill or unable to work and fielded sports teams to compete in recreational leagues. Immigrants altered the religious practices and rituals in their churches to meet their own needs and expectations, many times over the objections of their clergy. Various ethnic groups challenged the orthodox practices of the Catholic Church and insisted that their parishes adopt religious icons that they had worshipped in the old country. These included patron saints or protectresses from Old World towns, such as the Madonna del Carmine, whom Italian Catholics in New

York's East Harlem celebrated with an annual festival that their priests considered a pagan ritual. Women played the predominant role in running these street festivities. German Catholics challenged Vatican policy by insisting that each ethnic group have its own priests and parishes. Some Catholics, like Mary Vik, who lived in rural areas that did not have a Catholic church in the vicinity, attended services with local Christians from other denominations.

Religious worship also varied among Jews. German Jews had arrived in the United States in an earlier wave of immigration than their eastern European coreligionists. By the early twentieth century, they had achieved some measure of economic success and founded Reform Judaism, with Cincinnati, Ohio, as its center. This brand of Judaism relaxed strict standards of worship, including absolute fidelity to kosher dietary laws, and allowed prayers to be said in English. By contrast, eastern European Jews, like Beryl Lassin, observed the traditional faith and went to *shul* (synagogue) on a regular basis, maintained a kosher diet, and prayed in Hebrew.

With few immigrants literate in English, foreign-language newspapers proliferated to inform their readers of local, national, and international events. Between the mid-1880s and 1920, 3,500 new foreign-language newspapers came into existence. These newspapers helped sustain ethnic solidarity in the New World as well as maintain ties to the Old World. Newcomers could learn about social and cultural activities in their communities and keep abreast of news from their homeland. German-language tabloids dominated the field and featured such dailies as the *New Yorker Staatszeitung,* the *St. Louis Anzeiger des Westens,* the *Cincinnati Volkesblatt,* and the *Wisconsin Banner.*

Like other communities with poor, unskilled populations, immigrant neighborhoods bred crime. Young men joined gangs based on ethnic heritage and battled with those of other immigrant groups to protect their turf. Adults formed underworld organizations—some of them tied to international criminal syndicates, such as the Mafia—that trafficked in prostitution, gambling, robbery, and murder. Tongs (secret organizations) in New York City's and San Francisco's Chinatowns, which started out as mutual aid societies, peddled vice and controlled the opium trade, gambling, and prostitution in their communities. A survey of New York City police and municipal court records from 1898 concluded that Jews "are prominent in their commission of forgery, violation of corporation ordinance, as disorderly persons (failure to support wife or family), both grades of larceny, and of the lighter grade of assault."

Crime was not the only social problem that plagued immigrant communities. Newspapers and court records reported husbands abandoning their wife and children, engaging in drunken and disorderly conduct, or abusing

their family. Boarders whom immigrant families took into their homes for economic reasons also posed problems. Cramped spaces created a lack of privacy, and male boarders sometimes attempted to assault the woman of the house while her husband and children were out to work or in school. Finally, generational conflicts within families began to develop as American-born children of immigrants questioned their parents' values. Daughters born in America sought to loosen the tight restraints imposed by their parents. If they worked outside the home, young women were expected to turn their wages over to their parents. A young Italian woman, however, displayed her independence after receiving her first paycheck. "I just went downtown first and I spent a lot, more than half of my money," she admitted. "I just went hog wild." Thus the social organizations and mutual aid societies that immigrant groups established were more than a simple expression of ethnic solidarity and pride. They were also a response to the very real problems that challenged the health and stability of immigrant communities.

**Explore**

See Document 18.1 for a depiction of one immigrant family's intergenerational conflict.

## Hostility toward Recent Immigrants

On October 28, 1886, the United States held a gala celebration for the opening of the Statue of Liberty in New York harbor, a short distance from Ellis Island. French sculptors Frédéric-Auguste Bartholdi and Alexandre-Gustave Eiffel had designed the 151-foot-tall monument, *Liberty Enlightening the World,* to appear at the Centennial Exposition in Philadelphia in 1876. Ten years overdue, the statue arrived in June 1885, but funds were still needed to finish construction of a base on which the sculpture would stand. Ordinary people dipped into their pockets for spare change, contributing to a campaign that raised $100,000 so that Lady Liberty could finally hold her uplifted torch for all to see. In 1903 the inspiring words of Emma Lazarus, a Jewish poet, were inscribed on the pedestal welcoming new generations of immigrants.

Give me your tired, your poor,
Your huddled masses yearning to breathe free,
The wretched refuse of your teeming shore,
Send these, the homeless, tempest-tossed to me,
I lift my lamp beside the golden door!

Despite the welcoming inscription on the Statue of Liberty, many Americans whose families had arrived before the 1880s considered the influx of immigrants from southern and eastern Europe at best a necessary evil and at

## Anzia Yerzierska | Immigrant Fathers and Daughters, 1925

Anzia Yerzierska, a Jewish immigrant who came to the United States from Poland around 1890, wrote about the struggles of immigrant families in adjusting to their new world. Her novel *Bread Givers* focuses on the conflict of a Jewish daughter, Sara Smolinski, patterned after herself, and the girl's father, Reb Smolinski, a Talmudic scholar. Intent on taking advantage of new opportunities in America, Sara resists her father's attempts to impose his Old World beliefs about the traditional duties of a subservient female.

**Explore**

As I came through the door with my bundle, Father caught sight of me. "What's this?" he asked. "Where are you going?"

"I'm going back to work, in New York."

"What? Wild-head! Without asking, without consulting your father, you get yourself ready to go? Do you yet know that I want you to work in New York? Let's first count out your carfare to come home every night. Maybe it will cost so much there wouldn't be anything left from your wages."

"But I'm not coming home!"

"What? A daughter of mine, only seventeen years old, not home at night?"

"I'll go to Bessie or Mashah."

"Mashah is starving poor, and you know how crowded it is by Bessie."

"If there's no place for me by my sisters, I'll find a place by strangers."

"A young girl, alone, among strangers? Do you know what's going on in the world? No girl can live without a father or a husband to look out for her. It says in the Torah, only through a man has a woman an existence. Only through a man can a woman enter Heaven."

"I'm smart enough to look out for myself. It's a new life now. In America, women don't need men to boss them."

"*Blut-und-Eisen!* ["blood and iron"] They ought to put you in a madhouse till you're cured of your crazy nonsense!" . . .

Wild with all that was choked in me since I was born, my eyes burned into my father's eyes. "My will is as strong as yours. I'm going to live my own life. Nobody can stop me. I'm not from the old country. I'm American!"

"You blasphemer!" His hand flung out and struck my cheek. "Denier of God! I'll teach you respect for the law!"

I leaped back and dashed for the door. The Old World had struck its last on me.

Source: Anzia Yerzierska, *Bread Givers* (New York: Persea Books, 1975), 136–38.

### Interpret the Evidence

- How does Sara's father view the father-daughter relationship? How does Sara see it?
- Why does Sara's father object to her working in the city? What role does religion play in shaping his point of view?

### Put It in Context

What values and beliefs does Sara associate with the Old World? What new values does she associate with America?

worst a menace. Industrialists counted on immigrants to provide the cheap labor that performed backbreaking work in their factories. Not surprisingly, existing industrial workers saw the newcomers as a threat to their economic livelihoods. In their view, the arrival of large numbers of immigrants could only result in greater competition for jobs and lower wages. Moreover, even though most immigrants came to America to find work and improve the lives of their families, a small portion antagonized and frightened capitalists and middle-class Americans with their radical calls for the reorganization of society and the overthrow of the government. Of course, the vast majority of immigrants were not radicals, but a large proportion of radicals were recent immigrants. During times of labor-management strife (see chapter 17), this fact made it easier for businessmen and their spokesmen in the press to advance the notion that anti-American radicalism was a chronic immigrant disease.

Anti-immigrant fears linked to ideas about race and ethnicity had a long history in the United States. In 1790 Congress passed a statute restricting citizenship to those deemed white:

> Any Alien being a free white person, who shall have resided within the limits and under the jurisdiction of the United States for the term of two years, may be admitted to become a citizen thereof on application to any common law Court of record in any one of the States wherein he shall have resided for the term of one year at least, and making proof to the satisfaction of such Court that he is a person of good character, and taking the oath or affirmation prescribed by law to support the Constitution of the United States.

This standard excluded American Indians, who were regarded as savages, and African Americans, most of whom were slaves at the time. In 1857 the Supreme Court ruled that even free blacks were not citizens. From the very beginning of the United States, largely Protestant lawmakers debated whether Catholics and Jews qualified as whites. Although lawmakers ultimately included Catholics and Jews within their definition of "white," over the next two centuries Americans viewed racial categories as not simply matters of skin color. Ethnicity (country or culture of origin) and religion became absorbed into and intertwined with racial categories. A sociological study of Homestead, Pennsylvania, published in 1910 broke down the community along the following constructed racial lines: "Slav, English-speaking European, native white, and colored." Russian Jewish immigrants such as Beryl Lassin were recorded as Hebrews rather than as Russians, suggesting that Jewishness was seen by Christian America as a racial identity.

Scores of races were presumed to exist based on perceived shades of skin color. In 1911 a congressional commission on immigration noted that Poles are "darker than the Lithuanians" and "lighter than the average Russian." These were not neutral judgments, however. Natural scientists and social scientists had given credence to the idea that some races and ethnic groups were superior and others were inferior. Based on Darwin's theory of evolution (see chapter 16), biologists and anthropologists constructed measures of racial hierarchies, placing descendants of northern Europeans with lighter complexions—Anglo-Saxons, Teutonics, and Nordics—at the top of the evolutionary scale. Those with darker skin were deemed inferior "races," with Africans and Native Americans at the bottom. Scholars attempting to

make disciplines such as history more "scientific" accepted these racial classifications. At Johns Hopkins University, the leading center of academic training in the social sciences in the 1880s, historian Herbert Baxter Adams argued that the influx of southern European immigrants threatened the capacity for self-government developed in the United States by early settlers originating from Great Britain and Germany. The prevailing sentiment of this era reflected demeaning images of many immigrant groups: Irish as drunkards, Chicanos and Cubans as lazy, Italians as criminals, Hungarians as ignorant peasants, Jews as cheap and greedy, and Chinese as drug addicts. These characteristics resulted supposedly from inherited biological traits, rather than from extreme poverty or other environmental conditions.

Newer immigrants, marked as racially inferior, became a convenient target of hostility. Skilled craftsmen born in the United States viewed largely unskilled workers from abroad who would work for low wages as a threat to their attempts to form unions and keep wages high. Middle-class city dwellers blamed urban problems on the rising tide of foreigners. In addition, Protestant purists felt threatened by Catholics and Jews and believed these "races" incapable or unworthy of assimilation into what they considered to be the superior white, Anglo-Saxon, and Protestant culture. In 1890 social scientist Richard Mayo Smith wrote, "It is scarcely probable that by taking the dregs of Europe, we shall produce a people of high social intelligence and morality."

**Nativism**—the belief that foreigners pose a serious danger to one's native society and culture—arose as a reactionary response to immigration. New England elites, such as Massachusetts senator Henry Cabot Lodge and writer John Fiske, argued that southern European, Semitic, and Slavic races did not fit into the "community of race" that had founded the United States. In 1893 Lodge and fellow Harvard graduates established the Immigration Restriction League and lobbied for federal legislation that would exclude adult immigrants unable to read in their own language. In 1887 Henry F. Bowers of Clinton, Iowa, founded a similar organization, the American Protective Association, which claimed a total membership of 2.5 million at its peak. The group proposed restricting Catholic immigration, making English a prerequisite to American citizenship, and prohibiting Catholics from teaching in public schools or holding public offices. Obsessed with the supposed threat posed by Catholics, Bowers directed the expansion of the organization throughout the Midwest.

**Explore**

See Document 18.2 for a nativist perspective on immigration.

DOCUMENT 18.2

## "The Stranger at Our Gate," 1899

Critics of late-nineteenth-century immigration often relied on the germ theory of disease in their arguments for stricter immigration laws. However, nativist objections to immigrants went far beyond issues of public health. According to nativists, immigrants were sources of both biological and cultural "contamination." In the following cartoon, "The Stranger at Our Gate," the "germs" carried by immigrants are not limited to those associated with disease.

**Explore**

What do the inscription on the gate and the caption below the cartoon tell us about the specific policies the cartoon supports?

How would you interpret Uncle Sam's body language in facing the would-be immigrant?

What does the cartoon suggest about the role of religion in anti-immigrant sentiment?

What specific "threats" does the immigrant appear to pose to the United States?

THE STRANGER AT OUR GATE.

EMIGRANT.—Can I come in?　　UNCLE SAM.—I 'spose you can; there's no law to keep you out.

The Ohio State University Billy Ireland Cartoon Library & Museum

**Put It in Context**

What does this cartoon tell us about prevailing attitudes toward immigration at the end of the nineteenth century?

Proposals to restrict immigration, however, did nothing to deal with the millions of foreigners already in America. To preserve their status and power and increase the size of the native-born population, nativists embraced the idea of **eugenics**—a pseudo-science that advocated "biological engineering"—and supported the selective breeding of "desirable" races to counter the rapid population growth of "useless" races. Accordingly, eugenicists promoted the institutionalization of people deemed "unfit," sterilization of those considered mentally impaired, and the licensing and regulation of marriages to promote better breeding. In pushing for such measures, eugenicists believed that they were following the dictates of modern science and acting in a humane fashion to prevent those deemed unfit from causing further harm to themselves and to society. Alexander Graham Bell (see chapter 16), the inventor of the telephone, was one of the early champions of eugenics and immigration restriction.

Others took a less harsh approach. As had been the case with American Indians (see chapter 15), reformers stressed the need for immigrants to assimilate into the dominant culture, embrace the values of individualism and self-help, adopt American styles of dress and grooming, and exhibit loyalty to the U.S. government. They encouraged immigrant children to attend public schools, where they would learn to speak English and adopt American cultural rituals by celebrating holidays such as Thanksgiving and Columbus Day. In 1892 schools adopted the pledge of allegiance, written by Francis Bellamy, which recited American ideals of "liberty and justice for all" and affirmed loyalty to the nation and its flag. Educators encouraged adult immigrants to attend night classes to learn English. Ben Lassin tried this approach sporadically, but he did not prove to be an apt pupil. Like many immigrants, he made only limited progress toward assimilation.

## The Assimilation Dilemma

If immigrants were not completely assimilated, neither did they remain the same people who had lived on the farms and in the villages of Europe, Asia, Mexico, and the Caribbean. Some sought to become full-fledged Americans, like Mary Vik, or at least see that their children did so. Writer Israel Zangwill, an English American Jew, portrayed this goal and furnished the enduring image of assimilation in his 1908 play *The Melting-Pot*. Zangwill portrayed people from distinct backgrounds entering the cauldron of American life, mixing together, and emerging as citizens identical to their native-born counterparts. This representation of the **melting pot** became the ideal as depicted in popular cartoons, ceremonies adopted by business corporations, and lessons presented in school classrooms.

However, the melting pot worked better as an ideal than as a mirror of reality. Immigrants during this period never fully lost the social, cultural, religious, and political identities they had brought with them. Even if all immigrants had sought full assimilation, which they did not, the anti-immigrant sentiment of many native-born Americans reinforced their status as strangers and aliens. The same year that Zangwill's play was published, Alfred P. Schultz, a New York physician, provided a dim view of the prospects of assimilation in his book *Race or Mongrel*. Schultz dismissed the melting pot theory that public schools could change the children of all races into Americans, which he found absurd. **See Document Project 18: "Melting Pot" or "Vegetable Soup"?, page 582**.

Thus most immigrants faced the dilemma of assimilating while holding on to their heritage. Sociologist W. E. B. Du Bois summed up this predicament for one of the nation's earliest transported groups. In his monumental *The Souls of Black Folk* (1903), Du Bois wrote that African Americans felt a "two-ness," an identity carved out of their African heritage together with their lives as slaves and free people in America. This "double-consciousness . . . two souls, two thoughts, two unreconciled strivings" also applies to immigrants at the turn of the twentieth century. Immigrants who entered the country after 1880 were more like vegetable soup—an amalgam of distinct parts within a common broth—than a melting pot.

### REVIEW & RELATE

- What challenges did new immigrants to the United States face?
- What steps did immigrants take to meet these challenges?

✓ **LEARNINGCurve** bedfordstmartins.com/hewittlawson/LC

## Becoming an Urban Nation

In the half century after the Civil War, the population of the United States quadrupled, but the urban population soared sevenfold. In 1870 one in five Americans lived in cities with a population of 8,000 or more. By 1900 one in three resided in cities of this size. In 1870 only Philadelphia and New York had populations over half a million. Twenty years later, in addition to these two cities, Chicago's population exceeded 1 million; St. Louis, Boston, and Baltimore had more than 500,000 residents; and Cleveland, Buffalo, San Francisco, and Cincinnati boasted populations over 250,000. Urbanization was not confined to the Northeast and Midwest. Denver's population jumped from 4,700 in 1870 to more than 107,000 in 1890. During that same period, Los Angeles grew nearly fivefold, from 11,000 to 50,000, and Birmingham leaped from 3,000 to 26,000. "We live in the age of great cities," the Reverend Samuel Lane Loomis, a Massachusetts schoolteacher, remarked in 1886. "Each successive year finds a stronger and more irresistible current sweeping in towards the centers of life." This phenomenal urban growth also brought remarkable physical changes to the cities, as tall buildings reached toward the skies, electric lights brightened the nighttime hours, and water and gas pipes, sewers, and subways snaked below the ground.

## The New Industrial City

Urban growth in America was part of a long-term global phenomenon. Between 1820 and 1920, some 60 million people globally moved from rural to urban areas. Most of them migrated after the 1870s, and as noted earlier, millions journeyed from towns and villages in Europe to American cities. Yet the number of Europeans who migrated internally was greater than those who went overseas. As in the United States, Europeans moved from the countryside to urban areas in search of jobs. Many migrated to the city on a seasonal basis, seeking winter employment in cities and then returning to the countryside at harvest time. Whether as permanent or temporary urban residents, these migrants took jobs as bricklayers, factory workers, and cabdrivers.

Before the Civil War, commerce was the engine of growth for American cities. Ports like New York, Boston, New Orleans, and San Francisco became distribution centers for imported goods or items manufactured in small shops in the surrounding countryside. Cities in the interior of the country located on or near major bodies of water, such as Chicago, St. Louis, Cincinnati, and Detroit, served similar functions. As the extension of railroad transportation led to the development of large-scale industry (see chapter 16), these cities and others became industrial centers as well.

Industrialization contributed to rapid urbanization in several ways. It drew those living on farms, who either could not earn a satisfactory living or were bored by the isolation of rural areas, into the city in search of better-paying jobs and excitement. One rural dweller in Massachusetts complained: "The lack of pleasant, public entertainments in this town has much to do with our young people feeling discontented with country life." In 1891, a year after graduating from Kansas State University, the future newspaper editor William Allen White headed to Kansas City, enticed, as he put it, by the "marvels" of "the gilded metropolis." In addition, while the mechanization of farming increased efficiency, it also reduced the demand for farm labor. In 1896 one person could plant, tend, and harvest as much wheat as it had taken eighteen farmworkers to do sixty years before.

Industrial technology also made cities more attractive and livable places. Electricity extended nighttime entertainment and powered streetcars to convey people around town. Improved water and sewage systems provided more sanitary conditions, especially given the demands of the rapidly expanding population. Structural steel and electric elevators made it possible to construct taller and taller buildings, which gave cities such as Chicago and New York their distinctive skylines. Scientists and physicians made significant progress in the fight against the spread of contagious diseases, which had become serious problems in crowded cities.

Although immigrants increasingly accounted for the influx into the cities, before 1890 the rise in urban population came mainly from Americans on the move. In addition to young men like William Allen White, young women left the farm to seek their fortune. The female protagonist of Theodore Dreiser's novel *Sister Carrie* (1900) abandons small-town Wisconsin for the lure of Chicago. In real life, mechanization created many "Sister Carries" by making farm women less valuable in the fields. The possibility of purchasing mass-produced goods from mail-order houses such as Sears, Roebuck also left young women less essential as homemakers because they no longer had to sew their own clothes and could buy labor-saving appliances from catalogs.

Similar factors drove rural black women and men into cities. Plagued by the same poverty and debt that white sharecroppers and tenants in the South faced, blacks suffered from the added burden of racial oppression and violence in the post-Reconstruction period. From 1870 to 1890, the African American population of Nashville, Tennessee, soared from just over 16,000 to more than 29,000. In Atlanta, Georgia, the number of blacks jumped from slightly above 16,000 to around 28,000. Richmond, Virginia, and Montgomery, Alabama, followed suit, though the increase was not quite as high.

Economic opportunities were more limited for black migrants than for their white counterparts. African American migrants found work as cooks, janitors, and domestic servants. Work in cotton mills remained off-limits to blacks, but many found employment as manual laborers in manufacturing companies—including tobacco factories, which employed women and men; tanneries; and cottonseed oil firms—and as dockworkers. In 1882 the Richmond Chamber of Commerce applauded black workers as "easily taught" and "most valuable hand[s]." Although the overwhelming majority of blacks worked as unskilled laborers for very low wages, others opened small businesses such as funeral parlors, barbershops, and construction companies or went into professions such as medicine, law, banking, and education that catered to residents of segregated black

**African American Family, 1900**

Despite the rigid racial segregation and oppression that African Americans faced in the late nineteenth century, some black families found ways to achieve economic success and upward mobility. With its piano and fine furniture, the home of this African American family reflects middle-class conventions of the period. The father is a graduate of Hampton Institute, a historically black university founded after the Civil War to educate freedpeople.   Library of Congress

neighborhoods. Despite considerable individual accomplishments, by the turn of the twentieth century most blacks in the urban South had few prospects for upward economic mobility.

In 1890, although 90 percent of African Americans lived in the South, a growing number were moving to Northern cities to seek employment and greater freedom. Boll weevil infestations during the 1890s decimated cotton production and forced sharecroppers and tenants off farms. At the same time, blacks saw significant erosion of their political and civil rights in the last decade of the nineteenth century. Most black citizens in the South were denied the right to vote and experienced rigid, legally sanctioned racial segregation in all aspects of public life (see chapter 16). Between 1890 and 1914 approximately 485,000 African Americans left the South. By 1914 New York, Chicago, and Philadelphia each counted more than 100,000 African Americans among their population, and another twenty-nine northern cities contained black populations of 10,000 or more. An African American woman expressed her enthusiasm about the employment she found in Chicago, where she earned $3 a day working

in a railroad yard. "The colored women like this work," she explained, because "we make more money . . . and we do not have to work as hard as at housework," which required working sixteen-hour days, six days a week.

Although many blacks found they preferred their new lives to the ones they had led in the South, the North did not turn out to be the promised land of freedom. Black newcomers encountered discrimination in housing and employment. Residential segregation confined African Americans to racial ghettos, such as the South Side of Chicago and New York City's Harlem. Black workers found it difficult to obtain skilled employment despite their qualifications, and women and men most often toiled as domestics, janitors, and part-time laborers.

Nevertheless, African Americans in northern cities built their own communities that preserved and reshaped their southern culture and offered a degree of insulation against the harshness of racial discrimination. A small black middle class appeared in Washington, D.C., Philadelphia, Chicago, and New York City consisting of teachers, attorneys, and small business people. In 1888 African Americans organized the Capital Savings Bank of Washington, D.C. Ten years later, two black real estate agents in New York City were worth more than $150,000 each, and one agent in Cleveland owned $100,000 in property. The rising black middle class provided leadership in the formation of mutual aid societies, lodges, and women's clubs. Newspapers such as the *Chicago Defender* and *Pittsburgh Courier* furnished local news to their subscribers and reported national and international events affecting people of color. As was the case in the South, the church was at the center of black life in northern cities. More than just religious institutions, churches furnished space for social activities and the dissemination of political information. The Baptist Church attracted the largest following among blacks throughout the country, followed by the African Methodist Episcopal (AME) Church. By the first decade of the twentieth century, more than two dozen churches had sprung up in Chicago alone. Whether housed in newly constructed buildings or in storefronts, black churches provided worshippers freedom from white control. They also allowed members of the northern black middle class to demonstrate what they considered to be respectability and refinement.